Methodist Heritage a

Brian Beck has had a long and distinguished career in Methodist studies, having additionally served as President of the UK Methodist Conference and helped lead the international Oxford Institute of Methodist Theological Studies. This book is the first time that Beck's seminal work on Methodism has been gathered together. It includes eighteen essays from the last twenty-five years, covering many different aspects of Methodist thought and practice.

This collection is divided into two main sections. Part I covers Methodism's heritage and its implications, while Part II discusses wider issues of Methodism's identity. The chapters themselves examine the work of key figures, such as John Wesley and J. E. Rattenbury, as well as past and present forms of Methodist thought and practice. As such, this book is important reading for any scholar of Methodism as well as students and academics of religious studies and theology more generally.

Brian E. Beck is a Fellow and former Principal of Wesley House in Cambridge, UK. He was the Secretary of the Methodist Conference in Britain from 1984 to 1998 and President 1993 to 1994, and from 1969 to 2007 he shared in the leadership of the international Oxford Institute of Methodist Theological Studies. Now retired, Brian teaches the theology and history of Methodism, and New Testament Greek. He also looks after the college archives and serves on the library committee.

Routledge Methodist Studies Series

Series Editor: William Gibson, Director of the Oxford Centre for Methodism and Church History, Oxford Brookes University, UK

Editorial Board:

Ted A. Campbell, Professor of Church History, Perkins School of Theology, Southern Methodist University, USA

David N. Hempton, Dean, Harvard Divinity School, Harvard University, USA

Priscilla Pope-Levison, Associate Dean, Perkins School of Theology, Southern Methodist University, USA

Martin Wellings, Superintendent Minister of Oxford Methodist Circuit and Past President of the World Methodist Historical Society, UK.

Karen B. Westerfield Tucker, Professor of Worship, Boston University, USA

Methodism remains one of the largest denominations in the USA and is growing in South America, Africa and Asia (especially in Korea and China). This series spans Methodist history and theology, exploring its success as a movement historically and in its global expansion. Books in the series will look particularly at features within Methodism which attract wide interest, including: the unique position of the Wesleys; the prominent role of women and minorities in Methodism; the interaction between Methodism and politics; the 'Methodist conscience' and its motivation for temperance and pacifist movements; the wide range of Pentecostal, holiness and evangelical movements; and the interaction of Methodism with different cultures.

For a full list of titles in the series, please visit https://www.routledge.com/religion/series/AMETHOD

Methodism in Australia
A History
Edited by Glen O'Brien and Hilary M. Carey

British Methodist Hymnody
Theology, Heritage, and Experience
Martin V. Clarke

Image, Identity and John Wesley
A Study in Portraiture
Peter S. Forsaith

Methodist Heritage and Identity
Brian E. Beck

Methodist Heritage and Identity

Brian E. Beck

Routledge
Taylor & Francis Group

LONDON AND NEW YORK

First published 2018
by Routledge

2 Park Square, Milton Park, Abingdon, Oxfordshire OX14 4RN
52 Vanderbilt Avenue, New York, NY 10017

Routledge is an imprint of the Taylor & Francis Group, an informa business

First issued in paperback 2019

Copyright © 2018 Brian E. Beck

The right of Brian E. Beck to be identified as author of this work has been asserted by him in accordance with sections 77 and 78 of the Copyright, Designs and Patents Act 1988.

All rights reserved. No part of this book may be reprinted or reproduced or utilised in any form or by any electronic, mechanical, or other means, now known or hereafter invented, including photocopying and recording, or in any information storage or retrieval system, without permission in writing from the publishers.

Notice:
Product or corporate names may be trademarks or registered trademarks, and are used only for identification and explanation without intent to infringe.

British Library Cataloguing-in-Publication Data
A catalogue record for this book is available from the British Library

Library of Congress Cataloging-in-Publication Data
Names: Beck, Brian E., 1933– author.
Title: Methodist heritage and identity / Brian E. Beck.
Description: New York : Routledge, 2017. | Series: Routledge Methodist studies series | Includes bibliographical references and index.
Identifiers: LCCN 2017016695 | ISBN 9781138636194 (hardback : alk. paper) | ISBN 9781315206127 (ebook)
Subjects: LCSH: Methodism.
Classification: LCC BX8217 .B43 2017 | DDC 287–dc23
LC record available at https://lccn.loc.gov/2017016695

ISBN: 978-1-138-63619-4 (hbk)
ISBN: 978-0-367-88733-9 (pbk)

Typeset in Bembo
by Out of House Publishing

Contents

General introduction

The articles collected here were originally written over a period of some 20 years up to 2010, and represent my reflections on a number of Methodist and ecumenical questions. They vary in style, some having begun life as addresses, others as contributions to the *Epworth Review* or to collections of essays on particular subjects. Two are the fruit of pieces of research I had the opportunity to undertake. Each chapter looks at a specific topic but many require reference to the same historical background and some repetition has been inevitable. I have tried to limit it by editing where possible. The issues are discussed from the standpoint of a British Methodist but the wider Methodist scene is also taken into account. The last chapter in particular began life in an American context. It is included here because of the wider relevance of the issues discussed.

British Methodism has changed in some particulars over the period during which these pieces were written, making some references less obvious to today's reader. In particular, the central administrative structure has changed from a cluster of Divisions to a single Team, a new hymn book has been introduced and 'presbyter' has come into general use, replacing 'minister', now reserved as a collective term for presbyters and deacons. So far as possible these changes are accommodated in the notes.

The collection has been divided into two parts, the first primarily concerned with Methodism's past and its implications for the present, the other with wider issues, especially Methodism's place in the ecumenical scene. But an absolute distinction between the two parts cannot be sustained. What Methodism is depends greatly upon what it was.

I am grateful to the many friends who have encouraged me to undertake this venture, and in particular to Professor William Gibson for his generous help and advice. My thanks go also to the publishers who have allowed me to use work to which they hold the copyright.

Part I

Heritage

Introduction to Part I

All Christian churches carry the evidence both of their shared origins in the events and the faith to which the Scriptures bear witness and of their subsequent historical journey, that journey often marked by moments of disruption and consequent division: the Great Schism of 1054; the Protestant Reformation of the sixteenth century; the Act of Uniformity of 1662; and, in the eighteenth century, the Evangelical Revival, in which John Wesley and his associates played a major part. Such moments leave their mark.

In Methodism's case the legacy is manifold: a distinctive tradition of hymnody, an emphasis on personal experience of God's grace and commitment to discipleship epitomised in the annual Covenant Service, an expectation of relationships in the Church that support personal faith, an emphasis on lay as well as ordained leadership and ministry, a distinctive organisational structure (connexionalism), the memory that Methodism began as a movement to proclaim the gospel and a commitment to social service. Behind all this stand the figures of John Wesley and, in relation to hymnody, his brother Charles, both often remembered in isolation from their many other associates and out of their eighteenth-century context.

Attachment to the memory of John Wesley has fluctuated over the years. Early nineteenth-century writing and portrayal in ceramics and other media border on the hagiographic. By the twentieth century attitudes had changed. While Wesleyan Methodists were still strongly attached to his memory, the other branches that survived from the multiple divisions of the first half of the nineteenth century were less so (the Primitive Methodists had their own heroes in Hugh Bourne and William Clowes). One of the sticking points in the negotiations for the reunion of the separate bodies was the Wesleyan insistence that the doctrinal standards of the united Church should include a reference to John Wesley's Forty-Four Sermons and his Notes upon the New Testament.[1] Many non-Wesleyans felt that it would condemn the Church to being backward-looking and out of touch with contemporary biblical scholarship. It was only by hedging the reference round by qualifying phrases that it got through. It is the 'evangelical doctrines' 'contained' in them to which 'the preachers of the Methodist Church are pledged', and they 'are not intended to impose a system of formal or speculative theology...but to set up standards of preaching and belief which should secure loyalty to the fundamental truths of the gospel of redemption and ensure the continued witness of the Church to the realities of the Christian experience of salvation'.[2] One can make of that what one will.

Serious critical historical scholarship concerning John Wesley can be said to have begun in the second half of the twentieth century, with the pioneering work of Frank Baker, whose textual researches are the bedrock of the definitive Bicentennial Edition of his writings, still in progress, and the equally important work of Albert Outler. Others have followed their lead, and there is now an extensive bibliography of studies of his life and of aspects of his theology. Indeed, one of Outler's major contributions was to insist on studying Wesley as a theologian. Significantly, there are many fewer studies of his brother Charles, although Charles' influence, even today, through the medium of his hymns is far greater than that of John through his sermons.

It remains a puzzle to many ecumenical partners, especially to those in traditions that do not look back to a particular founding figure, why Methodism is so preoccupied with John Wesley, and there are many Methodists, more concerned with the mission of the Church in the present day than with the legacy of the past, who would share their disenchantment. In effect, they share the fears of those in 1932 who resisted reference to Wesley in the doctrinal standards. Is not the gulf between the Church and Western society already wide enough without deepening the divide by references to a bygone age? Is John Wesley still relevant?

Methodism's inherited legacy is more than that of the Wesley brothers, however, and it is important not to treat them in isolation either from their historical context or from the developments that followed their deaths. These also have shaped modern Methodism. The chapters that follow in the first part of this book also look therefore at the wider inherited legacy. One explores the history and theology of the idea of connexionalism. It is the earliest of the essays included in this book, first published in 1991. Since that time more attention has been given to the topic. In particular, the new official statement on the doctrine of the Church, *Called to Love and Praise*, adopted in 1999, devotes several pages to 'the connexional principle', and its ecclesiological significance is now more widely understood, particularly in ecumenical discussions. It has seemed appropriate to include alongside it a consideration of the concept of *koinonia*, now much employed in ecumenical discussions, even though, strictly speaking, it might be thought to belong to the second part of the book, which considers other ecumenical questions. But connexion and *koinonia* approach the same issues in different terms and belong together.

This part of the book concludes with a study of a significant lay servant of the church and of the anti-slavery movement in the period up to 1854, much respected in his time but barely known subsequently, and remembered only by his descendants, and in the village of his birth only by the chapel named after him. He is included here as an example of many, now largely forgotten, who have contributed to Methodism's heritage, and whose work has endured longer than their memory.

Notes

1 For this and other doctrinal issues involved in Methodist union, see John Kent, *The Age of Disunity* (London: Epworth Press, 1966), especially pp. 20–43.
2 See clause 4 of the Deed of Union, in *The Constitutional Practice and Discipline of the Methodist Church*, vol. 2, 7th edn, 2016 rev. (London: Methodist Publishing, 2016), p. 213.

1 John Wesley

Encounter or embarrassment?[1]

I once visited a newly opened Methodist church in the United States. It was on the grand scale, capable of seating 2,000. The vestibule, appropriately, was on the same scale. What caught the eye as one came in was a pedestal with a bust of John Wesley, the only piece of Christian symbolism – indeed, the only piece of furniture – in that vast space. To be fair, the place was new. Perhaps they intended to acquire other furnishings. But what they had started with spoke volumes about their priorities and their sense of identity. John Wesley somehow defined that church. It is not a unique case. In many British Methodist churches one can find, if not prominently displayed or in stained glass, then tucked away, in the preacher's vestry perhaps, some reminder of the one who is sometimes referred to as 'the Founder of Methodism'.

It is true that it is less common than it once was. The nineteenth century abounded in mugs, plates, teapots, loving cups, ceramic statuettes and busts, framed silhouettes, engravings and samplers. It was typical of the age. The library that W. E. Gladstone gave to the nation at Hawarden in north Wales has his image displayed on every available space. But even now celebrations of key moments in John Wesley's life can spawn a vast array of pottery and glass, pencils, erasers, pens, books, bookmarks, tea towels, T-shirts, even soap, embellished with his image or some quotation – or misquotation – from him. Every year on or around May 24th a posy of flowers is laid at his statue in St Paul's Churchyard in London. Annually there are heritage tours arranged for people to visit sites associated with him: Epworth (his birthplace), Oxford, Bristol and, of course, Aldersgate Street and his chapel in City Road London. Many Methodist churches are named after him, and an examination of the address list of ministers in the *Minutes of Conference* will reveal a fair collection of 'Epworths' and 'Wesley Manses'. Why is Methodism so obsessed with this man?

Of course we cannot escape history. Methodism, now a family of churches of some 38 million members worldwide, owes its origin to the eighteenth-century movement John Wesley led, and still bears the marks of the character he stamped upon it. The official doctrinal standards in Britain include reference to 44 of his sermons and his notes on the New Testament. There is no escaping the fact that Methodism would not now exist if he had not been the man he was and did the things he did. But that would be true of other branches of the

Christian Church, which yet do not exhibit this seemingly obsessive preoccupation with their founding figure.

Perhaps it is Methodism's equivalent of the more catholic tradition of the veneration of the saints. Of course Methodists do not invoke him for assistance, but there are plenty of examples in the catholic tradition of veneration of the memory of some saintly figure of the past whose work lives on: St Francis, St Benedict, St Ignatius Loyola – indeed, many religious orders are named after saints, as are parish churches and cathedrals. But all that is set against a background that Methodism largely lacks, a sense of the wider communion of the saints. The individual is one of many, and the many are not excluded from popular consciousness by attention to the one. But in Methodism John Wesley stands alone, and that produces a foreshortening of historical perspective. I suspect that, in the imagination of many Methodists, nothing of significance happened in the interval between Paul the apostle and John Wesley, with the possible exception of Martin Luther and the Reformation. Methodism at the popular level is seriously detached from its deeper roots.

The historical reality, as recent historians have tended to stress, is that Wesley was not alone. Of course there was always his brother Charles, who, for the Methodist in the pew, has had the greater influence. His hymns are widely sung, in the English-speaking world at least, while few read John's sermons. But the fact is that alongside the Wesley brothers in the eighteenth century there were other clergymen – Fletcher, Grimshaw and others – and hundreds of lay preachers without whose work the movement Wesley led could not have spread as it did. And alongside his movement were others. The Countess of Huntingdon, George Whitefield and Howell Harris at least must be named. Then there were the nineteenth-century figures whose work also left its mark upon British Methodism, but whose names, apart perhaps from the Primitive Methodists, Hugh Bourne and William Clowes, are largely forgotten.

So it is not surprising that since the mid-twentieth century there has been a reaction, a sense of boredom, of irrelevance, of embarrassment with the traditional Methodist fixation. One reason has been the feeling that he had nothing to say to the problems facing the modern Church and that he was making Methodism backward-looking in a secular age when radical changes were called for. So much of his writing starts from the assumption that the central problem for human beings to address is the problem of personal sin and guilt and how to be sure of going to heaven. The twentieth and twenty-first centuries have seen plenty of wickedness and the appalling suffering of war, which have seemed to dwarf the agonies of personal conscience over breaking the sabbath or using the odd swear word. And wasn't it all a bit neurotic? Had we not, with our scientific and technological achievements, grown up, come of age? Another factor was the developing ecumenical scene, calling, it was felt, for Christians to look outwards rather than inwards and backwards, to stress what they hold in common, not what makes them different.

This reaction has been mirrored at the professional level among historians by a certain debunking tendency. It has been observed that the early biographies of John Wesley were really hagiographies. Modern studies are more detached, more critical, drawing attention to his difficulties with women, his obsessive perfectionism, his authoritarianism, his obstinacy, the ambiguities and contradictions in his thinking that he refused to recognise, the fact that his band of preachers did not universally think him wonderful or simply eat out of his hand (though they rarely got away with it). Modern studies have tried to set him in his eighteenth-century background, drawing attention to his indebtedness to others for key elements in his ideas, and to stress the wide sweep of those ideas, and his development of them over his long life, rather than getting stuck with a few stereotypes of what he thought, such as the warmed heart or the world parish: two popular slogans, neither of which does justice to what he experienced or said.

What relevance, then, if any, does John Wesley have for today? Can we still encounter him? The key word is 'encounter'; it is not a matter of submission. Wesley was irredeemably an eighteenth-century figure, and he cannot simply be transplanted into the twenty-first and treated as the oracle to settle all our controversies or the pattern of life, to be slavishly followed. But many of the issues that deeply concerned him have their counterpart today, and I draw attention, in no particular order, to some aspects of his work that may stimulate us or make us feel uncomfortable.

Christ for all

I begin from the fact that, in the postmodern world, religion – and Christian religion in particular – is seen as a minority interest. A surprisingly large proportion of the population of Britain responds to surveys by saying that they believe in God but a remarkably small number profess active Christian allegiance. For all but about 5 per cent of the population, church is what one stays away from, and there are effectively two generations who have no understanding of the basic vocabulary of Christianity. It is seen as a minority interest: some collect stamps, or play golf; some are hooked on sailing or country dancing; vast numbers are mad about football; and some get religion. It depends on temperament, perhaps even, though to a diminishing extent, on upbringing. Should Christians then accept the role that society has cast for them, or is there a significant sense in which faith in Jesus Christ is an option on offer for all?

In the eighteenth century the same question was being posed in different terms. Belief in the existence of God was pretty universal, but what sort of God and with what consequences? Is faith in Jesus Christ genuinely an option on offer for all, or is there a predetermined split in the human race, between responders and non-responders, based this time not on temperament or upbringing but on a decision made by God – a divine decree – that some have been created for salvation, and are guaranteed to attain to it, and others to damnation, try what they may? Election and reprobation – what Wesley called 'the horrible decree'.

In theological terms Wesley was an Arminian. He held that all could be saved. The life, death and resurrection of Jesus as the action of the Son of God for the rescue of the human race made no sense if the outcome had been decided in advance when God drew up the blueprint for creation. 'Christ died for all, therefore all died'; Paul's words meant what they said, and were echoed in the hymns the early Methodists sang:

> The world he suffered to redeem
> For all he hath the atonement made
> For those that will not come to him
> The ransom of his life was paid.[2]

It was theological campaign material: a fierce ideological battle that split Wesley from many of his contemporaries.

The dust of that particular battle has now, happily, settled. But the underlying issue remains. In modern society we have the added challenge that Wesley barely faced: the presence of members of ancient and vibrant communities of faith that do not acknowledge that Christian claim. The question of Christ for all is no longer simply 'Is Christian faith a live option for those of no faith?' but 'Is there a significant sense in which even those other world faiths might be enhanced by what Jesus of Nazareth has brought to the world?'. The challenge of John Wesley is not to let go of the question; not to acquiesce in the easy get-out of saying that religion does not deal with truth but is all a matter of taste and choice or inherited culture.

Fellowship

Then contemplate the increasing isolation that many people experience in their lives, at least in the West. It is to be seen in many ways: the shrinkage in family size and the instability of many families; the impersonality of many neighbourhoods in towns and cities, with shifting populations; the addiction to the television or computer screen; online shopping and entertainment; personal stereos; working from home. The redeeming feature of the ubiquitous mobile phone is that it marks a resurgence of the human spirit against isolation; human interaction matters – genetically we are gregarious. But it is still not face to face; there is no warmth of body, no human scent in a text message.

Isolation was hardly the problem of Wesley's day but social dislocation was. Often in the towns people were crammed together in overcrowded slum dwellings. Throughout his lifetime there was movement from countryside into towns, with consequent uprooting, loneliness and loss of values.

One of the major strengths of the Wesleyan movement was the way it brought people together in groups, large and small, in close and sustaining relationships. Quarter by quarter they were numbered off and accounted for, given a ticket of membership that said they belonged. And, while some of that was the result of practical responses to practical problems, it was undergirded by a conviction: 'Christianity is essentially a social religion…to turn it into a solitary religion is indeed to destroy it.'[3] 'The gospel of Christ knows of no religion but social: no holiness but social holiness.' '"Holy solitaries" is a phrase no more consistent with the gospel than holy adulterers,'[4] as Wesley expressed it in 1739 – a little hard on the Desert Fathers and the monastic tradition, but a conviction nonetheless.

What, then, is the Christian church on a Sunday morning? A random gathering of individual believers who assemble to enjoy God, like the audience at a concert or play, sitting side by side in the same place at the same time because it is the most convenient arrangement? Or a fellowship; something analogous to a family, containing, like any other family, married and single members, young and old, but with an identifiable bond between them? Are baptism and eucharist individual events or, rather, the rite of entry into and the sustaining meal of a community, because it is as we are related to others in openness, love and trust that we begin to discover our true humanity – begin to be saved, in other words? That is Wesley's challenge, and if it is true of the church it has wider implications too, as we shall see.

The service of the mind

Next I draw attention to another, often commented on, feature of the society we live in: what is often referred to as 'dumbing down' – the tendency in public debate to polarise everything, set things off in stark contrasts of black and white, want yes/no answers, reduce complicated issues to soundbites. We see it not only in politics and the media, but also in religion. It is a phenomenon with many causes. There is a swing in culture from thought to feeling, a demand for everything to be simple and effort-free ('easy' is a word that sells products) and a suspicion of complex answers. Such attitudes apply to religious matters. People are wary of 'doctrine' and prefer platitudes.

Sometimes John Wesley is portrayed as 'the apostle of the warmed heart', as though he had reduced Christianity to states of religious feeling. We forget the Oxford don with the disciplined and enquiring mind, who reduced everything to order, with carefully numbered paragraphs and sub-paragraphs, published books and pamphlets, and produced edited extracts of many other writers' works in order to educate his people. Charles too could pray, in a hymn for the opening of Kingswood School, 'Unite the pair, so long disjoined, knowledge and vital piety.'[5] We lose that emphasis at our peril. Over the long history of the human race it is the thinkers, the philosophers, the scientists, the inventors – those who have used their brains – who have had most impact, for good or ill, in the development of our cultures. One of the reasons, among many, for the decline in Christianity's grasp upon the West has been the fact that we have not properly addressed the philosophical questions of the day and have allowed popular misconceptions, such as 'Science has disproved religion', to go unchallenged and form popular attitudes. Wesley never lost sight of the fact that the call to love God with our whole being includes the disciplined service of the mind. In that insistence he still speaks today.

The 'optimism of grace'

Then I refer to a prevailing pessimism. It comes at two levels. We see it in the personal life story of so many individuals, who see little point in trying to get anywhere because there seems nowhere to go, who fall into depression or escape into drugs because the future seems to hold so little. It is met with on a broader scale in those who manage their personal lives reasonably well but see little to be optimistic about in the world at large. The seeming unwillingness of human beings – particularly the wealthy and powerful, it would appear, and especially when acting corporately – to do anything except serve their own interests is profoundly depressing. Suppose we manage to police the world against international terrorism; do we have the will to tackle its causes? Can there be a resolution of the many conflicts in the world? We can be astonishingly moved by world poverty and respond to televised appeals, but do little or nothing to change a lifestyle that perpetuates such conditions. We are capable of recognising the causes of global warming and the long-term effects of damaging the ecosystem but at the same time resist every measure that might bring change if it impinges on us.

Can anything change? In Wesley's thinking and lifelong work there was a threefold emphasis – not new or unique, just classical Christianity reaffirmed – that we would do well to maintain. First, everyone has worth; not because they are interesting or gifted or clever or great achievers, but because they are loved by God; loved whether they are good or bad, prosperous or totally deprived, with disability or without, on a high or in the depths, innocent or guilty of the worst; loved and valued, known by name and offered forgiveness. Second, there is no limit to what God can do, with the individual or the situation, to change things. We may not be able to predict what may be achieved or how change may come about, but there is in the gospel of the resurrection of Jesus Christ a transforming energy that derives not from human capacity or ingenuity, nor from human self-confidence, but from faith in the capacity, and will, of God to bring about a new deal. Gordon Rupp referred to it as the optimism of grace. But, third, Wesley always insisted that to be loved, forgiven, changed by God is not a passive matter. The heart of his much-controverted and perhaps muddled doctrine of Christian perfection was the double insistence: God can bring about change, but we too must change. In place of self-interest and apathy must grow wholehearted love of God and neighbour, expressed not just in benign feelings and limp gestures but in active work for the good of others. That is why, throughout his life, Wesley was to be found working for the poor, visiting prisoners, supporting the campaign against slavery, protesting against economic exploitation. This too was social religion, and, if today our understanding of the causes of the world's ills is more complex than his general belief that most things could be set right if only individuals had the will to change, we dare not abandon his insistence that the Christian is called to serve the coming of God's kingdom in the world, for it is through such service that God graciously brings it about. But the motivating power of such efforts remains the optimism of grace. The God of the resurrection is a God who springs surprises.

Commitment to the poor

I elaborate a little on that last point by referring to Wesley's total commitment to the poor. He was a cultured, affable man, who had an amazing gift of rapport with all manner of people, but he was ill at ease with the rich. He thought wealth one of the greatest hindrances to entering the kingdom of God, and he severely limited his personal wealth throughout his life, giving the surplus away. It is no accident that the text he took for his first ever sermon in the open air, the beginning of that public ministry that more than anything else brought about the eighteenth-century religious revival, was the one taken by Jesus in Luke's gospel in his opening sermon in Nazareth: 'The Spirit of the Lord is upon me, because he has anointed me to preach the gospel to the poor.'[6] Consider too this passage from his journal:

> In the afternoon I visited the sick... On Friday and Saturday I visited as many more as I could. I found some in their cells underground, others in their garrets, half-starved both with cold and hunger, added to weakness and pain. But I found not one of them unemployed that was able to crawl about the room. So wickedly, devilishly false is that common objection, 'They are poor only because they are idle.' If you saw these things with your own eyes, could you lay out money in ornaments and superfluities?[7]

Perhaps Wesley did have a blind spot so far as the upper classes went. Perhaps his idea of frugal living was too spartan and denied the value to the human spirit of art, music and culture. Certainly he had only the sketchiest notion of what we would now regard as the systemic causes of poverty. Perhaps historians are right that he was not so successful in communicating with the really poor, the destitute and brutalised, as the later idealised portrait suggests. Servants and tradespeople were those who responded in numbers. But this man's commitment to the underprivileged was not ivory-towered. He met them face to face and saw the reality rather than the myth.

In our day we are aware that poverty is global as well as local; sometimes we are more aware of global poverty than local. We know that the global economy that brings such benefits – not the least of them our televised awareness of global suffering – also is a cause of that suffering. But the middle classes to which Methodism largely appeals rarely really understand what it is like to be poor: to have neither credit cards nor creditworthiness, no secure home, no address opening the door to benefits, no regular doctor or dentist, no loose change to give access to a public toilet; or, if we are a little better off, no ability to buy in bulk and so save on price, only weekly benefits from which to meet monthly bills, and so on. Wesley's face-to-face commitment puts a question to all. Read his writings carefully and it comes home how often it is the interests of the poor that drive his thinking and his understanding of the gospel.

Lifestyle

Last, I pose a question about Christian lifestyle. Wesley inherited through his parents something of the Puritan tradition of Christian living. And he was not alone in reacting against the breakdown of values in his day. Drunkenness, swearing, sabbath-breaking, adultery, deceit, idleness and luxury were for him sins to be denounced and avoided. They get frequent mention in his sermons. A Christian was to be different from the world around, and early Methodists were often brutally persecuted for that very thing.

Over the years that tradition became stereotyped, so that Methodism often came to be seen negatively in terms of no alcohol, no gambling, no card-playing or dancing. The lifestyle of many contemporary middle-class Methodists is often little different from that of their non-Methodist, non-believing neighbours, however, except perhaps in supporting Christian Aid and going to church. The distinction between church and world is not so sharp as once it was. Is that a good thing?

No reference has been made in this discussion to John Wesley's so-called conversion in 1738. One reason is that to describe his May 24th Aldersgate experience as a conversion is to use the word in a very special sense, for he had been a practising believer long beforehand. But even in that more limited sense it was one of two conversions, the first being in 1725 when he first heard the call to holy living, to give his all to the love of God and his fellow human beings with heart and soul and mind and strength. That marked a decisive change in his lifestyle. Aldersgate changed the motivation and the driving power for it, but the quest for holiness never left him, and it is the driving force of all his evangelism. 'Our main doctrines, which include all the rest, are three – that of Repentance, of Faith and of Holiness. The first of these we account, as it were, the porch of religion; the next, the door; the third, religion itself.'[8] What has that to say to contemporary Methodism or any other Christian tradition? Is the blurring of the distinction in lifestyle between church and world today due to the widening influence of Christian values on society, or is the church losing its grip on its vocation to be holy? And, if that is the case, by what sort of distinctive lifestyle should Christian holiness be expressed today? That, I am sure, is a question Wesley would be asking of us were he suddenly to return.

Notes

1   Adapted from a lecture given at Muswell Hill, London, on 24 May 2003.
2   George Osborn (ed.), *The Poetical Works of John and Charles Wesley*, 13 vols. (London: Wesleyan-Methodist Conference, 1868–72) (hereafter 'Osborn'): vol. 3, p. 4 [as later amended]; see also II Cor. 5:14.

3 Sermon 24 [Sermon on the Mount IV], § I 1, in Albert C. Outler (ed.), *The Works of John Wesley*, vol. 1, *Sermons I: 1–33*, bicentennial edn (Nashville, TN: Abingdon Press, 1984), pp. 533f.

4 Osborn, vol. 1, p. xxii, para. 5.

5 Osborn, vol. 6, p. 408.

6 Journal for 2 April 1739, in W. Reginald Ward and Richard P. Heitzenrater (eds.), *The Works of John Wesley*, vol. 19, *Journal and Diaries II (1738–1743)*, bicentennial edn (Nashville, TN: Abingdon Press, 1990), p. 46.

7 Journal for 8 February 1753, in W. Reginald Ward and Richard P. Heitzenrater (eds.), *The Works of John Wesley*, vol. 20, *Journal and Diaries III (1743–1754)*, bicentennial edn (Nashville, TN: Abingdon Press, 1991), p. 445.

8 'The Principles of a Methodist Farther Explained', §VI 4, in Rupert E. Davies (ed.), *The Works of John Wesley*, vol. 9, *The Methodist Societies: History, Nature, and Design*, bicentennial edn (Nashville, TN: Abingdon Press, 1989), p. 227.

2 Rattenbury revisited

The theology of Charles Wesley's hymns[1]

Ernest Rattenbury published *The Evangelical Doctrines of Charles Wesley's Hymns* in 1941,[2] part of a three-volume project that included the *Eucharistic Hymns*[3] but, because of the conditions of the war, was never completed. Comparatively little seems to have been done in detail on the theology of the hymns since then.[4] Much more attention has been devoted to their literary and poetic aspects. That may well be a tribute to the thoroughness of Rattenbury's work, but it is at least worth asking whether the last word has been spoken or whether more work ought to be done. If it ought, then it needs to be done by one more qualified and better read in the subject than I, who count only as, in the true sense, an amateur. My purpose is only to ask the question, and to indicate some directions in which I think further work might be done. Whether, therefore, this chapter is to be considered a genuine revisiting of Rattenbury or a mere pit stop on the way is for others to decide.

The question is important because, arguably, Charles Wesley is for British Methodism a more important theologian than his brother, John. John is of structural importance. Without him, the Methodist movement as we know it would not have begun. Without the organisational fabric he gave it the movement would almost certainly not have survived. Nevertheless, in spite of the fact that in the 1784 Deed of Declaration he gave the Notes upon the New Testament and the first four volumes of the Standard Sermons the status of doctrinal standards, and never gave any such status to any of the hymn books, it was Charles' hymns that built into the Methodist psyche the theological character that even now, much diluted though it is by the passing of the generations, remains the most potent force holding Methodism together as a church. And this is true not merely in a devotional sense. As Rattenbury observes,[5] it was Charles' hymns more than anything else that destroyed the power of eighteenth-century Calvinism.

What I have said applies to Britain. The hymns have not exported well. Their use has never been so widespread across the Atlantic, where frontier hymnody had proportionately greater influence. There are only 51 hymns by Charles Wesley out of 734 in the current *United Methodist Hymnal*. And, of course, the hymns do not easily translate. It needs a poet to translate a poet adequately, and some of Charles' distinctive English defies any translation. This is perhaps the main reason why attempts in the international Oxford Institute of Methodist Theological Studies to get Charles' theology studied alongside that of John have so far been unsuccessful. Little is known and the full corpus is so inaccessible.

A follow-up to Rattenbury could therefore be important. Rattenbury's work is based by his own admission on a limited range of the published material. Considering the extent of the entire corpus, some 9,000 pieces, that is not surprising. But few of them, apart from those in the Large Hymn Book of 1780, have received critical treatment. And there is now the addition of the hitherto unpublished material edited by Kimbrough and Beckerlegge.[6] All that awaits the enterprising Ph.D. student. Still more important, however, is the task that is never definitively done but must be repeated in every generation: that of theological appraisal. It is on this question of evaluation that I offer these remarks.

First, let me return to the point to which I have already drawn attention, Charles Wesley's theological contribution to the Evangelical Revival. We deceive ourselves if we imagine that John Wesley's extensive theological writings were the decisive influence in the formation of the Methodist preachers or their hearers. Their importance in the controversies of the time cannot be denied, but the words that lingered in the minds of the society members as they made their way back to their homes, and in the minds of the preachers as they rode on to the next stopping place, were not snatches from *A Plain Account of Christian Perfection* or *Thoughts upon Slavery* but

> Died he for me, who caused his pain?
>   For me, who him to death pursued?
> Amazing love! How can it be
> That thou, my God, shouldst die for me?[7]

If you want proof of that remark, consider the printing statistics, for example, of *Hymns on the Lord's Supper* (ten editions in just under 50 years) or the Large Hymn Book of 1780 (seven editions in 12 years). That John, who edited most of the hymn books, acknowledged them to be theological statements is clear from his censorship of the texts; not all the changes are merely matters of taste. And, if you want further confirmation, consider the fate of the doctrinal standards today. All preachers are expected to have read the Forty-Four Sermons and the Notes upon the New Testament. How many can remember them a year later? Yet most can make a fair fist at singing at least some of the hymns from memory.

All hymns, if they qualify for the name at all, express some theology, however naïve. Few, comparatively speaking, could be claimed to offer coherent theological teaching. The majority of Charles' hymns do that, and those characteristics that qualify them to rank also as English poetry contribute to it, with their careful use of language and their ordered presentation of ideas. Unlike so many religious songs, which can only be sung, for in a words-only edition they stand out as no more than a string of repeated words, these hymns bear regular use in private reading and meditation. Although of course there are many out of the 9,000 or so productions that do not deserve a second look, at their best they are not mere versifications of passages of scripture but written with intensity of feeling and depth of spiritual experience, and with a poetic quality that speaks to the depths. How often, simply turning the pages of a hymn book, one is struck by this. So, while one would not regard these hymns in the strict sense as systematic theology, they are powerful theological statements, and behind them lies the theological understanding of their author. They are the more powerful for avoiding some of the niceties of John's careful distinctions, and their influence has not been confined to Methodism.

The influence diminishes

Nevertheless, their influence is diminishing, even here in Britain, which has largely been their home. One can trace the fact in the reducing number of Charles Wesley hymns in successive editions of various books: about 480 out of 525 in 1780, expanded to 700 or so in the later supplemented editions; 443 out of 981 in the Wesleyan book of 1903; 254 out of 984 in 1933. With that may be compared 275 out of 1,052 in the Primitive Methodist book of 1889, 183 out of 980 in the United Methodist Free Churches (UMFC) book of the same year. In *Hymns and Psalms* it came down to 156 out of 823, about the same proportion as the UMFC. Now, in *Singing the Faith*, the figures are 79 out of 790, exactly 10 per cent. There is a necessary connection between a hymn book and the community that uses it, and few things illustrate so well the changes in both taste and spirituality as the changes in successive editions of a hymn book designed for use by the same community. British Methodism is not now so deeply rooted in Wesleyan theology as our nineteenth-century predecessors were, at least among the Wesleyans.

The reasons for this are complex. Methodist Union in 1932 will, I think, have played a part. Changes in musical taste have also contributed. Modern songs are simpler, use fewer ideas, simpler language and more repetition and generally avoid rhyme, and much modern hymnody follows the trend. We could debate endlessly whether we are better or worse for it. I simply make the point that the mantra-style repetition of a few words, which has a Christian history stretching back through the *Kyrie eleison* to the psalms ('for his mercy endures for ever'), has a valid place in the repertoire of Christian worship and private devotion, as Taizé and Iona have illustrated for us afresh. That is not the same, however, as the hymn, with its ordered content, and they fulfil different functions. Some of the polemics that fill the pages of the *Methodist Recorder* on this subject seem to me to be about as fruitful as an argument about the relative merits of a symphony concert and a set of door chimes. One would never use the one in place of the other. Nor, one may add, in spite of its instant critics, would one expect *The Big Blue Planet*, produced especially for the young, to supersede established hymnals.

But we must look deeper for the causes of the shrinking range of Charles Wesley hymns in use, for the root causes are theological and spiritual, and that takes us straight into a theological evaluation.

There is a further point, however, before we do so. One of the striking features of Charles' hymns is their biblical basis. All the standard studies draw attention to this. Both in verbal allusions and in their imagery they draw heavily on the Bible. That is a commonplace. It is a commonplace too that today there is nothing like the widely shared and extensive knowledge of the Bible that was a feature of the eighteenth and nineteenth centuries. This is not just the fault of our public educational system – none existed for most eighteenth-century Methodists – but a fault of the church's own teaching. Our task is made more difficult because there is no longer a standard text to echo; but the problem goes deeper. The place of the Bible in popular devotion has changed. And that takes us back to the theological and spiritual issue. So to some comments on the theology of the hymns and their impact today.

The great strength of the hymns, in spite of what I shall go on to say, is their theological range, too wide to do them justice in a single chapter. Rattenbury's book uses Bunyan's pilgrim as a model and divides the hymns into those that belong to the pilgrim way – conversion and its results, justification by grace, adoption, assurance, new birth, the quest for love, the band of pilgrims – and on the other hand what he called the hymns of the hinterland – the backdrop of the journey, consisting in the classical doctrines of God, the Trinity, the incarnation and atonement, the Spirit, eucharist, Church, Bible, last things. These are analysed with care and well illustrated.

Ecumenically speaking, one might say that the hymns of the hinterland have survived better than those of the pilgrim way. A limited number at least have found their way into the standard repertoire of hymn books of every tradition. So have a few that, strictly, belong to the pilgrim way: 'O for a thousand tongues', for example, 'O thou who camest from above', 'Forth in thy name, O Lord, I go', 'Come, O thou traveller unknown' (better known outside Methodism, sadly, than within) and, of course, 'And can it be that I should gain?'. But the bulk of those that belong to the pilgrim way are known only within Methodism, and a diminishing number of these.

For Rattenbury was right to speak of the *evangelical* doctrines. Everything is written within the framework of an eighteenth-century Arminian evangelical theology. That is not to say that every hymn sets it out. But where there is a conscious setting forth of truths of the faith the cross is central and the theme is personal salvation. Perhaps only in the hymns on the nativity of Christ does the incarnation supplant the atonement as the central doctrine of the gospel. Consider, for example, 'Let earth and heaven combine', which celebrates the joining of the two natures in Christ:

Our God contracted to a span,
Incomprehensibly made man.

This is the basis of the confidence

> And we the life of God shall know
> For God is manifest below.[8]

Even with some of these hymns, however, the focus shifts before the end to the cross, which in other hymns is the centrepiece, as in a great altar triptych, to which all other features direct the eye. Consider one of the great unknowns among the *Hymns for the Nativity*:

> O mercy divine
> How couldst thou incline
> My God, to become such an infant as *mine*?

It continues:

> Like him I would be,
> My Master I see
> In a stable; a stable shall satisfy me.

> And here I will lie,
> Till raised up on high,
> With him on the cross, I recover the sky.[9]

Evangelical theology still lives, though it is not the evangelicalism of the eighteenth century. But it is not the only theological framework embraced by contemporary Methodism. The theology of the hymns therefore addresses us, as it were, from a distance, and some of us more strongly than others; some elements of it, as I try to show in a moment, make most contemporary Methodists uncomfortable.

But that is true not only of their theology but also of their spirituality. As John Wesley's arrangement of the 1780 hymn book shows, they assume a pattern of spiritual experience, consciously felt and actively sought after, which begins with the conviction of personal sin, moves to an assurance of justifying grace and the awakening of love in the heart through the Holy Spirit and from there moves on towards holiness, that entire renewal of heart and life in the love of God and neighbour, experienced both as imperative and as gift, that has its consummation in the life of heaven. John and Charles did not see eye to eye on all the details of this (John, for example, saw perfection in one sense as a stage on the way, attainable in this life, and insisted that one could be assured of having reached it; Charles disputed that). But John's contents page of the 1780 book (describing the nature of religion, and providing for the penitent, for backsliders, for believers and for the society) was no artificial schema forced on the material; that is what the bulk of the hymns are about.

Today, however, that spirituality has been much diluted. While elements of it remain, I doubt whether many ordinary Methodists today see themselves as embarked on a pilgrimage to be described in those formal terms; indeed, many might find any notion of pilgrimage strange. The evidence is there in the successive modifications of the contents pages in the line of hymn books since 1780, down to *Hymns and Psalms*, from which it has entirely disappeared. There the word 'holiness' remains, though even 'repentance' has gone. But that illustrates what we all know by observation anyway.

When we pick up the hymns today, therefore, we are taking them out of their spiritual context and applying them, sometimes with reduced force, to a rather different spiritual and theological tradition. We edit out some of the verses, not just because they make the hymn too long but because they find no echo with us; and we gloss over particular lines that we otherwise sing. Who takes literally the fifth and sixth lines of that otherwise magnificent hymn 'Jesus the first and last',

> Thou wilt the root remove
> And perfect me in love,

which, as verse two shows, is part of the work of grace done here below?[10]

Part of this general shift in theological and spiritual perspective has been a shifting of the ground on particular subjects. An interesting example would be the double movement in eucharistic theology, which had a prominent place in early Methodism, receded in the nineteenth and early twentieth centuries and has advanced again in the last few decades. For this we have to thank not only the ecumenical liturgical movement but Rattenbury's own published work on the eucharistic hymns. One could cite other shifts. The place of total commitment in the service of Christ remains central to much Methodist spirituality, as the continued use of the Covenant Service shows, yet the formal language of perfection is much less in use among us. I have heard many exhortations from the tribunes of the Methodist Conference about social engagement, upholding Christian values, maintaining our witness, doing evangelism. I do not recall anyone calling us to press on to perfection. The preachers in the early Conferences would have found that strange.

Again, one could point to the shift in the understanding of the atonement. There are still those among us who hold to a substitutionary theory, but they are in a minority. Many are made uncomfortable by

> Never love nor sorrow was
>   Like that my Saviour showed:
> See him stretched on yonder cross,
>   And crushed beneath our load,[11]

which we do sing; and by

> He dies to atone
> For sins not his own
> Your debt he hath paid and your work he hath done…

> He purchased the grace
> Which now I embrace:
> O Father, thou knowest he hath died in my place,[12]

which we used to sing; and still more uncomfortable by

> The bread dried up and burnt with fire
> Presents the Father's vengeful ire,
>   Which my Redeemer bore:
> Into his bones the fire he sent,
> Till all the flaming darts were spent,
>   And Justice asked no more,[13]

which for that very reason we don't sing at all.

But perhaps the point at which the deepest gulf arises between us and Charles is in our response to illness, dying and death – somewhat cursorily treated, as it happens, by Rattenbury. This topic is also one of the most poignant to study, because so many of the hymns on the subject, which are no longer published, are written out of personal bereavement for a friend or a child, or in the agony of seeing a friend or a child suffer and waste away. Not only do we easily forget how common premature death was and how high the death rate in childbirth and among infants, we forget also how great a part unrelieved pain played in most people's experience of illness. Expectations have dramatically changed with the advance of medical science. For us, the general assumption is of recovery from most forms of illness unless something goes wrong, and we may even resort to litigation if it does. In the eighteenth century things were much more in the balance, even for relatively minor ailments, and prayer the most obvious resort – with no guarantee, however (so experience taught), that recovery would follow. For this experience a whole theology was constructed, with its roots deep in the Old Testament, which spoke of God testing by suffering those whom he loves, of death in God's good time as a joyful and long-awaited deliverance from a vale of tears, and of recovery as an indication that God had further work for his servant to do, or further purification by suffering to undergo before he or she was fit to drop into an unchangeable eternity. Consider this one-verse hymn, 'for all sick persons'

> Who languish on a bed of pain,
>   With various maladies of soul,
> Healer divine, in life detain,
>   Till thou hast made their spirits whole;
> Or let them here thy goodness see,
> Or fit, or take them up to thee.[14]

Anaesthetics and antibiotics have not only changed medicine, they have transformed theology. The notion of natural causes now plays a much greater part in accounting for disease and death, and we hesitate to attribute them to the direct hand and plan of God. Today if we go down with flu we think of the person who coughed at us in the tube, not of the inscrutable providence of God. I am not sure that that shift has made it any easier for us to discern where God is to be found in the experience. The whole topic of the theology of suffering and its relation to Charles' understanding of atonement deserves more analysis than it often receives.

The noticeable gaps

Along with these shifts in theological climate it is fair also to draw attention to what must be regarded as gaps on the shelves of Charles' storehouse, as viewed from the perspective of today. I draw attention to three.

There is, first, the lack of attention to the social impact of the gospel – that is, the recognition that the proclamation of the kingdom of God has prophetic implications, negatively and positively, for the ordering of public life, the conduct of nations and the behaviour of the individual citizen. There are 51 hymns in the section of *Hymns and Psalms* entitled 'The Social Order'. Only four are by Charles Wesley. This is indicative of his cast of mind.

Of course, there are hymns that echo his brother's compassionate concern for the poor:

> Outcasts of men, to you I call,
> Harlots and publicans and thieves.[15]

But that is in terms of the gospel message, not addressing material need. One that comes closer is 'Holy Lamb, who thee confess':

> Pass we thus our happy days
> 'Twixt the mount and multitude,
> Doing or receiving good.[16]

But that is at the level of private charity.

When we think we have come nearest to statements that seem to echo the biblical emphasis on the macro-impact of the coming of God's kingdom we suddenly find ourselves in the realm of allegory. 'Omnipotent Lord, my Saviour and King' takes up the apocalyptic passages in the gospels:

> O who can explain this struggle for life,
> This travail and pain, this trembling and strife:
> Plague, earthquake, and famine and tumult, and war.
> The wonderful coming of Jesus declare.[17]

But they are all struggles in the believer's soul, 'floods of temptation and flames of desire'. Similarly, 'O thou whom once they flocked to hear',[18] which meditates on Christ the physician, particularly in relation to John 5, concludes with a call to 'O my soul's physician thou', which may (or may not) be true to John's gospel, but is certainly not adequate in relation to the gospel tradition generally. The great Christmas hymn 'All glory to God in the sky' only just makes it, in my opinion, as a statement of what the coming of Christ (the first or the second) implies for the world order:

> Thou only art able to bless,
>   And make the glad nations obey,
> And bid the dire enmity cease,
>   And bow the whole world to thy sway.
> [...]
> All sorrow before thee shall fly,
>   And anger and hatred be o'er,
> And envy and malice shall die,
>   And discord afflict us no more.[19]

Here Charles was way behind John, who did, for all his limitations, more readily recognise what I have just called the macro-impact of the gospel – its implications for slavery, for example – though of course he lacked the analytical tools available to later generations to pinpoint causes and remedies. Perhaps a house in fashionable Marylebone was not the best vantage point from which to reflect on the gospel and the social order. Certainly, the many hymns on public affairs that poured out on every occasion of national crisis, from the Jacobite rebellion to the Lisbon earthquake and the threat of war with France, provide nothing to inspire us in this respect, offering little more than exhortations to national repentance in the style of the Book of Joel combined with high Tory loyalty to the Crown, defects and all.

The second gap is allied with the first. For all the emphasis in the experience of Methodists on the society and the class meeting, and the excellent contribution made by the hymns, which celebrate the fellowship of the church on earth and the communion of saints, Charles' theology is essentially individualistic. The starting point is that provided by the evangelical framework, the individual delivered from sin, and set, with others, on the way to salvation. In spite of the one-to-one encounter of Jesus with disciples in the gospels, this is not the starting point of much of the Bible. When Adam or Abraham is portrayed it is for the sake of those they represent. When Christ is set forth as our salvation it is in him that we attain it. Something of this is to be found in the hymns:

> See where our great High Priest
>   Before the Lord appears...

Never without his people seen,
The head of all believing men,[20]

but it is not dominant.

Third, there is the whole area of creation and the natural world. One looks in vain for hymns that celebrate the created order. Creation is assumed; the focus of interest is the fall, because we are involved in it, but wonder at the beauty of the world and the variety of its peoples is wanting, as is our responsibility for the planet. Here Isaac Watts and more modern writers offer more.

These are gaps that Charles Wesley does not fill, and a modern hymnal will rightly look elsewhere. They are partly the reason why the grip of Charles' hymns on Methodist thought and spirituality is less than it was. Occasionally a new item is added to the contemporary repertoire, as when six appeared in *Hymns and Songs* in 1969, and *Hymns and Psalms* has reintroduced some verses and language omitted from earlier editions (but not gone as far as the *United Methodist Hymnal* of 1992, in printing 17 out of the original 18 verses of what we know as 'O for a thousand tongues to sing'). Nevertheless, statistics speak for themselves. We are singing less of Charles than we used to do. The well-known injunction of a previous warden of the New Room in Bristol, that every Methodist service should contain at least four Charles Wesley hymns, seems now even less likely of universal observance than when it was first uttered.

The future?

So, what is the future for these hymns? Is the selection in use to continue to diminish until it dwindles to nothing, sometime in the middle of the twenty-first century? Will there be a Charles Wesley festival in 2095, or 2195? Idle questions, perhaps, but some predictions and suggestions may not be out of order.

First, there will surely remain in the general usage of the church a relatively small selection of those hymns that express the central truths of the faith and are universal to all Christians. They are already to be found in most hymn books. They have passed the test of catholicity and stood the test of time. There is no reason why they, any more than many more ancient hymns, should fall from use altogether. They include those general hymns on the doctrine of God, the Church and the eucharist that Rattenbury considered under the heading 'hymns of the hinterland'.

Second, there will surely also remain a number of those hymns that speak of Christian faith and life, of the grace of God and the gift of His love, of the longing for a heart fully made new, of the mutual caring of Christian fellowship and of the joys of heaven. Many of these too are also to be found outside Methodist circles, though they are most likely to speak to those who find themselves within that tradition. Whether that circle of users will still be the

Methodist Church in 2095 or some united church that has inherited the gifts that Methodism will have brought, time alone will tell.

I base that judgement not on any forecast of trends in taste for hymnody but on their theological content. They express, and express well, those basic truths that are central to the Christian faith, whether considered as a system of belief or as a personal spiritual experience. To suggest that even these will become unused and unknown is to suggest that Christianity will in decades to come be so transformed as to have no continuity with the present. That I do not believe. I do not hold the formal doctrine of the indefectibility of the Church, but I do believe that God will preserve the faith once delivered to the saints. That surely cannot be a more difficult task for the Almighty in the third millennium than it was in the previous two.

Whether the hymns in either of these groups will remain unmutilated, still in the state in which Charles Wesley left them to us, is a more difficult question. Much will depend on whether the next generation finds a means of accommodation between the legitimate desire for inclusiveness in the language we use for the worship of God and the equally legitimate desire to hear the witnesses of the past speak to us of our common faith in their own words.[21] In any event, the risk that will attend the survival of a limited selection of hymns in public use, such as I am envisaging, is that it will not be the whole register of Charles' theology that our successors will hear but only certain notes within it. That is true for us now, though, as I have tried to show.

The real future for the wider range of these hymns, however, so it seems to me, lies in their private devotional use. For many, that is an important part of their use now. Some are more suitably used in this way in any case: 'When quiet in my house I sit, Thy book be my companion still',[22] 'Open, Lord, my inward ear and bid my heart rejoice',[23] 'Come, O thou traveller unknown'.[24] The demand is likely to grow, though mostly among the reflective classes. Already there is a considerable store of Christian classics available for devotional use, and John Wesley, who published *The Christian Library*, would certainly have recognised and welcomed the phenomenon. There could be a much larger selection, or selections, of Charles' hymns for various purposes. But for that to happen, of course, there needs to be a readily accessible edition of the complete works. Osborn's 13-volume set, published over 100 years ago, is hard to obtain. A modern edition is overdue. It would not of itself meet the need I have in mind, but it would be a stimulus to the anthologist, for the sheer quality of some of the material would demand wider circulation.

The purist will argue that to use hymns solely in private devotion is a frustration of their purpose, for hymns are essentially communal and are designed to be sung. The music is a necessary element in their use. To take them out of the public arena into the privacy of the home or the retreat cell is to emasculate them, though it begs the question how many of the hymns Charles ever expected to be sung. But for the hymns to be sung by a congregation, however small, implies a community of purpose, a shared theology and spirituality, that is difficult to obtain in an increasingly diversified church. I have just said that there will remain a relatively small core of hymns that will continue to serve this purpose, but I do not think that extensive use will ever again be true of whole churches as it was of the Wesleyans in the eighteenth and nineteenth centuries. The most one can hope for, for most of the hymns that have been in use for the last hundred years or so, even for that proportion of them that remain in *Hymns and Psalms* (and a still smaller portion in *Singing the Faith*), is that they will live on in the use of small groups and, largely unsung, in private devotion. Even that, let us remind ourselves, is but a fraction of those our eighteenth-century fore-bears knew, and a smaller proportion still of those Charles actually produced. Indeed, in private devotion, there could be a much more representative selection of the range of Charles' writing than would ever be possible in a selection designed for popular public use.

Perhaps the Wesley brothers themselves would welcome this. As Oliver Beckerlegge points out,[25] John perhaps hinted at it in his 1780 preface when he referred to the new collection as 'a little body of experimental and practical divinity' to be *read*, and Charles might have said there is no reason, after all, why what was written on horseback may not be prayed on one's knees.

Notes

1 Lecture given in Bristol in November 1995 as part of the Charles Wesley Festival and published in the *Epworth Review*, vol. 26, no. 2, 1999, pp. 71–81. Copyright Trustees for Methodist Church Purposes, reprinted by permission.

2 J. Ernest Rattenbury, *The Evangelical Doctrines of Charles Wesley's Hymns* (London: Epworth Press, 1941).

3 J. Ernest Rattenbury, *The Eucharistic Hymns of John and Charles Wesley* (London: Epworth Press, 1948).

4 See also now the introduction to Franz Hildebrandt and Oliver A. Beckerlegge (eds.), *The Works of John Wesley*, vol. 7, *A Collection of Hymns for the Use of the People Called Methodists*, bicentennial edn (Nashville, TN: Abingdon Press, 1989), pp. 1–22.

5 Rattenbury, *The Evangelical Doctrines*, p. 121.

6 S. T. Kimbrough, Jr and Oliver A. Beckerlegge (eds.), *The Unpublished Poetry of Charles Wesley*, 3 vols. (Nashville, TN: Abingdon Press, 1988–92).

7 *Hymns and Psalms: A Methodist and Ecumenical Hymn Book* (London: Methodist Publishing, 1983) (hereafter '*HP*'), 216; *Singing the Faith* (London: Methodist Publishing, 2011) (hereafter '*StF*'), 345; Osborn, vol. 1, p. 105.

8 *HP* 109; *StF* 208; Osborn, vol. 4, pp. 109f.

9 Osborn, vol. 4, pp. 122f., emphasis in original.

10 *HP* 735; compare with *StF* 329; Osborn, vol. 13, p. 221.

11 *HP* 166; Osborn, vol. 3, p. 229; not in *StF*.

12 *The Methodist Hymn Book* (London: Methodist Conference Office, 1933) (hereafter '*MHB*'), 188; Osborn, vol. 4, p. 371.

13 Osborn, vol. 3, p. 216.

14 Osborn, vol. 4, p. 133.

15 *HP* 706; Osborn, vol. 1, p. 93; rewritten in *StF* 454.

16 *MHB* 598; Osborn, vol. 7, p. 46.

17 *MHB* 502; Osborn, vol. 2, p. 197.

18 *HP* 150; Osborn, vol. 4, p. 376.
19 *HP* 400; Osborn, vol. 4, p. 125.
20 *HP* 622; Osborn, vol. 3, p. 313.
21 *Singing the Faith* contains numerous examples of attempts to make the language more inclusive; by no means all are successful.
22 *MHB* 310; Osborn, vol. 9, p. 94.
23 *HP* 540; Osborn, vol. 2, p. 263 – not the first verse.
24 *HP* 434; *StF* 461; Osborn, vol. 2, p. 173.
25 Hildebrandt and Beckerlegge, *The Works of John Wesley*, vol. 7, p. 66.

3 The eucharistic hymns

An appreciation[1]

In 1745 John and Charles Wesley, 'presbyters of the Church of England,' as they described themselves, published in Bristol a book entitled *Hymns on the Lord's Supper*.[2] The book is important, not just as evidence of the strong sacramental quality of the Wesleyan Revival but because so many of the hymns have come into regular use in the churches across ecumenical boundaries. Seven of them find their place in the eucharistic section of the 1983 Methodist book *Hymns and Psalms*, and ten more in other sections.[3]

That most of the hymns, if not all 160 of them, were by Charles Wesley there can be little doubt. The book was prefaced, however, by extracts from a devotional work of a century before by Daniel Brevint, Dean of Lincoln: *The Christian Sacrament and Sacrifice*. Comparing hymns and preface gives an interesting insight into the way Charles worked. One is reminded again and again of the phrases Brevint had used, and can see how the hymn writer's own meditation had built upon them.

But Charles was no mere versifier of other people's thoughts. Over and over one comes to those typical phrases that capture the essence of the Wesleys' understanding of what God is about: 'pardon and holiness and heaven', for example, or – in the duller language of the theologians – justification, sanctification and glory. We have here the distillation of the Wesley brothers' own devotion.

The book was immensely popular in the Wesleys' lifetime. It had run to ten editions by 1792. But the intense devotion of these hymns proved strong meat in the nineteenth century. One reason, no doubt, was the relative infrequency with which the sacrament was celebrated in the Methodist societies, and the general drift, as the century wore on, away from the sacramental emphasis of Methodism's early beginnings, a drift only beginning to be reversed in recent times. Even today many Methodists would find themselves far from home.

Partly the problem is one of language and taste. Frankly, it must be said that some of the hymns could not now be sung. Sensitivities have changed, and I cannot imagine any congregation now coping with

> Come then thou Saviour of mankind,
> Bring back that last tremendous hour,
> And stand in all thy wounds confest,
> And wrap us in thy bloody vest.[4]

In any case, Wesley lived in an age that was able to handle symbolism more easily than our more literal minds can manage. So the thought that occurs more than once, that we rise in the flames or smoke of Christ's sacrifice to heaven, is not an easy one for us.

But, for many, the problem is more than the language or the imagery. Wesley worked, for example, with a substitutionary understanding of the atonement in its fiercest form. The bread, made of wheat, beaten and bruised, speaks of the injury to the Lord's body, and the subsequent baking and charring of the loaf points to the flames of God's wrath that he endured for us.[5] This does not speak easily to our age.

Then there is the sacrificial language:

> With solemn faith we offer up,
> And spread before thy glorious eyes,
> That only ground of all our hope,
> That precious bleeding sacrifice,
> Which brings thy grace on sinners down,
> And perfects all our souls in one.[6]

As early as 1761 that had been given a more general setting in another publication, and even in *Hymns and Psalms* it appears in the section on prayer.[7] For Protestants generally, the Tractarian controversies of the nineteenth century made the eucharistic sacrifice a difficult doctrine to recover.

There is also the fact that, under the influence of the liturgical movement, the emphasis in eucharistic theology has shifted. We now see the whole celebration much more clearly as a corporate act of the people of God, made Christ's Body by receiving his body – though we should note how often Charles differed from Brevint in using 'we' rather than 'I'.

We have moved on too in that we see the eucharist more clearly as the commemoration of the whole of Easter, Christ crucified and risen. We treat more seriously the literal meaning of the word 'eucharist': thanksgiving. The eighteenth century – and, indeed, the nineteenth – still lived under the shadow of the medieval distortion of the eucharist as almost exclusively a commemoration of Maundy Thursday and Good Friday. Yet who can read the hymns in this book and not declare them joyful and full of gratitude?

What, then, is there to say about this book? First, there is its range, and its depth. There is no question that, for Wesley, the eucharist is the supreme act of Christian worship.

> Fasting he doth, and hearing bless,
> And prayer can much avail,
> Good vessels all to draw the grace
> Out of salvation's well.

> But none, like this mysterious rite
> Which dying mercy gave,
> Can draw forth all his promised might
> And all his will to save.[8]

It thus gathers to itself all the central themes of the doctrine of salvation. In the eucharist the love of God, poured out for us on Calvary, is made visible in bread and wine. We stand before the cross and our sins are taken away. In receiving the bread and wine we receive Christ and are nourished by him. We offer up the only sacrifice we can offer, Christ himself, already offered for us, and in his offering he takes up ours. Past, present and future are joined and heaven is already experienced. So, all the moods are expressed: penitence, submission, dedication, gratitude, hope, joy. This is no narrow, tunnel-vision view of what the eucharist means but a complex interweaving of many strands.

And yet, if there is perhaps one dominant note struck throughout, it is the note of presence:

> Jesus, we thus obey
> Thy last and kindest word;
> Here in thine own appointed way,
> We come to meet our Lord.
>
> Our hearts we open wide,
> To make the Saviour room;
> And lo! The Lamb, the Crucified,
> The sinner's Friend, is come![9]

For this is no mere memorial, no mere remembrance of a past event. It is a living encounter through the Holy Spirit with Christ crucified and risen:

> Ye faithful souls, who thus record
> The passion of that Lamb Divine,
> Is the memorial of your Lord
> A useless form, and empty sign?
> Or doth he here his life impart?
> What saith the witness in your heart?[10]

And so it is truly a feast:

> O what a soul-transforming feast
> Doth this communion yield!
> Remembering here thy passion past,
> We with thy love are fill'd.[11]

Or:

> We need not now go up to heaven,
> To bring the long-sought Saviour down;
> Thou art to all already given,
> Thou dost even now thy banquet crown:
> To every faithful soul appear,
> And show thy real presence here![12]

How that comes about is a mystery, but we know it to be true:

> O the depth of love divine,
> Th' unfathomable grace!
> Who shall say how bread and wine
> God into man conveys!
> *How* the bread his flesh imparts,
> *How* the wine transmits his blood,
> Fills his faithful people's hearts
> With all the life of God!
> [...]
>
> Ask the Father's Wisdom *how*;
> Him that did the means ordain!
> Angels round our altars bow
> To search it out in vain.
>
> Sure and real is the grace,
> The manner be unknown;
> Only meet us in thy ways,
> And perfect us in one.
> Let us taste the heavenly powers;
> Lord, we ask for nothing more:
> Thine to bless, 'tis only ours
> To wonder and adore.[13]

Second, I draw attention to the book's basic idea: the use of hymns for eucharistic devotion. It is significant that Wesley turned a book of private meditation into a volume of hymns to be sung. It is too crude to say there were so many people at the celebrations the Wesleys held in their heyday that they had to be given something to do while people were communicating. What they were given was a book of devotions for the illiterate: theology they could learn by heart; theology they could meditate on and celebrate together; words that would tell abroad, as the Great Thanksgiving tells abroad, the meaning of the event; words that would turn a time of waiting into prayer. How many communicants today, I wonder, come to receive bread and wine so prepared, or return to their places to hold in their minds the meaning of what they have done?

Yet, to put it like that lays all the stress on thinking and understanding. It is an ancient tradition of the Church to sing the liturgy, and the essential thing about the hymns is that they are *sung*. If the words strike a chord within us when they are read or heard, evoke our 'Amen', uplifting our hearts in a moment of speech, the music prolongs the response. Singing is the sostenuto of praise.

So gratitude is due, not just for the book and its contents but, in the communion of the saints, for the one who wrote it. These hymns are full of anticipation of the joys of heaven. There is a characteristic touch at the end of one of the hymns that transforms a conventional reference to our joining the church above into a celebration of friendship broken and renewed – that fellowship that was, for the early Methodists, the experienced reality of the church of Christ:

> Lo, on thy bloody sacrifice
> For all our graces we depend;
> Supported by thy cross arise,
> To finish'd holiness ascend,
> And gain on earth the mountain's height,
> And then salute our friends in light.[14]

Among those friends is the one who in the offering of his own poetic gifts exemplified his own words:

> Take my soul and body's powers,
> Take my memory, mind, and will,
> All my goods, and all my hours,
> All I know and all I feel,
> All I think, and speak, and do;
> Take my heart – but make it new.[15]

A gift the Lord accepted and returned to us for our benefit.

But, last, we come to the heart of things. The 1745 edition of *Hymns on the Lord's Supper* carried a text on the title page; it was a common custom. In this case, the text was 'Do this in remembrance of me'.

The hymns are full of feeling: such wonder at the undeserved grace of God given us in the self-giving of his Son should surely move us to wonder and joy. All the things that the eucharist stands for – judgement, atonement, grace, forgiveness, presence, gift and promise – are *felt*.

> The tokens of thy dying love
> O let us all receive,
> And feel thy quickening Spirit move,
> And *sensibly* believe.[16]

But what if there is no feeling, no awakened perception? What if the sacrament leaves us unmoved and cold – a complaint voiced then as often as it is now?
   No matter.

> And shall I let him go?
> If now I do not feel
> The streams of living water flow,
> Shall I forsake the well?

The answer is clear:

> Because he saith, *Do this,*
> This will I always do;
> Till Jesus comes in glorious bliss,
> I *thus* his death will show.[17]

And always there is the prayer

> Come Holy Ghost, thine influence shed
> And realise the sign;
> Thy life infuse into the bread,
> Thy power into the wine.[18]

'Do this in remembrance of me.' It is an invitation:

> He bids us drink and eat
> Imperishable food,
> He gives his flesh to be our meat,
> And bids us drink his blood:
> What'er th' Almighty can
> To pardon'd sinners give,
> The fulness of our God made man
> We here with Christ receive.[19]

Notes

1 Originally given as an address in Bristol Cathedral on 18 June 1995 to mark the 250th anniversary of the publication of *Hymns on the Lord's Supper*, and published in the *Epworth Review*, vol. 24, no. 2, 1997, pp. 12–17, under the title 'A Sermon for Charles'. Copyright Trustees for Methodist Church Purposes, reprinted by permission.

2 See Osborn, vol. 3, pp. 181ff.; and Rattenbury, *The Eucharistic Hymns* (hereafter 'Rattenbury').

3 In *Singing the Faith*, its 2011 successor, the numbers are four and two, respectively.

4 Rattenbury, no. 25.
5 Rattenbury, no. 2.
6 Rattenbury, no. 125.
7 It is omitted altogether from *Singing the Faith*.
8 Rattenbury, no. 42.
9 Rattenbury, no. 81.
10 Rattenbury, no. 89.
11 Rattenbury, no. 94.
12 Rattenbury, no. 116.
13 Rattenbury, no. 57.
14 Rattenbury, no. 52.
15 Rattenbury, no. 155.
16 Rattenbury, no. 30.
17 Rattenbury, no. 86.
18 Rattenbury, no. 72.
19 Rattenbury, no. 81.

4 Reflections on Methodism after Wesley[1]

There are two reasons, apart from general fascination, for looking at the age after Wesley. In spite of the renewed interest in John and Charles Wesley in recent decades it is impossible to understand contemporary British Methodism simply by reference to their legacy; one also has to take account of the way the movement evolved after them and the legacy that evolution has left. Moreover, the issues with which those early Methodists were grappling remain contemporary; they are issues that all the churches, not just Methodism, still have to confront, which is why this chapter offers reflections and questions but no answers.

There is no space here for a full historical survey of the nineteenth century, but we do need some background. The Methodist story is set in the context of massive forces for change in British society: the challenge to the old order; the pressure for political reform and democratic government; the social dislocation involved in the Industrial Revolution and the growth of the cities and city slums; in the early part of the century the military threat of France and the spectre of a French-style revolution; in the later decades growing prosperity and the consolidation of the British Empire; running through the years the thread of social reform movements – the abolition of slavery, the gradual improvement of conditions in the prisons and in working conditions, especially for women and children; improvements in education and in public health; and towards the end of the century the movement for women's suffrage. We also have to remember the considerable civil disabilities that Christian communities outside the Established Church suffered, at least until the 1870s, the suspicion with which they were often regarded and the unofficial discrimination they often experienced. On the ecclesiastical scene we have to take account of the considerable change in the landscape brought about by the Tractarian Movement and the gradual erosion of confidence in received theological ideas caused by scientific discovery. All that would be a challenge for any community, even if they were superbly equipped to deal with it. Through no fault of their own, the Methodists were not.

The Methodist story in the nineteenth century can be characterised as one of expansion in the first half and contraction in the second. That is true simply of numbers. The growth in the movement overall was very impressive, from around 95,000 in 1800 to over half a million by 1860, but thereafter, although numbers continued to increase, they did not keep pace with population growth, so that in effect the movement was contracting. More dramatic, however, were the schisms. In the 60 years after Wesley's death the core body, the Wesleyans, who were the legal successors to his movement, saw six major secessions and other smaller ones, the last costing the Wesleyans something like a third of their membership. Then, roughly from 1850 onwards, there began a gradual process of reintegration, culminating in the reunions of 1907, to create the United Methodist Church alongside the Wesleyan and Primitive Methodists, and of 1932, leading to the Methodist Church as it is today. Even now, two bodies, the Independent Methodists and the Wesleyan Reform Union, remain separate. Those divisions have left their legacy in contemporary Methodism, not so much because there are people still alive who remember the pre-1932 churches but because, in local churches, the emphases and convictions of those earlier days are handed on from generation to generation, and ministers and lay preachers brought up in those congregations imbibe them and spread them more widely.

John Wesley's death in 1791 left his successors with a number of problems; indeed, by dying he let the cork out of a bottle that had been fermenting for some decades. Underlying them was the rising prosperity and social aspirations of a proportion of Methodists. Three problems came to a head very quickly: what was to be the relationship to the Established Church; what was to be the status of the predominantly lay body of travelling preachers; and who was to control the Methodist movement? Entangled in these was the question: who is to preside over the sacrament of Holy Communion? But these questions were quickly joined by others. Rather than going chronologically through the controversies, however, it will be more useful to try to identify some of the issues that they raise. There are six, each pointing to a tension.

Movement and Church

I have used the word 'movement' of the early Methodists so far, because that is clearly how it began: as a clerically led lay movement for personal piety and reform of life within the Established Church. To the end of their lives John Wesley and, still more vehemently, his brother Charles resisted notions of separation. But it has to be said that, because he consciously placed the imperative to proclaim the gospel above church rules, John took a series of steps that made separation inevitable, such as creating a network of local groups and travelling preachers under his personal pastoral supervision, and, by 1784, claiming the right to ordain. Increasingly the movement took on the trappings of church, though it resisted the name. Chapels were built, organisation was formalised, Holy Communion was celebrated. Not all Methodists welcomed all the changes. Through to the 1850s some Wesleyans attended their parish church in addition to the Methodist meetings, and still preferred to be married in church. To this day Methodism retains some of the features of a movement, such as a recorded membership and the annual issue of a membership ticket.

But gradually the Wesleyans and the other Methodist bodies came to think of themselves as churches. The growth of the Tractarian Movement accelerated the process; it was too much for Methodism's inherited Protestantism to digest, and it sharpened attitudes on both sides of the Anglican–Methodist divide. By the end of the nineteenth century Methodism as a whole was firmly in the Free Church camp.

The advantage of a movement is its flexibility. It is not in the same way tied to buildings; it can adapt to changing circumstances; it need not be encumbered by elaborate organisation; it can avoid high overhead costs; it can set more stringent membership criteria; it does not have to be tied by tradition – indeed, its tradition may precisely be to be adaptable. There is no doubt that, in evolving from movement to church, Methodism lost something; each of the nineteenth-century secessions were due in part to the failure of the Wesleyans to adapt. On the other hand, all movements that manage to survive do so in part because they develop sustaining structures.

Today it is sometimes suggested that the path to recovered Christian unity points to Methodism once again becoming a movement within an encompassing church. I have yet to be convinced. Methodism has come too far down the road to being a church to revert to being a movement. It would imply loss of recognition of ecclesial status.

But all churches in Britain are looking for ways to become a movement again. We ask for fresh expressions of being church. We suggest that the inherited pattern of formal buildings and Sunday worship need not be invariable, and may even be a hindrance to the church's mission. How does such experimental flexibility mesh with inherited church structures? Will any of the churches succeed in owning such movement-like developments, or will they too in the end lead to further divisions?

Outreach and open doors

John Wesley's movement took off with the open-air preaching that he began in 1739. Throughout his life he issued calls for the practice to continue. The fact that he felt the need to do so in itself suggests that the other aspect of his work, the gathering and sustaining of converts in small groups, increasingly took precedence. As the movement grew in numbers it was inevitable that more and more of the preachers' time would be taken up in nurturing the membership. The trend continued throughout the nineteenth century – not that the Wesleyans lost their emphasis on evangelism and conversion, but the expectation increasingly was that it could be effected indoors, as people were attracted, especially in the towns, to ever larger and more prestigious buildings. Even in the countryside the work seems to have progressed by gathering people in cottages and barns rather than by going into the fields.

In the ten years 1810 to 1820 two similar movements, one in the potteries of Staffordshire and the other in Devon and Cornwall, independently arose in protest against this domestication of the work, both re-emphasising open-air preaching. Neither set out to be a breakaway movement, but both flourished the more the Wesleyan Conference, fearful that the authorities would regard them as seditious, tried to suppress them. The two movements separated from the Wesleyans as the Primitive Methodists and the Bible Christians. They grew at a rapid rate, and spread to other parts of the country. They had other features in common. Both were grass-roots movements, not officially sponsored, and both appealed to orders of society that the Wesleyans were no longer particularly reaching: farm labourers, tin miners, journeymen cobblers, potters and carpenters. Both were further removed from the Established Church that the Wesleyans were still to some extent cultivating. In both the emphasis was on revivalist preaching and singing, and, not surprisingly, since so many would be barely literate, the use of any kind of liturgical book was regarded as a sign of the absence of the Holy Spirit.

Sociologists will not be surprised that, as the decades passed, both Primitive Methodists and Bible Christians became more middle class and institutionalised, eventually thinking of themselves as national churches. Some of the late nineteenth-century gothic chapels the Primitive Methodists put up, especially in the north-west, rival anything produced by the Church of England. But they never lost, either in folk memory or to some extent in practice, the outreach emphasis of their early days.

It was not until the 1880s that the Wesleyans themselves began to break the mould in what was known as the Forward Movement. Especially under the leadership of Hugh Price Hughes the Wesleyans developed a new form of outreach, based on central halls, large, seemingly secular buildings that in more modern times we would call 'dual-purpose', combined with practical social work, soup kitchens, clinics and the like. Open-air preaching was revived, and the central halls themselves were sometimes referred to as 'open-air meetings with the roof on'. A typical Sunday pattern would be a devotional service for the faithful in the morning, Sunday school in the afternoon and a large meeting in the evening, with the emphasis on popular hymns and evangelical preaching.

The story illustrates a continuing tension in church life. Does the church exist to nourish the faithful or to attract the faith-less? Is worship to sustain faith and understanding at a deep level, or to be readily accessible to those who happen to come in from outside? Arguments about Bach and Charles Wesley versus Graham Kendrick and Betty Pulkingham or the Authorised Version versus the Good News Bible illustrate the point. And what about those who come in from outside? I guess most churches open their doors on Sunday and prepare to welcome visitors. Few receive them, except as migrants from other congregations. An open-door policy by itself will not lead to church growth. How is the church today to reach those outside its doors, effectively excluded by cultural difference and sheer unfamiliarity?

It is an ironic footnote to this section to observe that another breakaway Methodist group, the New Connexion, in 1865 experienced its own secession because of its resistance to experiments in reaching the unchurched poor, when William Booth left it to form what became the Salvation Army.

Piety and social engagement

I have already touched on the this. John Wesley is notable, especially in his later years, for his published comments on a number of social evils, his criticism of accumulated wealth and his support of the anti-slavery movement. The Wesleyans who succeeded him were less outspoken. Some individuals played a committed, if not too prominent, part in the anti-slavery movement, and most of the Tolpuddle Martyrs were Wesleyans. But on the whole they were silent on the emerging social issues of the day. They had little to say about working conditions in the mines, factories or prisons. When they engaged with government on educational issues it was largely to protect their own turf, such as resisting concessions to Roman Catholics over the version of the Bible to be used in religious instruction, rather than to address the wider educational needs of the day. The travelling preachers were forbidden to engage in political comment. Not until the 1880s did the Wesleyans really begin to be heard on the theme of social justice and political issues generally, High Price Hughes again taking the lead. The Primitive Methodists were less inhibited, and became involved in support for the Liberal Party, and later for Labour, and many Primitive Methodists withheld the educational component in the rates in protest at the 1902 Education Act – though that, again, is later on.

For the Wesleyans, I think the reluctance was twofold. There was the pietistic conviction that the world's business should be left to others, and that the purpose of Methodism was to nurture souls in faith and personal holiness. But there was also, especially at the beginning of the nineteenth century, the desire to keep their heads down. They were desperate not to be seen as agitators. The danger was real. In 1811 Lord Sidmouth introduced a Bill in the House of Lords that would have required all those licensed as dissenting preachers or teachers to be certified as ministers of a particular congregation and vouched for by persons of substance. It was aimed at suppressing what Sidmouth perceived to be the danger of uneducated wandering political agitators, but it would have destroyed at a stroke the entire Methodist system of circuits and itinerant preachers. By dint of massive protest, not only from Wesleyans, the Bill was quietly dropped. The early Methodists were vulnerable. The social engagement that came in the 1880s rode on the back of numerical and financial strength and social acceptance.

The issues are still with us, in Methodism as in other churches. How far should the church go out on a limb in the name of social protest? Its voice is welcome in support of the state, less welcome in criticism. Churches need to be more aware than they sometimes are that overmuch engagement in political matters could put their charitable status at risk, with disastrous financial consequences. That spectre was raised in the 1980s over support for the World Council of Churches' Programme to Combat Racism. Should the church confine its interventions to those matters that affect its own life – Sunday trading and Sunday parking fees, for instance? How far *can* the churches go out on a limb and still carry their members, of diverse political allegiances, with them?

There will always be those who say that politics and religion don't mix, and, opposing them, those who want to turn the church into a single-issue campaigning group on whatever happens to be the cause of the moment.

Centrality and locality

So far I have directly described only two of the secessions from the Wesleyan body and some of the reasons for them. Some of the others – the United Methodist Free Churches; the Wesleyan Reformers; and the earliest of them, the still existing Independent Methodists – were formed, in part at least, around the conviction that in terms of the locus of church government the Wesleyans had got it wrong.

In the eighteenth century, partly because of John Wesley's own authoritarian character, partly because – objectively speaking – the movement would not have survived without it, the national movement was centrally governed, by Wesley himself, through the mouthpiece of the Conference, which was (in his eyes at least) purely consultative. At his death that government legally passed, by virtue of a deed poll drawn up in 1784, to the Conference. More about its composition later. The first thing to note is that technically it exercised total control over the Methodist movement through the travelling preachers (increasingly referred to as ministers) as its agents.

In practice, though, the situation was more complex. In each local Methodist society there was a small group of lay leaders, and they often had very clear views about the way local affairs should be handled. Those views might not coincide with the views of the Conference and its ministerial representatives. Also, for each chapel building – not every society, of course, had a building in the early days – there was a group of trustees, often different people from the leaders, and often from a more prosperous class of person. They too had ideas about how things should be handled. A classic issue from the 1790s was whether Holy Communion should be celebrated in the Methodist chapel – and, if so, by an unordained Methodist preacher – or only at the parish church. Many saw it, rightly, as a further step towards separation from the Established Church. The Conference settled that by a compromise, but also at the price of a secession, the New Connexion. A notorious case arose in Leeds in 1827 when the trustees wished to install an organ in the new Brunswick Chapel and the leaders objected; the case went to the Conference, which, in defiance of its own rules, supported the trustees. Another secession followed.

The issue confronting them was: who has final authority in a local church? Is it the local church itself, or some wider, more comprehensive body? If so, is that the circuit, the network of geographically associated local churches or a wider network of all the circuits in a district – say, Yorkshire? Or is it the Conference itself? Many of the breakaway groups opted for the local church or circuit. The Primitive Methodists opted in the early days primarily for the district.

There were many pressures in this debate. This was an age of ferment over democratic rights. Should not democratic rights also be exercised in the church? How qualified is a remote central body to judge the particularities of a local situation? Today we would debate the question in terms of devolution or subsidiarity. There is the fact that all churches are, in the final analysis, voluntary associations, and there are limits to the compulsion that can be exercised upon them. But there is also a fundamental ecclesiological issue, not just for Methodists. I think it is the most intractable ecumenical question of all: to what extent does ultimate authority under God in the church lie with the local congregation, and to what extent with some wider (or, if you prefer, higher) authority? Most denominations come to some practical answer to this question; most local congregations, of whatever denomination, belong to a wider network, be it a diocese, a district association, a Conference or an Assembly. But that sometimes evades the issue of principle. When a congregation belongs to a wider body, is that body purely advisory or does it exercise authority, and, if so, does it do so because that authority has been voluntarily ceded to it by the local churches represented in it, or does it exercise authority in its own right? A diocese, like a Conference or presbytery, exercises authority in its own right; in the case of the Baptist Union or the Congregational Federation, authority is ceded by the local church. I see no theoretical bridge between those two alternatives.

Clericalism and lay ownership

Allied to the above issue is the composition of the central Wesleyan Conference. John Wesley of course kept a clear distinction in his mind between ordained and unordained, even if the Church of England would not have agreed with him about where to draw the line, for some of his preachers he had ordained himself. In his eyes, however, most of his preachers were laymen. In the years after his death the preachers themselves, for the sake of equality among themselves, chose to ignore the distinction. To put it crudely, they talked of themselves as laymen and behaved as if they were ordained. That inevitably generated tensions within the movement as a whole, in which many members began to see the preachers as fellow laymen who were giving themselves airs. Already by 1797 the Methodist New Connexion had been formed, partly on the basis of complete separation from the Established Church, but partly also on the basis that government in the Conference should be equally shared between the travelling preachers and other lay members of the movement representing the local churches. Other Methodist bodies later tackled the same question. All included rank and file elected members in their governing Conference as well as travelling preachers – two members to one preacher in the case of the Primitive Methodists.

But the Wesleyans went the other way. By the 1820s they had developed the doctrine of the Pastoral Office. As they read the Scriptures, those called to shepherd the flock of Christ were called to preach, to teach *and to rule*, and these responsibilities were exclusively theirs. So the Conference remained stubbornly clerical, not just because it is always more congenial to cling on to power than to let it go but because they believed authority was entrusted to them by God.

To concede would have been disobedience. This more than any other factor accounted for the secessions of the nineteenth century. Travelling about the country as they did, but never staying in one place for more than two years, or three at the outside, the travelling preachers gained a superficial knowledge of the whole movement, but at a deeper level were often out of touch, and by their authoritarian attitudes often did more harm than good. It was not until 1878 that lay representatives were admitted as members of the Wesleyan Conference.

The nature and authority of ordained ministry remains a live debate in contemporary Methodism. In it one may discern not only Wesleyan voices echoing down the years but also voices from the other traditions that united in 1932. To what are presbyters ordained, and how far is their ministry exclusive? There are those for whom, as in 1791, it is a matter of principle and a bulwark against clericalism and sacerdotalism that suitable lay persons should preside at Holy Communion. Others as fiercely hold the opposite view. People would generally concede to ordained ministers a voice in the counsels of the church, but on what grounds? On grounds of pastoral experience accumulated over years? Wider knowledge of the church gained through a succession of different appointments? Theological education and knowledge of the tradition? Or by divine right? Does ordination itself impart to the one ordained a voice and vote in the church's affairs? If so, is that an exclusive right? If not, what weight does that voice carry alongside others? Other churches may debate these questions in terms of the authority of bishops. All traditions have practical arrangements for allowing different voices, lay and ordained, to be heard in debate, but Methodism differs on the authority accorded to such voices and on the theological question involved; and, while Methodism strives to present to the world a coherent statement of its position, it would be a bold Methodist who claimed that all Methodists see things the same way.

Church and society

My last reflection is a comment on the pressures I have already mentioned. Just before this chapter was written, in 2007, the world heard the news of the terrible massacre of children in an Amish school in the United States. They are a community that has tried to resist social change and remain encapsulated within societal practices that once were virtually universal. It is not easy to do, and there come moments when the wider society, which has moved on and left them behind, breaks in upon them, whether in the form of modern weapons of destruction or of helicopters and medical facilities coming to the rescue.

The nineteenth century was a period of massive social change, and none of the Methodist bodies I have mentioned kept pace with it. Some deliberately turned back to a perceived golden age. The Primitive Methodists chose their name in echo of John Wesley's plea in the last year of his life for Methodism to return to the simplicity of its earliest days. All the Methodist branches hung on for as long as they could to pre-Darwinian attitudes to the Bible. It is said that the biblical scholar Arthur Samuel Peake single-handedly saved Primitive

Methodism from fundamentalism in the period before the First World War. In 1933 the newly united churches produced a new hymn book, which has been rightly criticised in a recent study as backward-looking, containing virtually no contemporary hymns.[2]

But the lesson of nineteenth-century Methodism is that contemporary voices cannot be shut out of the church. The call for democracy, and later the call for women's participation (and eventually for women's ordination), clamoured to be heard. Willy-nilly, surrounding culture influences church thinking and practice. The Wesleyans up to 1850 saw that as a bad thing, unaware that they were themselves perpetuating the paternalistic attitudes of a previous age. How far is the voice of society around us the voice of the world, in the Johannine sense, and how far is it the voice of God? Clearly, the church must in some respects differ from contemporary society if it is to have any identity at all. But at no stage in its existence, not even in New Testament times, has the church been entirely free from the influence of the surrounding culture. Early worship was modelled, among other things, on the synagogue. After Constantine, church government reflected imperial patterns, and so on. The supreme task of the church, perhaps, if it is to be true to its calling, is to evaluate the voices and discern the spirits. We know in our own day, with our current theological and ethical dilemmas, how difficult this can be. It may make us a little more sympathetic towards the successors of John Wesley.

Notes

1 These reflections on the story of Methodism were first shared with an informal ecumenical discussion group, and later printed in the *Epworth Review*, vol. 34, no. 2, 2007, pp. 6–16.

2 Andrew Pratt, *O for a Thousand Tongues: The 1933 Methodist Hymn Book in Context* (London: Epworth Press, 2004).

5   Reflections on connexionalism[1]

'Connexion' and 'connexionalism' are words that trip so lightly off Methodist tongues that we rarely give them much thought. Yet they are distinctive of our language about ourselves, and it is at least worth asking what ecclesiological convictions lie behind them.

Surprisingly, the question does not seem to have been often considered in recent times.[2] The 1937 Conference Statement on the Nature of the Church, for example, failed to refer to it.[3] Apparently, something so fundamental to our practice was judged to have no implications for our theology. Now may be a good time to take it up.[4]

It is no simple matter from within the system even to list the constitutive features of a connexional church. From the local perspective the most obvious are surely the circuit (shared ministers, invited and supported by the circuit; local preachers; the preaching plan; the assessment; the superintendent), in property matters 'Manchester', and, with reference to membership, the fact that it is transferable, never purely local. For the presbyters, the key items will be stationing, itinerancy, the presbyteral synod and their presbyteral identity 'in full connexion'. With all this there is the central authority of the Conference and the all-pervading Standing Orders.

There are other things, of course: connexional grants, a flood of literature, 'our' hymn book and service book, committees and synods, and the Divisions,[5] but these could be the fruit of a looser association. The list, interestingly, would be a little different across the Atlantic (no circuits, but bishops and several tiers of conferences). Just as important as the identifiable items, however, are the intangibles, the genes (or perhaps viruses?) in our make-up, which determine distinctive responses in particular circumstances, particularly our tendency – sometimes resented, sometimes welcomed, sometimes used as an excuse – to think in terms of central authority. These things others may see more clearly than we do ourselves. Is such connexionalism a concept of ecclesiological importance, or a relic of our past, as archaic in its meaning for the twenty-first century as in its spelling?

The eighteenth century

Historically, the word is not peculiar to Methodism. In the eighteenth century it was a term in general use to refer both to the circle of those connected to some person or group or to the relationship itself. It could be employed in political and commercial as well as religious contexts. In the religious sphere it was used, not only by Wesley and his associates but by other leaders of the Evangelical Revival, such as Howell Harris and the Countess of Huntingdon, and its specific connotations depended on the forms of the associations they developed. But it was the particular character of the connexion Wesley maintained with his societies and preachers that gave the term the technical significance it has come to have, earning it a special entry in the *Oxford English Dictionary*.[6] 'In connexion with us' naturally became 'our connexion', and eventually 'the connexion', leading to the abstract noun 'connexionalism'.

In Wesley's usage the term primarily has three applications: to members, societies and preachers. All are connected to or in connexion with him. His view of it was clearly, if somewhat disingenuously, set out in the 'Minutes' of 1766. After describing how people took the initiative in asking to join him, first as members of society and later as preachers, he explains the power he exercises over them:

> It is a power of admitting into and excluding from the Societies under my care; of choosing and removing Stewards; of receiving or not receiving Helpers; of appointing them when, where and how to help me; and of desiring any of them to meet me, when I see good.[7]

There are secondary applications. Through their connexion with Wesley, the preachers are connected with each other. So, similarly, are the societies. Indeed, their unity is all-important. 'I have only one thing in view, to keep all the Methodists in Great Britain one connected people.' 'The Methodists are one people in all the world; and…it is their full determination so to continue.'[8] But there is no question that, while he lives, Wesley is the linchpin that holds them together. Addressing the 'Travelling Preachers in our Connexion' in 1769 he writes:

> You are at present one body. You act in concert with each other, and by united counsels. And now is the time to consider what can be done in order to continue this union. Indeed, as long as I live, there will be no great difficulty: I am, under God, a centre of union to all our Travelling as well as Local Preachers. They all know me and my communication. They all love me for my work's sake: and, therefore, were it only out of regard to me, they will continue connected with each other. But by what means may this connexion be preserved when God removes me from you?[9]

The bonds that give substance to this connectedness are manifold. All societies, their constituent bands and classes, and their leaders and stewards are furnished with the same rules. They are subject to the same discipline as to personal godliness and the quest for perfection. Members can be transferred from one society to another. The preachers similarly are held under obedience to Wesley and act in his name in the discipline of the societies. They are furnished with their own rules, and answerable to him for faith, personal behaviour, doctrine and the conduct of their ministry. By having their station changed each year they travel widely among the societies and help to give them a sense of belonging to a single family. As time goes on other factors enter into the picture, such as Wesley's publications and the hymns. Central funds are raised, for the general debt on the chapels, for Kingswood School and to assist the preachers. All is under the supervision of the annual Conference of the preachers, which meets to consider points of doctrine and discipline, receive reports of the societies and station the preachers. Wesley regarded the Conference as advisory (so that the connexion is with him, not, at this stage, with the Conference), though not all the preachers saw it in quite the same terms.

It is possible to chronicle the significant steps in the development of the system from 1739 to 1791, by which time all the basic ingredients were in place, but they were created in response to need. There was no grand plan at the outset; as later writers were fond of pointing out, unlike some other denominations Methodism did not come into existence to bear witness to any principle of ecclesiastical polity. Like Topsy, the connexion just grew.

Yet convictions about the nature of the church underlie the system and were influential in giving it its distinctive shape. Wesley's views about the church changed over the years and were never fully coherent, and assessment is complicated by this and by the gradual process by which the Methodist societies came to be, and to recognise themselves as, a separate church.[10] The whole movement is motivated by three convictions about the gospel, however: Christ died for all; all are called to a life of holy love; and there is no such thing as solitary religion. They had immediate implications for the life of the church. Whatever else might be said about its purpose, it exists to proclaim universal redemption, to nurture growth in holiness and to provide for every seeker after salvation to be joined to others in fellowship. It was the failure of the churches, established and non-conformist alike, to fulfil this God-given programme that was believed to demand and justify the Methodist preachers and societies.[11]

These convictions explain, for example, the tenacity with which Wesley and his successors on both sides of the Atlantic held on to the idea of ministerial itinerancy. If the preachers cease to travel and become associated with particular congregations, they will become absorbed in pastoral care and the nationwide mission will cease, for there will be none to go to new areas. Localised ministers may become prey to the prejudices of local leaders so that preacher and congregation alike go astray doctrinally or lose their original fervour.[12] What actually happened to societies that left Wesley's connexion, and the subsequent story of some of the other eighteenth-century connexions, show that these fears had some justification.

These convictions explain too the tight discipline and the role of the conference. Only central authority, it was believed, along with the itinerancy, can guard against the doctrinal dangers of latitudinarianism, Calvinism or antinomianism, or the spiritual dangers of growing cold. Only the constant watchfulness of preachers and local leaders could ensure that all the members of the societies press on to perfection.

They also explain the other institutional features: the model deed, to ensure that chapels are retained in service for their original purpose; the Deed of Declaration, setting up the Legal Conference for Britain and Ireland; and the ordinations for America, providing in both cases for the continuance of the work after Wesley's death.

Later developments

The system created by Wesley has survived to a surprising degree. At his death the authority passed to the Conference, technically the Legal Hundred, in practice a wider body. This now became fully the focus for ministerial loyalty and exercised the powers of admission, appointment and discipline. It was, similarly, the focus for the societies collectively, and for members individually, each of whom had the right (after 1835) of appeal to the Conference on a disciplinary matter. With Wesley removed from the scene, however, there tended to be more emphasis than before on the connexion as a system of mutual support by which the societies are related to each other. It was not just because it was so frequently disrupted by dispute that great stress was placed upon the unity of 'the body'. Richard Watson may be quoted in illustration:

> The religious body to which we belong is a Connexion; that is, a number of societies who have agreed to unite themselves in a common bond of doctrine and discipline, under a common code of regulations and usages, and under a common government... Our very union implies the submission of each society to the influence and opinion of the whole, to the Rules agreed upon...and to those authorities which...are appointed to maintain that Christian 'order' in which we have placed ourselves.[13]

There were repeated constitutional battles in the nineteenth century over the exclusively ministerial character of the Wesleyan Conference, and to a lesser extent the question of devolution of power to districts and circuits; but all branches retained some form of connexionalism, stronger or weaker according to one's point of view. Union in 1932 brought together features of all the branches, but with certain important exceptions it is the Wesleyan tradition that has prevailed. At the same time, in significant ways, the heartbeat has changed, particularly in the twentieth century, as the traditional tight spiritual discipline has given way to broader and more varied understandings of spirituality, and a greater openness to all comers, with 'church' gradually replacing 'society' in our self-understanding. All this underlines the need to consider what connexionalism might still mean.

The British pattern has reproduced itself in many parts of the world, the main variant being the institution of an executive presidency in many other conferences, sometimes with a form of episcopacy. In important respects, although it retains a strong emphasis on the connexional principle, the American pattern is different. The basic unit is the annual conference for each area, with which the ministers of that area are in connexion. The primary legislative authority, however, rests, by delegation from the annual conferences, in the four-yearly General Conference, of which alone the term 'connexional' tends to be used. The General Conference, moreover, embraces central conferences in countries outside the United States, which have agreed to a constitutional link in situations in which the British Conference would have granted autonomy. In addition, the United Methodist Church has retained a threefold ministry, and the bishops, though subject to the authority of the General Conference and each assigned to a particular jurisdiction, exercise collectively a general superintendency over the whole connexion.

Rationale

During the nineteenth century there was some reflection on the nature of connexionalism, particularly among the Wesleyans. Most of it took place in the context of controversy, provoked by internal disputes about the authority of the Conference and, externally, by the need to give an account of Methodism to the rest of the Christian world. Systematic treatises on the nature of the church tended to have somewhat less to say about it.[14] Because of the pressures involved, most attention was given to episcopal claims for a threefold ministry, legal establishment, the authority of pastors in the church and the case for congregational independency. In general, the conclusion was that for Wesleyans connexionalism was a distinct form of polity, nearest to presbyterianism, but as distinct from it as from episcopacy or independency. The New Connexion, on the other hand, saw itself more clearly as presbyterian (admitting lay elders to the government of the church) with a congregational element at local level. It is instructive to try to sift out the theological arguments, as distinct from practical advantages, that tended to be advanced in favour of a connexional form of polity.

Scripture

The most straightforward line was simply to argue that the principle of congregational independency lacked scriptural support. Since congregationalism appealed for support to scripture as decisive for polity, it was fair to point out biblical evidence on the other side. It was not felt necessary, however, to look for the same level of detailed scriptural evidence to support connexionalism.

No detailed plan of church government is laid down in the New Testament, and Methodism did not come into existence as a matter of conscience on an issue of polity. All that was needed, therefore, was to show that the connexional principle did not conflict with scripture. That was not difficult to do. Indeed, some Wesleyan writers managed to argue that most of the features of their system were consonant with the Bible.[15]

Nevertheless, many of the presentations of this argument are surprisingly offhand, considering the tenacity with which the central authority of the Conference was being defended in the period. Often they amount to little more than a *nihil obstat*. The societies form a voluntary union. The obligations upon them derive not from scriptural warrant so much as from the fact that, having chosen to accept a given system, they ought subsequently to abide by it. Thomas Jackson gives the flavour:

> There is nothing in the New Testament that forbids distinct churches or societies to unite with others in even the closest alliance, especially if, by this unity, they can for themselves secure important religious advantages, and acquire a greater power to benefit and bless the world.[16]

Pragmatism, one might think, rather than principle.

Itinerancy

There were more positive arguments, however. One related to ministerial itinerancy. As in Wesley's day it is stressed that the call to mission can be fulfilled only if the church has the capacity to expand into new areas. The congregational principle of the 'gathered church' is seen to militate against this. A minister cannot fulfil his calling to preach to the unconverted if he is tied to the care of a particular congregation. Feeling ran very deep on this matter. Ministers must function where there is no congregation as yet, or where the congregation is too weak or too poor to support them.

But itinerancy has to be organised. The preachers must be stationed where they can be most effective. Strong churches must be enabled to help the weak in poorer (urban and rural) areas. All this presupposes that ministers and congregations alike accept allegiance to a superior body that is responsible for such oversight. It is admitted that independent churches may form associations to promote mission at home and abroad – as, indeed, they did – but this is seen as an admission of the weakness of the theory of independency and a covert form of connexionalism.

Itinerancy is also important if the fidelity of preachers and congregations to the gospel is to be maintained. The argument is carried forward from Wesley's day that frequent changes of ministerial appointment guard both pastor and congregation against collusion in heresy or decline, and have the added advantage of providing a varied ministry to meet different needs in each congregation, and a varied stimulus to the pastor to keep him at his best.

Discipline

This aspect of thinking about itinerancy leads to what amounts to a further argument, for it is not merely frequent change in the stations that is required to maintain standards but firm central discipline. J. H. Rigg gives it perhaps its most forceful expression:

> Wesleyan Methodism is a connexional system; there subsists in it an absolute intercommunity of interests; a united people…a united and circulating pastorate. This renders it absolutely necessary that both ministers and people should have distinctly adopted or accepted one doctrine and one discipline. No minister can be required to teach and enforce, nor any people to receive and submit to, a system of doctrine and discipline which he or they cannot in conscience approve… There *must*…be an authority and power in the whole united society to enforce the conditions of the union in every circuit and upon every minister.[17]

Fellowship

In the latter half of the nineteenth century a further argument was developed, starting from the broad principle of fellowship (Rigg), or the communion of saints (Benjamin Gregory). 'Unless a Christian Church in some effective measure makes provision for real individual fellowship, – fellowship which joins into one loving brotherhood the general society of believers, so that each believer may have actual spiritual comradeship with some company of other believers, and be linked to the whole body in vital and organic connexion, so that all may have an opportunity of using their spiritual faculties and gifts, – that Church is essentially defective.'[18] It is perhaps surprising that this form of argument should have taken so long to surface. One reason may be the time taken to develop a church rather than society consciousness. It may also have been linked to the erosion of confidence after 1850 in the fifth argument, to which I now turn.

The Pastoral Office

With many of the preceding arguments the non-Wesleyans would have heartily agreed. They differed on the extent of lay representation in the Conference and at other levels, and in the degree of authority over their own affairs to be retained by circuit and district meetings. But, as has been noted, all accepted some form of connexionalism, and, as Wesleyan critics pointed out, even the circuit embodies the principle.[19]

A distinctive Wesleyan argument, however, and for that body by far the most important, derived from the nature of the pastoral office. Pastors (the elders or shepherds of the New Testament) are appointed for the church by God, to teach, to feed and to rule. The source of their authority and the nature of their office are both significant. They cannot be dependent on the congregation to whom they minister. If there is to be a ministry in accordance with the will of God there must be a body of presbyters independent of particular congregations. Pastors are chosen and appointed by pastors. Sometimes the point is simply that a presbytery is needed for the appointment and oversight of ministers, each of whom has authority to rule in the church. At other times the point lies in the collective rule of the presbyterate in Conference. Either way, the scriptural concept of pastoral ministry was held to require a body of pastors jointly responsible for the government of the whole church and free of dependence on any particular congregation. In the eyes of Wesleyan ministers, all of whom – with the permission of their district meetings – were entitled to attend, there is no doubt that connexionalism meant primarily their collective oversight of all the societies and their answerability to one another in the Conference.

Evaluation

In reviewing these arguments, it is difficult even now to separate wheat from chaff. The 'dust of a thousand pamphlets' to which John Kent once referred[20] still tends to cloud the vision. Today's debate between the churches is subtly different, not least in the way it appeals to scripture. What is immediately striking, however, is the limitations of the arguments advanced. Theory does not match up to practice.

Concerning scripture

The emphasis on voluntary union, for example, and the conclusion, echoing Wesley, that those who don't like the rules are free to go elsewhere, illustrate how far into the nineteenth century Methodism still thought of itself in terms of society rather than church. It is understandable in terms of the legal sanctions still attached to the establishment in the early part of the nineteenth century, to which all non-Anglicans objected, and the variety of denominations between which one might choose. Exclusion from the Methodist societies, it was insisted, did not necessarily imply exclusion from the church of God. Today it is even more evident that people exercise their civil liberties in choosing where they will worship, often without regard to denominational principles. But, while this line of argument will do for a religious society, it is hardly an adequate theological basis for the ordering of the church of Christ. Not even for an Arminian is church membership a voluntary matter, but a response to the compulsion of grace.

In any case, the argument that Methodism is free to adopt any polity that is consonant with the Bible was surely inadequate as a rationale of connexionalism as Methodism actually practised it. Whatever may be said of the freedom of individuals to join the connexion, it hardly applied to the societies. There was not much free choice available to them where their foundation was the work of a Methodist preacher, and certainly very little later; they could opt out only at the penalty of losing all claim to property on the model deed. The discipline was actually stronger and the divine authority for it presumed to be greater than this argument suggested.

Concerning itinerancy

There was greater strength in the argument from itinerancy. We should not forget the underlying difference of view affecting the argument in the early period, between Wesleyan Arminianism and the stricter version of Calvinistic predestination, that regarded evangelism as unnecessary. Today the need for mission beyond the bounds of the local congregation would be generally admitted. There are difficulties in the argument, however. It has its greatest appeal to the imagination when it can be seen geographically in terms of unreached areas, at home or overseas. Here the individual congregation is at its weakest and the need for collaboration clearest. But what if there are no vacant geographical areas, and the country can be divided formally or informally into parishes, each the responsibility of its congregation? Perhaps its application today lies in the need of unreached areas that are not geographical but defined in other ways (trades unions, commerce, the arts, etc.), and that are beyond the scope of any one local congregation. However that may be, the strongest element lies in the fact that undergirding itinerancy is an outlook that addresses nothing less than the whole nation in terms of mission.[21]

Even so, the argument does not go far enough. These needs could be met by a relatively loose form of association, such as churches in the Independent tradition actually adopted. What was required was justification for the tighter, more directive form of connexionalism embodied in Methodism, in which the central body exercises authority over local churches and does not exist merely to advise on and facilitate what they independently wish to do.

Concerning discipline

This justification the argument from the need for discipline was intended to provide. Rigg's plea for uniformity in doctrine and practice does not have the same bite today. It is yet another sign of a 'society' mentality, and the intellectual xenophobia of many Wesleyans (and other Methodists) in relation to the emerging new ideas shows all too sadly what it could produce. A society can set its criteria for membership more narrowly than a church (although on paper they were astonishingly wide in Methodism: not conversion, but 'desire to flee from the wrath to come'). There is, of course, a question about the limits of doctrinal and ethical pluralism tolerable in the Christian church, for which all the churches must find an answer, but the difficulty in the idea of central discipline (in practice, the discipline of the Conference over the preachers, and the preachers over the societies) is that discipline, to be effective, needs wherever possible to be self-imposed.

What the argument does do, however, is highlight the fact that the central issue in connexionalism concerns jurisdiction. From where, or by whom, are local churches ultimately governed? Who takes the final decisions, and lays down the rules for decisions taken by others? In our tradition it is the Conference, but only because jurisdiction lies there. It is possible for there to be more than one conference within the same connexion, as in Britain and Ireland until 1928, and the United Methodist Church today. What finally determined that British and American Methodists became two connexions was not Wesley's plan, nor his ordinations for America, nor the existence of the American Conference (which in fact existed before 1784) but the decision of the Christmas Conference in 1784, against Wesley's expectations, to elect its own bishops and determine their titles, and the decision of the 1787 Conference to decline Wesley's nomination of Richard Whatcoat for the superintendency. By these acts it asserted an independent jurisdiction.[22]

Concerning the Pastoral Office

This is perhaps the best point at which to discuss the argument from pastoral authority. Central to it is the concept of 'rule' in the church. Alfred Barrett indeed begins his *Ministry and Polity of the Christian Church* in 1854 from the idea of God as ruler and its implications for civil and ecclesiastical government. The church does not govern itself; God does, through its pastors. A congregation cannot appoint its minister, for that implies that the governor is subject to the will of the governed. Church does not precede ministry.

For much of the century the Wesleyans argued, against successive waves of protest, that such rule belongs exclusively to the pastors, as 'those who must give account'. It was the main point that differentiated them from the other bodies. Even the admission of laypeople to the Conference in 1878 did not really alter things.[23]

There were of course 'non-theological factors'. The Wesleyans were afraid of 'levelling' influences and some of the other bodies perhaps unduly driven by them.[24] There was prejudice too. Independency was judged by appearances rather than by theory. There is no logic in the argument that ministers ordained by the decision of a congregation are humanly appointed but those ordained by a presbytery are appointed by God, but there was much anecdotal evidence to give rise to the fear. In fact, the basis of congregational independency is the claim that this alone allows Christ to rule in his church without interference by politicians or prelates.

They were not helped by the memory, confirmed by developing overseas work, that the societies arose through the ministry of travelling preachers. The New Testament tells a similar story: the apostles are commissioned before the first conversions at Pentecost. The dependence of immature societies on leaders from outside was taken as the norm for a mature church. Temporal priority was interpreted as theological precedence.

The chief objection to the Wesleyan case is that church and ministry are set over against each other. Even the anti-Wesleyan arguments tended to assume the disjunction. What was needed was a recognition, familiar enough today, that any discussion of ministry must begin with Christ and continue with the church, before considering how ministry in its various forms, of which presbyteral ministry in only one, is distributed.[25]

I now review these questions from the vantage point of the Union of 1932 and the doctrinal clauses of the Deed of Union, but there are strands in the nineteenth-century debate that remain to be unravelled. No one, I imagine, would want to employ the heavy language of 'ruling' any longer, with the implication that some in the community are born or called only to 'be ruled'. But the discussion in the 1980s[26] of the role of the Ministerial Session of the Conference, and continuing comment from time to time on the principle of equal numbers of presbyters and lay representatives in the Conference, reveal that we still have not settled in our collective mind how to relate pastoral responsibility for the life of the church to the structures of representative government, nor how to affirm that the responsibility given in ordination is shared with laypeople without being taken away from ministers.

However those questions are resolved, there remains a point of importance in the Wesleyan pastoral argument for connexionalism. It lies not in any pastoral exclusiveness but in the fact that presbyteral ministry bears witness to the catholicity of the church. Ministry of word, sacrament and pastoral care, in whatever form or forms they are exercised, are a constitutive feature of the church, part of its givenness. Those who are called to enter it enter a ministry that, in its essence, belongs to the church as a whole. This fact is adequately acknowledged only to the extent that ordination is a representative act of the wider church. The strength of that argument, however, is more likely to be recognised by those who have already accepted the case for a connexional view of the church, of which ordination is then a sign. It follows from connexionalism, rather than establishing it. Moreover, it hardly leads us of necessity to all the central powers of the Conference. In traditional Presbyterianism presbyteries have a smaller compass.

Concerning fellowship

The argument from fellowship has more potential. Its value lies in its stress on relatedness as essential to the concept of 'church', a relatedness expressed not just theologically in terms of a common Lord, faith and baptism but experientially in terms of human bonds, mutual interdependence and church organisation. 'In Methodism membership in the Church is membership "one of another"… We are often represented as no longer a Society but a Church; as if there were any incompatibility between the one and the other… The Church is itself essentially a Society.'[27] One key element in it fails to be addressed, however. It is easy to see the implications of fellowship within the life of the local church and the Methodist tradition of class meetings as a way of facilitating this. But the leap from local church to circuit, and thence to district and the Conference, is a large one, especially if fellowship is presented in personal, individual terms. It is true that the Methodist is a member of the whole connexion and not just of the local society, but one of the weaknesses of most nineteenth-century discussions is that the link between the local and the wider church is not adequately explored. Indeed, 'local church' and 'national church' or 'denomination' are often referred to in the same sentence in contradistinction to the church universal, as though they are equivalent expressions.

One comes away from nineteenth-century discussions of connexionalism, then, with a feeling that the practice is larger than the theory. A connexional view of the church was firmly held and its benefits widely appreciated. Indeed, some descriptions of its advantages over other forms of polity are almost nauseating in their complacency. No major branch of Methodism abandoned it altogether. But in ecclesiological terms the rationale, except in relation to the pastoral session of the Conference, fails to match the depth of conviction. The arguments offer some support to a looser understanding of the word 'connexional', in which the Wesleyans could use it to describe presbyterian and episcopal churches generally, but they are inadequate for the tighter understanding that actually informed Methodist practice. Are the arguments, then, merely the attempt to invest with theological dignity customs that are no more than pragmatic in origin and deeply entrenched in conservative practice? That is the issue to which we must now turn.

Towards a theology

Does the inadequacy of earlier arguments betray a lack of real justification for the practice, or was there, in the tenacity with which all branches of Methodism retained connexionalism in some form, a conviction struggling for expression? Can the theological implications of Methodist practice be stated more cogently? If that task could be more successfully undertaken, it might be easier to see what is readily negotiable, in church union conversations or discussions about internal reform, and what should be seen as central to our identity, to be abandoned, if at all, only after the gravest consideration.

The nineteenth century was much concerned with the argument against independency. In some ways that argument is now dated. But the debate is not closed. Ecumenically the tradition is still strong.[28] In addition to the Congregational and Baptist denominations that represent it, independency meets us in other ways. Local Ecumenical Partnerships understandably tend to think of themselves in this vein, especially when they lack a single wider ecclesiastical structure to which to relate. Many Methodist churches are congregational by outlook, partly because many members, welcome as they are, have never had any particular grounding in Methodist understandings, and have come to worship in a Methodist church by accident or for convenience. For all these reasons our self-understanding needs regularly to be set out afresh.

There are of course many aspects of Methodist tradition that reflect its understanding of doctrine that are not included here but would find their place in a full study of a Methodist doctrine of the church. The Conference, for example, in both the British and the American traditions, represents an exercise in corporate *episcope*. I doubt whether, on either side of the Atlantic, there would be willingness to surrender that principle. But it is not the essence of connexionalism. While, in the form we know it, the Conference has its setting in a connexional church, it is worth remembering, on the one hand, that there was a connexion before there was a conference (Wesley regarding himself as the one exercising oversight and the Conference only as advisory) and, on the other hand, that corporate *episcope* can be exercised by the church meeting in a strict congregational setting.

Again, it has been a persistent feature of Methodist history that church life has been organised to encourage growth in holiness. The structures (class meeting, membership ticket, quarterly review, etc.) have not always been well used, and have often been allowed to decline. Even though nineteenth-century writers argued strongly that the pursuit of holiness required a connexional discipline, such local pastoral structures are in fact compatible with a looser form of denominational association, or none at all. For this reason I do not include this factor here, but any statement of our doctrine of the church would have to include it.

I am not aware of any fresh arguments for connexionalism being advanced in British writing in the twentieth century. A recent line of argument in the United States, derived from the idea of covenant, deserves attention, however. Paragraphs were inserted into the 1988 *Discipline* of the United Methodist Church in the United States that employed that idea:

> Methodists everywhere have embraced the idea that as a people of faith we journey together in connection and in covenant with one another. Expressing the high degree of cohesiveness and centralized organization among Methodists, the connectional principle became the distinguishing mark which set them apart from the normal patterns of Anglican ecclesiastical organization as well as the more loosely organized Protestant bodies of the day. This acceptance of strong covenantal bonds among the Methodists was no accident. There were deep theological roots, including the concept and experience of covenant and the resulting emphasis on faith journeying in covenant with God and one another. The connectional idea is a style of relationship rather than simply an organizational or structural framework… It is in essence a network of interdependent relationships among persons and groups throughout the life of the denomination.

Another section of the *Discipline*, inserted at an earlier date, speaks of the ordained ministry: 'Members in full connection with an Annual Conference by virtue of their election and ordination are bound in special covenant with all the ordained ministers of the Annual Conference.'[29]

Once again, however, theory falls short of practice. The appeal to the covenant has the advantage of touching Methodist sensitivities, with its reminder of the covenant service. But there is also a well-established usage in the congregational tradition, in which a group of believers covenant with God and each other to form a church. It is significant that, in that tradition, the individual believer precedes the church, which is a local gathering of believers.[30] There is a danger of covenant being understood in Methodism in a similar way. The impression can be gained from the quotations that it is a matter of choice that ministers and congregations surrender their rights for the benefit of a connexional union. The essence of connexionalism, however, is not to concede the congregational principle. Theologically speaking, there are no such rights. A congregation *belongs* to the wider church, and only by virtue of this can it claim to be a church. Ordination does not mean for any minister a commission to a freelance exercise of presbyteral functions, which can then be voluntarily surrendered, but authorisation to minister within and on behalf of the church. Unless more explicit emphasis is laid on the biblical understanding of covenant *obligation*, as imposed by God upon us as overlord upon vassal, covenant can too easily be understood in terms of a voluntary surrender of autonomy for mutual benefit.

Underlying principles

The last paragraph points in the direction in which a more adequate statement of the case might perhaps be made. In fact, it seems to me that there are three principles undergirding the Methodist tradition and practice of connexionalism. Two arise from the tradition. The third is less familiar.

Catholicity

No local church (society, congregation) is a unit complete in itself and autonomous, but is *essentially* linked to the wider church. Circuit, district, connexion are circles of belonging that may take (and have taken) different forms in different circumstances, but the essential thing is the belonging.

This is in principle the nineteenth-century argument, derived from Wesley, that Christian believing is societary in character. Baptism is incorporation into the church. Membership in Christ inescapably involves membership in his body, and this will be only a token membership unless it is 'enfleshed' in face-to-face meeting and mutual responsibility. Such membership is not an option, though in practice individuals may decline to exercise it. It is not possible to believe in Christ for salvation without being incorporated by him into his people, for salvation involves such incorporation. The critical point, however, is that what is true of the Christian individual is also true of the local community in which his or her membership is primarily worked out.

Much of the nineteenth-century discussion was surely prejudiced from the outset by an uncritical acceptance of dichotomy between local and universal church. If one simply counts instances of the word *ecclesia* in the New Testament one easily comes to the conclusion that its use was limited either to the local church or to the church universal. Then, of course, the application of the term to a national church or a nationwide connexion is hard to justify biblically for lack of appropriate texts. We have seen that nineteenth-century writers dodged this issue. In fact, all that the linguistic evidence shows is the absence at the New Testament stage of any development of regional or met-ropolitan structures to which *ecclesia* could be applied, rather than a doctrinal reluctance to do so.

But the uses of the *word* are not determinative for the *idea*. If the doctrine of the church is properly rooted in the Old Testament, one begins with the peo-ple of God (indeed, with creation, and God's purpose for the created order, of which the people of God are sign, sacrament and promise). Every assembly of Israelites, however small, and for whatever purpose, is an assembly of God's peo-ple, but Israel is not the people of God only when assembled. This remains true in the Christian dispensation. Every small gathering in Christ's name, however small, the two or three, is a gathering of the church, promised his presence in the Spirit. So is a representative gathering in synod or conference. It does not follow that any and every such gathering is invested with all the powers and responsibilities that belong to the church as a whole, or that to use the word 'church' of the whole Christian community in a region is illegitimate. What is illegitimate, but unavoidable in our present state, is the use of 'church' for a denomination. Of that all are guilty.

The discussion is thus about the catholicity of the church. A claim to catho-licity is a claim both to belong to the church universal, in its historical suc-cession and its contemporary spread among the nations, and to be open to all the world. It is hard to see how such a claim can be made with integrity unless 'belonging' has the implication of being bound by a network of mutual obligation and jurisdiction. A voluntary association of (essentially autonomous) churches is not enough, for it is not a confession of what *is*. The issue is not mutual self-help but acknowledgement of a larger identity.

To press the point: wider relationships of a congregation with other con-gregations in the church is not an option, or a matter of covenant or free asso-ciation. The relationships exist, if indeed it is a congregation of the one holy catholic church. They are denied unless they are expressed structurally. It is not just a matter of the voluntary surrender of autonomy, for there is no autonomy to surrender. It is a matter of the acceptance of mutual responsibility, and sub-mission to mutual jurisdiction.

Mission

The church is to be structured for mission. Although it was a driving force of Wesley's ministry, Methodism has no monopoly of this conviction. There have been other periods in history when the structures developed in the church have been particularly adapted to its missionary task. Once again, it is not the particular expressions so much as the underlying principle that is important.

It would, of course, be a severe impoverishment to make the missionary task the only criterion for ordering the life of the church. It is no more than a half-truth to declare that 'the church exists for mission'. The church exists for the glory of God, and that must include provision for worship and nurture as well as mission. But it would be an equal impoverishment to make worship and the care of the faithful the criteria for the church's order. Mission is one mode in which God is worshipped.

The danger is that, in the strongly traditional environment of a religious community, structures adapted to one missionary situation become perpetuated as hindrances to missionary activity in another. A still greater danger is that, in replacing them, the church allows itself to be guided exclusively by the pastoral needs of settled congregations turned in on themselves.

These points can be illustrated from the ordained ministry. Historically, the distinction between itinerant and local preachers was that the former offered themselves full-time for work, which involved evangelism as well as pastoral oversight and required their freedom from secular occupations in order to travel. This distinction gave rise to the assumption that ordained ministers could be defined as those who devote themselves full-time to specifically ministerial duties, seen as duties with a church base, and created problems when other missionary pressures suggested a need for ordained ministers to serve outside the organisation of the church. 'Sector ministry' became a battleground between different applications of the same basic principle, that the church's structures should be determined by the missionary task.

A similar comment can be made about itinerancy. We have seen that it was regarded as essential to mission and the support of work in deprived areas. As a system it is now undergoing considerable change. Many question the principle of annual stationing and periodic changes, though some argue as strenuously in favour of centralised stationing as others argue against any stationing at all. Change of some sort is probably inevitable, but the danger is that the original motivation may be lost. Ministry is not just pastoral care of congregations, nor even leading the local church in witness and service in its local community; it is concerned with the furtherance of the total mission of the church, and the church's ability to deploy human resources to best advantage to that end.

Subsidiarity

A third principle needs to be articulated, and here we break new ground, for, so far as I am aware, the question was not addressed in theoretical terms in the past, though practical solutions were found to problems as they arose. We have stated the principle undergirding connexional practice, that no church is an independent unit but a member in a wider network, in which it finds its identity. The difficulty, if such a principle is accepted, is to draw the outer limit. If churches as well as individual Christians are 'members one of another', and there is no hard shell surrounding the local church but each is interpenetrated by its neighbours, where does one draw the boundary? Why not a world connexion, a world Conference with legislative powers and a polyglot *Constitutional Practice and Discipline* in seven volumes? Is not the American tradition, which incorporates the Central Conferences of Europe, Africa and Asia within the jurisdiction of the General Conference in the United States, more consistent than the British one, which has progressively allowed dependent districts and conferences to detach themselves into independent jurisdictions (Australia; Canada; South Africa; Ireland, in surprisingly recent times; latterly other conferences in Africa, Asia and the Caribbean)?[31]

It is not a problem peculiar to Methodism. In the episcopal tradition it presents itself in the identification of the diocese with its bishop as the 'local' church, and the debate about provinces, autocephalous churches and universal primacy.

I have just considered some of the implications of the principle that the church is to be structured for mission. It is also relevant to the question of the outer boundaries of ecclesiastical jurisdiction. A church must be structured effectively to respond in mission to the society in which it is set. From the beginning Methodism has been concerned with mission to the nation – that is, to the widest reachable horizon of civic and political community. 'Reachable' is a key word, however, and there comes a point at which distance or political factors demand that horizons be defined more narrowly if mission is to be effective. So it was with America in 1784 and has often been elsewhere since then. In some settings only a more limited jurisdiction has been able to authenticate the mission. Social, political and geographical boundaries are thus natural guides when drawing boundaries of ecclesiastical jurisdiction.

A further principle that can be invoked, however, is that of subsidiarity. Originally articulated in Roman Catholic discussion of social philosophy, it has come recently to be applied to questions of church order.[32] Decisions ought not to be taken on any issue in the church at a higher level than they need be. The more local the problem, the more local the jurisdiction that applies to it. It denies the full stature of the people of God to take out of their hands decisions for which they themselves should be answerable. This is not a very common line of thought in Methodism, although the United Methodist Free Churches, in allowing relative autonomy to circuits and districts, were giving expression to it. As a principle, subsidiarity has the advantage in offering a rationale for autonomous national churches. It is appropriate that there should be national jurisdictions, to deal with national matters. It is double-edged, however. It raises the questions whether, on the one hand, purely regional and local matters should both be dealt with at a lower level and, on the other, whether national jurisdiction should not be limited in respect to international issues, over which the churches should be acting together not just by consent but by mutual obligation.

Conclusions

This chapter has not attempted to defend the Methodist constitutional system in its detail but to explore the abiding principles that might inform it. It may be useful to conclude with a few rather general observations arising from what has been discussed. I do not pretend to envisage how precisely they might be implemented in practice.

(1) It will be readily seen that the above arguments represent a case for structural unity in ecumenical, not just Methodist, terms. Certainly, they underline the extent that disunity in the church denies the nature of the church itself. The present phase of ecumenical discussion in Britain, as a result partly of disillusionment with the past and partly of the sheer complexity of the present situation, is tending to talk of commitment and collaboration in mission. Sooner or later, however, questions of structural unity will have to be addressed again, and this will no doubt raise again all the old fears about unity and uniformity. But (whatever the Wesleyans may have thought) uniformity is not desirable, nor is it inevitable with union. The nub of the matter is the question of jurisdiction. Churches are not united until they submit their autonomy to one another in matters of mutual concern, not as a generous gesture but in recognition of belonging. It is not surprising that a Methodist should take that view. The connexional tradition implies it.

(2) Methodism has inherited a system with a strong central authority. One way in which the Wesleyan system dominated the others at Union in 1932 is that, in spite of the changes that were accepted, the church has still not learned well how to devolve responsibility. Not enough responsibility is given to district synods, with the inevitable consequence that, when they meet, time may be wasted trying to justify the expense.[33] Locally not enough weight has been given to the church meeting, so that the privileges of (full) membership tend to be seen simply in terms of qualification for holding office or electing others to do so. What does subsidiarity imply for the church's Standing Orders?

(3) In relation to structures, connexion historically was between the Conference and local churches. Circuits and districts were later comers on the scene. Circuits are more important in the economy than districts, in that they are the basis of the ministry of local preachers and, in theory and varying degrees of reality, they are the unit to which ministers are stationed. In America the circuit has virtually disappeared. Some congregationally minded British Methodists would like to see it go here. Yet there is potential in the circuit for all kinds of developments, not least in shared ministry and in sharing diversity in church life. If along with districts they are to be preserved in the future, the criterion must surely be whether they serve the mission of the church, and enable, as intermediate stages, each local church to be aware of its relatedness within the whole. If they are retained, circuit and district must be given a proper place in the scheme of things, each with its own range of responsibilities.

(4) The connexion is of churches with each other as much as with the Conference. The Conference is the servant of that connexion, not its master. It is a means by which the church corporately takes counsel, exercises jurisdiction over itself, makes reciprocal sharing possible and furthers its mission

(in other words, exercises *episcope*). There will always be difficulty about government in the church, because the basis for decision is never simply a majority (or even consensus) view, but fidelity to the gospel and discernment of the leading of the Spirit. With such criteria there is always the potential for clash between those making decisions and those affected by them, who may imagine that all that is at stake is the majority opinion. The difficulty underlines the need for the major judgements of any responsible body, the Conference included, to be tested against a wider constituency, and for its decisions to be disseminated and assimilated (and thus owned or disowned) by the church as a whole.

(5) For Wesleyans, the pastorate was a leading argument for connexionalism. If the comments offered above have any validity we must now turn the argument upside down. It is connexionalism that determines the corporate nature of the ministry. Ordained by resolution of the Conference and admitted into full connexion with it, presbyteral ministers are a sign and instrument of the connexional nature of the church. They are a representation locally of the *episcope* of the wider people of God. The ministry of superintendent, chairman and president highlights in wider spheres the representative character of every minister. An important indicator of this representative character is the fact that, in some sense, ministerial appointments are made by the will of the church as a whole, by the Conference, and not just by local contract – a fact to be borne in mind in any future reconsideration of stationing.

(6) Last, aside from any specific question of church union, we need to learn how to surrender authority to the wider church. The connexional principle that denies autonomy to the local church applies equally to the Conference in its relations both to ecumenical partners in this country and to other embodiments of the church outside Great Britain. We belong with them in the one holy catholic and apostolic church, and partnership is not a matter of choice but of obligation. 'Ecumenical sharing of resources' is a piece of jargon that has awakened a certain amount of resistance in British Methodism recently, both because it employs terminology invented by others and because it has been offered to us by the World Council of Churches in a package that also contains many weird and provocative things. But we must learn to work with it. At root it is pure connexionalism.

Notes

1 Originally published in two parts in the *Epworth Review*: vol. 18, no. 2, 1991, pp. 48–59; and vol. 18, no. 3, 1991, pp. 43–50. Copyright Trustees for Methodist Church Purposes, reprinted by permission.

2 But see Reginald Kissack, *Church or No Church? A Study of the Development of the Concept of Church in British Methodism* (London: Epworth Press, 1964).

3 The omission was amply rectified in the 1999 Statement on the Church, *Called to Love and Praise*, which is available in *Statements and Reports of the Methodist Church on Faith and Order*, vol. 2, *1984–2000*, pt 1 (Peterborough: Methodist Publishing House, 2000), pp. 1–59.

4 The context in 1991 included an invitation to the British churches, as part of the Inter-Church Process, to consider the nature and purpose of the church in the light of its mission, discussion of the question as to whether the Methodist and United Reformed Churches should open union negotiations, and the beginning of work on *Called to Love and Praise*.

5 Referring to the Church's central administration as organised in 1991.

6 Vol. 2, p. 839. 'Connexion' is the original spelling. It began to give way in the eighteenth century as the verb 'connect' replaced 'connex'. American Methodist usage is 'connection'.

7 *Minutes*, 1766, in Henry D. Rack (ed.), *The Works of John Wesley*, vol. 10, *The Methodist Societies: The Minutes of Conference*, bicentennial edn (Nashville, TN: Abingdon Press, 2011), p. 329.

8 John Telford (ed.), *The Letters of John Wesley*, vol. 8, *July 24, 1787, to February 24, 1791* (London: Epworth Press, 1931), pp. 205, 260.

9 *Minutes*, 1769, in Rack, *The Works of John Wesley*, vol. 10, p. 377. The ultimate answer to his question was of course the Conference, legally established.

10 For Wesley's views, see Frank Baker, *John Wesley and the Church of England* (London, Epworth Press, 1970), pp. 284ff.; and Kissack, *Church or No Church?*, p. 61.

11 See *Minutes*, 1746, in Rack, *The Works of John Wesley*, vol. 10, p. 177: 'In what view are we and our helpers to be considered? Perhaps as extraordinary messengers designed of God to provoke others to jealousy.'

12 See Coke and Asbury's notes to *The Doctrines and Discipline of the Methodist Episcopal Church, in America* (Philadelphia: Henry Tuckniss, 1798), p. 42: 'Our grand plan, in all its parts, leads to an itinerant ministry. Our bishops are travelling bishops. All the different orders which compose our conferences are employed in the travelling line... Everything is kept moving as far as possible; ... next to the grace of God there is nothing like this for keeping the whole body alive from the centre to the circumference, and for the continual extension of that circumference on every hand.'

13 Richard Watson, 'An Affectionate Address to [the] Trustees, Stewards, Local Preachers and Leaders of the South London Circuit', 1828, *Works*, London, Wesleyan Conference Office, 8th ed. 1865, vol. 7, pp. 90f. Note the use of 'the body' for the connexion, and the evolution of the term 'United Societies'. Originally marking the union of two societies in Bristol, it was extended to other societies (as each comprising a union of bands and classes?); but in the nineteenth century it referred to the societies in union with each other, and is found in this sense also in the singular, 'United Society'.

14 See Richard Watson, *Theological Institutes*, 4 vols. (London: John Mason, 1823); William Burt Pope, *A Higher Catechism of Theology* (London: T. Woolmer, 1883); William Burt Pope, *A Compendium of Christian Theology*, 3 vols. (London: Wesleyan Conference Office, 1875–76).

15 Though only by stressing the financial responsibilities of leaders and stewards and classing them as 'deacons'.

16 Thomas Jackson, *The Institutions of Christianity Exhibited in Their Scriptural Character and Practical Bearing* (London: Wesleyan Conference Office, 1868), pp. 477f.

17 James Harrison Rigg, *The Principles of Wesleyan Methodism* (London: Partridge and Oakey, 1850), pp. 89f., emphasis in original.

18 James Harrison Rigg, *A Comparative View of Church Organizations, Primitive and Protestant*, 3rd edn (London: Charles H. Kelly, 1897), p. 11. See also Benjamin

Gregory, *The Holy Catholic Church, The Communion of Saints* (London: Wesleyan Conference Office, 1873).

19 Rigg, *The Principles of Wesleyan Methodism*, p. 96.

20 John Kent, *Jabez Bunting, the Last Wesleyan* (London: Epworth Press, 1955), p. 44.

21 See 'Large Minutes, 1763', in Rack, *The Works of John Wesley*, vol. 10, p. 845: God's design in raising up the Methodist preachers is 'to reform the nation, and, in particular, the church: to spread scriptural holiness over the land'.

22 This is true, notwithstanding the 1784 pledge of loyalty to Wesley, withdrawn in 1787. See Gerald F. Moede, *The Office of Bishop in Methodism: Its History and Development* (Zurich: Gotthelf-Verlag, 1964), pp. 44–62.

23 See the *Minutes* for 1876 (London: Wesleyan Conference Office, 1876), p. 197: 'The Conference records its judgement that the extension of the influence and co-operation of the laity in accordance of the preceding Resolution is not in any way inconsistent with the integrity and efficiency of the Pastoral Office…or any of the essential principles of Wesleyan Methodism.'

24 As late as 1879 Rigg was arguing against a 'false principle foolishly applied', that Christ's spiritual kingdom should be analogous to civil and political economy and that the latter should be republican. 'Wesleyan Methodists for the most part will deny them both.' James Harrison Rigg, *The Connexional Economy of Wesleyan Methodism in its Ecclesiastical and Spiritual Aspects* (London: Wesleyan Conference Office, 1879), pp. 90f.

25 See the Conference reports *Ordination in the Methodist Church* (1960), *Ordination* (1974) and *The Ministry of the People of God* (1988), all available in *Statements and Reports of the Methodist Church on Faith and Order*: respectively, vol. 1, *1933–1983* (Peterborough: Methodist Publishing House, 1984), p. 101; p. 108; and vol. 2, pt 1, p. 229.

26 A major overhaul of the relations between the Ministerial and the Representative Sessions of the Conference was adopted in 1989.

27 Benjamin Gregory, *A Handbook of Scriptural Church Principles* (London: Wesleyan-Methodist Book Room, 1888), p. 256.

28 See the contributions of the Baptist Union of Great Britain and Ireland and the Congregational Federation to *Reflections* (London: British Council of Churches and Catholic Truth Society, 1986), pp. 10ff., 29ff.

29 *The Book of Discipline of the United Methodist Church* (Nashville, TN: Abingdon Press, 1988), p. 116, para. 112; p. 228, para. 422. E. Dale Dunlap, 'The United Methodist System of Ministry', in Russell E. Richey and Kenneth E. Rowe (eds.), *Rethinking Methodist History: A Bicentennial Historical Consultation* (Nashville, TN: Kingswood Books, 1985), p. 18, refers to 'a covenanted commitment on the part of congregations, clergy and the connection…which involves the surrender of certain individual rights in order to benefit from the values of covenanted rights and principles, and in the interest of a common cause'.

30 See the statement of the Congregational Union of England and Wales in R. Newton Flew, *The Nature of the Church* (London: SCM Press, 1952), p. 171.

31 The first in this sequence of autonomy was of course the United States itself, and it is one of the ironies of history that the American Conference, somewhat to Wesley's regret, claimed an independence of British jurisdiction in 1784 that it has comparatively rarely negotiated with its own daughter churches overseas but that the British Conference has more frequently granted.

32 'Just as it is wrong to withdraw from the individual and commit to the community at large what private enterprise and endeavour can accomplish, so it is likewise unjust and a gravely harmful disturbance of right order to turn over to a greater society of higher rank functions and services which can be performed by lesser bodies on a lower plane. For a social undertaking of any sort, by its very nature, ought to aid the members of the body social, but never to destroy or absorb them.' Pius XI, *Quadragesimo Anno*, 1931, quoted in Walter M. Abbott, *The Documents of Vatican II* (London and Dublin: Geoffrey Chapman, 1966), p. 300.

33 I believe this is less true now than in 1991, when the article was written.

6 Connexion and *koinonia*

Wesley's legacy and the ecumenical ideal[1]

Probably no one would have been more surprised than John Wesley himself to find his connexion discussed as an ecclesiological concept. For him, it was essentially a practical and pastoral arrangement in the service of mission. Something had to be done to provide care for those who had discovered faith in Christ and to nurture them in their growth towards holiness. In the context in which the notion was developed, the religious societies of the eighteenth century, there was no reason to think of it in any other terms. The ecclesiological reality, it seemed, was the Established Church.

This has remained the case until comparatively recent times. Connexion has been regarded by all sides as a constitutional rather than an ecclesiological issue. Throughout the nineteenth century in Britain there were strenuous defences of the Wesleyan and other varieties of the connexional system, but when systematic theologies of these groups came to treat the doctrine of the church they were curiously silent on the subject of connexion. Only in 1999 in Britain was an ecclesiological statement adopted by the Conference that seriously addressed the subject.[2] A theological account of connexion for the United Methodist Church in the United States and its related conferences was first inserted in the *Book of Discipline* in 1988.[3]

Yet there have always been ecclesiological implications in the practice, and these became greater when the shift took place on his death from a connexion with John Wesley in person to a connexion with a conference. With this shift, the gradual move from existing as a union of societies to existing as a church was accelerated. Sadly, with this development the institutional aspects of connexion were accentuated, and other elements that in fact hold more ecclesiological value tended to become submerged.

This chapter attempts to tease out some of those ecclesiological values, and to set them alongside a recent articulation of the ecumenical ideal, *koinonia*, to see whether they have anything to say to one another.

Connexion

The previous chapter in this volume reviews the history of the concept in more detail than is necessary here. 'Connexion' was neither an exclusively Methodist word nor exclusively religious. Wesley gave the word a distinctive character, however, by the way he stamped his own personality and method upon his branch of the revival movement. In his usage there were three primary applications of connexion: to members, to societies and to preachers, all connected with himself and under his authority. From that vertical relationship, however, there developed a lateral one: the preachers with each other, forming a single body meeting in conference, and the societies with each other, giving rise to references to 'the United Societies'. The paramount importance of that unity for Wesley is seen in his last letter to the American church, in which he urges them to declare clearly that 'the Methodists are one people in all the world; and…it is their full determination so to continue'.[4]

The bonds of this connexion were developed pragmatically, in response to pastoral need or opportunity: band and class meetings, itinerancy of preachers, rules, hymns, sermons, Notes upon the New Testament and other publications, and conference; later the model deed and Deed of Declaration in Britain, and for the new church in America the Twenty-Five Articles of Religion (which have survived as a standard) and the *Sunday Service* (which did not). Underlying all these is discipline, exercised for the sake of three convictions out of which the entire movement sprang: that Christ died for all (so mission is the primary imperative), all are called to holy living (hence the discipline and the need for oversight) and there is no such thing as solitary religion (hence the societies and all that is designed to sustain them). It was these convictions and pastoral needs that prompted Wesley, in frustration at the unwillingness of the Church of England to act, to embark upon ordinations for America and later elsewhere, thereby, from the point of view of canon law, cutting the main hawser mooring the Methodist ship to the Established Church.

Since Wesley's death the movement has developed, in different ways on each side of the Atlantic, yet the organisational structure Wesley bequeathed to it has proved remarkably enduring. Its hallmarks are still conference, rules (in Britain, Standing Orders; in America, the *Discipline*), itinerancy, a common hymnal and, above all, the expectation that the local church and its common life are defined not by itself but by a central body that has the authority to make the rules by which it is governed, and that to be a (United) Methodist is to belong not just to a local congregation but – as of right – to the wider communion.

In many other ways, however, while the framework has remained, the inner life has changed. Not only do Methodist churches perceive themselves as churches and not simply as religious societies, the spiritual quest and the pastoral mechanisms for pursuing it have changed. Gone are the band meetings, the mutual cross-examination, the love-feasts and watch-nights. Week-by-week life in a local Methodist church is not likely to differ very much from a Presbyterian or Baptist church of similar social complexion. This has made it even more likely for connexion to be seen in institutional terms: as a benefit, if it makes grant aid possible; as a convenience, in that it guarantees a supply of accredited ministers; and as a constraint or imposition, if it is felt to inhibit local initiative or if the local church has to pay what it regards as an excessive amount for the benefits it receives. This description would have to be modified in various ways if one were to attend those churches in other parts of the world that have grown out of earlier British and American missionary expansion, but it is largely true of the British and American scene. The very insertion of the 1988 statement about the nature of connexionalism into the United Methodist *Book of Discipline* reflected the sense of a need to reclaim a heritage.

In fact, independency, whether consciously defined as such, or in the unreflective pragmatic form in which it is encountered among church members in many denominations, has always been the main target for apologists of connexionalism. Nineteenth-century British writers, for example, were willing to regard episcopalian and presbyterian polities as essentially connexional, albeit less centralised than the Wesleyan connexion. But they viewed congregationalism as another thing altogether. From the eighteenth century on, congregationalism was seen by Methodist writers as posing several serious dangers: the minster's primary function would be to serve the congregation rather than to engage in mission; because they were appointed by them, ministers would be more likely to be subject to the congregation's influence than the congregation to their leadership; this would make doctrinal heresy and spiritual slackness serious dangers; and if ministers kept their prophetic edge they would be in danger of being sacked, while if they did not they would be there for life and slowly sink – along with the church – into decline. If one picked on worst-case examples (as Methodist apologists did!) there was much in contemporary experience to sustain such fears.

A proper evaluation of connexionalism, however, must begin not from institutional arrangements nor from polemics but from the characteristics of the early period. The British and American traditions both have much to learn and to recover from their earlier heritage, even though (as we shall see) the wider ecumenical debate also poses some questions.

Ecclesiological values

What, then, are the ecclesiological values that lie behind Wesley's pragmatic and pastoral system? As we have already noted, it was a system for a voluntary society, not for a separate church. Yet it was developed out of assumptions about what the church should be, and for that reason it still has ecclesiological significance. I highlight six points that hold value for contemporary ecclesiological reflection.

Evangelism and spirituality

The connexion arose out of missionary and pastoral need, not out of a desire to make organisation more scriptural. Nineteenth-century Wesleyan apologists never tired of making the point that, unlike other churches in the Reformed tradition, church organisation was not of itself an issue for them. They assumed that the form of the church is dictated by the inner nature of the faith, not juridically by either scripture or tradition. Wesley's convictions on this point cannot be divorced from his Arminianism. He insisted that salvation must be offered to all, not just to the elect. The structures of the church must therefore serve this goal. Moreover, the church's mission has to do ultimately with holiness, in the person and in the wider society. God's design in raising up the Methodist preachers was 'not to form any new sect; but to reform the nation, particularly the Church; and to spread scriptural holiness over the land'.[5] The structures of the church must therefore serve both to evangelise and to develop spirituality.

To affirm such a principle today is not to deny the significance of tradition (indeed, to do so would be to render an examination of the Wesleyan heritage pointless). Still less does it deny the significance of scripture, from which the recognition of the imperatives of evangelisation and spiritual formation arise. But in an age when the historical relativity of both scripture and tradition is increasingly acknowledged, and the cultural conditioning of all our inherited structures is recognised, it is important to try to identify core values by which structures are to be assessed and retained or replaced. The mission of the church is one of them.

Personal relations

Connexionalism was essentially interpersonal. Members, societies and preachers were in union with Wesley and thus with one another. The constituent elements in the system – bands, classes, societies and conferences – were designed to enable people to meet.

> Christianity is essentially a social religion, and to turn it into a solitary religion is indeed to destroy it... I mean not only that it cannot subsist so well, but that it cannot subsist at all, without society, without living and conversing with other men.[6]

The structures were designed to serve these relationships. Yet, ironically, like all other church structures, they have become over time a hindrance to meeting. In our ecumenical age they will need to be overcome, modified or ignored to make wider meeting possible.

World perspective

Relationships were understood to be more than local. Potentially they were universal. I noted above Wesley's insistence that 'the Methodists are one people in all the world; and...it is their full determination so to continue'. His hopes of keeping the British and Americans in a single connexion after the War of Independence were soon dashed. The Americans showed themselves determined to go their own way in ecclesiastical matters, as in political. In the conditions of the time it was too much to expect otherwise. But note that Wesley's words were more than a declaration of an administrator struggling to hold his organisation together. They were rooted in the conviction that the call to 'that holiness without which no one shall see God' is a call to perfect love. Therefore, unity – unity without borders – is a gospel imperative.

Accountability

In all this there was a stress on accountability. The purpose of all the tiers of meetings that Wesley organised – bands, classes, society meetings, leaders' meetings, preachers' meetings and conferences – was to 'render strict account'. The primary concern of the meetings was not 'business', in the modern sense, but spiritual and theological oversight; they met to hold one another to the path in faith, prayer, obedience, faithful pastoring, doctrinal fidelity and continuing witness and mission. The agenda of the first Conference in 1744 reads: 'What to teach; How to preach; and What to do, i.e., how to regulate our doctrine, discipline, and practice.'[7] No one should think of him- or herself as autonomous. All answer to one another. (The only exception, of course, was John Wesley himself. He certainly did not think of himself as answering to the fellowship, though some of the preachers did and his brother, at least, was not afraid to take him on.)[8]

Oversight

Oversight, *episcope*, was thus in practice a matter of central importance. John Wesley can rightly compared with the Ignatian bishop, seen as the focus of unity for the church.[9] When he ordained for America, it was not just Richard Whatcoat and Thomas Vasey as preachers and pastors but Thomas Coke as superintendent; and to this day in the United Methodist tradition the general superintendency of the whole church is laid upon the collective shoulders of the bishops.

Covenant

Finally, Wesley's model of connexion carried some suggestion of the believer's relationship of covenantal obedience to God. Unfortunately, this suggestion has typically been obscured by the reality that his connexion originated as a voluntary association. In his own time and in the following century this voluntary status was often emphasised as a counter to charges that the connexion was too authoritarian. It was contended that, if people did not like the regime, they were free to take themselves off. Actually, it was not always so simple in practice. More importantly, this emphasis tended to undercut the ecclesiological dimension of covenantal obedience to God.

This danger remains in some modern accounts of connexion. The previous chapter in this volume quotes extensively the passage in the 1988 statement in the United Methodist *Book of Discipline* that employs the idea of covenant: 'Methodists…as a people of faith…journey together in connection and in covenant with one another… Here were deep theological roots, including the concept and experience of covenant and the resulting emphasis on faith journeying in covenant with God and one another.'[10]

Such an account of connexion will not quite do. It may be appropriate to a religious society but it is inadequate as a statement of relationships within the church. It treats connexion as a covenant analogous to our covenant with God, but does not delineate the relationship between the two. To see the problem, compare the comments on covenant in the report 'Costly Unity', published in 1993 after a World Council of Churches consultation on '*Koinonia* and Justice, Peace and the Integrity of Creation':

> A covenant between human beings carries the biblical sense only if it is made before God with the intention of obedience to God's covenantal requirements. To enter into a covenant means we accept the conditions under which God sets us in the midst of creation.[11]

In other words, connexion (at its best) is not a voluntary association but an ecclesiological discipline. It arises out of the nature of the gospel and the church.

Koinonia

When we turn to the concept of *koinonia* the most succinct statement is the World Council of Churches' Canberra Statement of 1991, 'The Unity of the Church as *Koinonia*: Gift and Calling'.[12] This can be readily supplemented by material in the report of the Fifth World Conference on Faith and Order, held in 1993 at Santiago de Compostela. Some of its flavour is given in the following extract:

> (2.1) The unity of the Church to which we are called is a *koinonia* given and expressed in the common confession of the apostolic faith; a common sacramental life entered by the one baptism and celebrated together in one eucharistic fellowship; a common life in which members and ministries are mutually recognized and reconciled; and a common mission witnessing to all people to the gospel of God's grace and serving the whole of creation… This full communion will be expressed on the local and universal levels through conciliar forms of life and action. In such communion churches are bound in all aspects of their life together at all levels in confessing the one faith and engaging in worship and witness, deliberation and action.[13]

Further quotations from the Santiago report illustrate that *koinonia* is a far more comprehensive and deeply rooted concept than connexion can hope to be:

> (4) '*Koinonia*' is above all a gracious fellowship in Christ expressing the richness of the gift received by creation and humankind from God. It is

a many dimensional dynamic in the faith, life and witness of those who worship the Triune God, confess the apostolic faith, share the Gospel and sacramental living, and seek to be faithful to God in Church and world... (10) The interdependence of unity and diversity which is the essence of the Church's *koinonia* is rooted in the Triune God revealed in Jesus Christ. The Father, Son and Holy Spirit is the perfect expression of unity and diversity and the ultimate reality of relational life... (14) The very structure of the Church is relational... No Christian can exist as an isolated individual exercising a privileged and direct communion with God... (15) Both unity and diversity are expressive of *koinonia*... (17) The *koinonia* of the Church is also universal.[14]

The manifest strength of this development of the notion of *koinonia* is its rooting in the doctrine of the Trinity. There is thus given to the ecumenical goal a central theological paradigm and a Godward dimension. The unity to which we are called is not a blending of structures, nor a reconciliation of human communities, but the drawing of human beings – and, ultimately, of all creation – into the life of God.

This poses a question not only for our contemporary expressions of ecumenical goals but for the life and structures of all the churches in our separation. Until that Godward dimension becomes central to our reflection on what the church is and our ordering of its life, our vision will remain distorted.

Engaging the notion of *koinonia*

With some sense of the notion of *koinonia* before us, I want to engage it now from a Wesleyan perspective. I will do so by examining both parallels and contrasts between the ecclesiological emphases of connexion and *koinonia*. I begin with some interesting parallels between the model of the church as *koinonia* and the connexional vision.

Parallels between *koinonia* and connexion

(1) *Koinonia*, like connexion, is not a mere option for the church. The parallel in sentiment between Canberra's 'No Christian can exist as an isolated individual exercising a privileged and direct communion with God' and Wesley's 'Christianity is essentially a social religion' makes the point.
(2) *Koinonia*, like connexion, is interpersonal. Again, we can pick up the Canberra statement, 'The very structure of the Church is relational'. It is spelled out there in terms of a common confession of faith, a shared sacramental life and mutual recognition of members and ministries. Although the emphasis would be placed somewhat differently, Wesley's connexion was essentially about people meeting. If Wesley failed to offer the Methodist people a satisfactory doctrine of the church, he certainly gave them an experience of the church – meeting in small groups together, sustaining one another – in which the eucharist took on a new significance.

(3) *Koinonia*, like connexion, is mission-oriented: '[A] common mission witnessing to all people to the gospel of God's grace and serving the whole of creation... The *koinonia* of the Church is...universal,' to quote Canberra again. So too, for Wesley, the connexion was potentially universal, embracing all who will.

If there is a difference between *koinonia* and connexion on these issues, apart from the language, it might be the starting point. Wesley began at the micro-level, with the needs and relationships of individual believers, and worked outward from them via the local church to the wider connexion. *Koinonia*, because the setting for the discussion is worldwide ecumenical relations, begins at the macro-level and works inward toward the local church. But we should make no mistake about the fact that what it says about relations between separated churches applies equally to particular congregations and to relationships in any local church.

The challenge of koinonia *to connexion*

When we turn from similarities to differences, perhaps the most important challenge to Methodist thinking in the concept of *koinonia*, apart from the Trinitarian framework already mentioned, lies in the insistence that *koinonia* embraces both unity and diversity. This would not have been obvious to Methodists of the eighteenth or nineteenth centuries, nor, indeed, in the first half of the twentieth. The most uncompromising statement of an attitude common in that era is perhaps that of J. H. Rigg, quoted more fully in the previous chapter:[15] 'Wesleyan Methodism is a connexional system; there subsists in it an absolute intercommunity of interests; a united people...a united and circulating pastorate. This renders it absolutely necessary that both ministers and people should have distinctly adopted or accepted one doctrine and one discipline.' I suspect that kind of statement needs to be made only when the rot has begun to set in. Now, of course, at least on the British scene, it is the chain stores that present a uniform front and uniform contents to the passer-by, not the Methodist churches. In British Methodism we have largely legalised diversity, I suspect more so than in the United States or continental Europe. As a result we struggle with the relationship between unity and diversity, with an inheritance strongly unsympathetic to the latter.

The challenge of connexion *to* koinonia

If a weakness is to be discerned in the exposition of *koinonia* summarised above, it is perhaps in the realm of accountability. I use that word rather than its obverse, jurisdiction, because the latter can too readily be seen as something extraneously imposed. Moreover, it is legal terminology, somewhat removed from the essentially interpersonal stress of *koinonia*. *Koinonia* negates autonomy, however, and poses the central question in the ordering of the church as to how individual members, congregations and wider groupings answer to one another. Documents on *koinonia* make much of conciliarity but very little of account-ability, except as an agenda item still to be addressed: 'Koinonia must not be interpreted as meaning acceptance of our present denominational structures so long as they are "in communion". That would make *koinonia* only a synonym for "reconciled diversity".'[16]

It has been one of the strengths of the connexional heritage that it offers an answer to the practical question of creating accountability in the form of the conference – the gathering of representatives of the churches to take counsel together in prayer to discern and declare the mind of God, whose conclusions are binding on the churches they represent. That is the setting in which local churches answer to each other and regulate one another in obedience to Christ. (The reality experienced may be very different; politicking enters in, though that is nothing new.)

Interestingly, the British and American traditions diverge in the application of this principle in ways that mirror more ancient divisions in other tradi-tions. Briefly, in the American tradition (although there are some exceptions) daughter churches outside the United States, while governed in many respects by their own conferences, are bound together by common membership in, and under the discipline of, the General Conference and a single Council of Bishops, which are global in character. In the British tradition, daughter churches (of which America was the first, enjoying 'that liberty wherewith God has so strangely made them free')[17] have become autonomous, linked by agreements about mutual support and cross-representation. Thus the American tradition is more centralist and globalist, akin to the Roman approach with its single college of bishops and universal primacy, while the British mirrors the Anglican and Orthodox traditions in recognising greater regional auton-omy (although, in the case of the Orthodox, we must not forget the bind-ing character of the truly ecumenical councils). Curiously, one can defend the British Methodist/Anglican position by appeal to a characteristically Roman principle: subsidiarity.[18]

Conclusion

It may seem strange that the contribution of John Wesley to ecumenism should be discussed under the very Methodist heading of connexionalism, rather than in connection with the more often quoted 'catholic spirit'. In 1749 – in Dublin, of all places – he published a document that has had renewed attention in recent decades: his *Letter to a Roman Catholic*. In it he pleads for tolerance, and sets out those convictions that Protestants and Catholics share – in essence, the doctrines of the Creed – and pleads:

> If we cannot as yet think alike in all things, at least we may love alike…
> Let us resolve, first, not to hurt one another…secondly, …to speak nothing
> harsh or unkind of each other…thirdly, …to harbour no unkindly thought,

no unfriendly temper…fourthly, endeavour to help each other on in whatever we are agreed leads to the Kingdom. So far as we can, let us always rejoice to strengthen each other's hands in God.[19]

The sentiments were echoed in a sermon of the same date, 'The Catholic Spirit'.[20] Certainly, in these documents Wesley enunciated an important theological principle, now often referred to as the notion of a hierarchy of truths. Central to this scale of values were the spiritual values of faith and love. But in his day that was, as it remains in ours, a programme for reaching across denominational barriers while those barriers remained, and possibly as a means by which we one day come to see that they are unnecessary and can be removed. But connexion, and its larger, theologically more adequate counterpart, *koinonia*, look forward to the day when there are no barriers and ask: shall we still live as though there were barriers? And, if not, how shall our common life be ordered?

Notes

1 Adapted from my contribution to Randy L. Maddox (ed.), *Rethinking Wesley's Theology for Contemporary Methodism* (Nashville, TN: Kingswood Books, 1998), pp. 129–41. Copyright 1998 Kingswood Books, an imprint of the United Methodist Publishing House. Used with permission; all rights reserved.

2 *Called to Love and Praise*: see *Statements and Reports*, vol. 2, pt 1, pp. 1ff.

3 See *The Book of Discipline* (1988), pp. 116–18, para. 112. The paragraph continues in a revised and much-abridged form in *The Book of Discipline of the United Methodist Church* (Nashville, TN: Abingdon Press, 1996), p. 109, para. 109.

4 Letter to Ezekiel Cooper (1 February 1791), in Telford, *The Letters of John Wesley*, vol. 8, p. 260.

5 Large Minutes, Q. 3, in Rack, *The Works of John Wesley*, vol. 10, p. 845.

6 Sermon 24, § I.1, in Outler, *The Works of John Wesley*, vol. 1, pp. 533–4.

7 Minutes, 25 June 1744, in Rack, *The Works of John Wesley*, vol. 10, p. 124.

8 See Wesley's comment 'I sent for them to *advise* me, not to *govern* me', in Minutes, 1766, in Rack, *The Works of John Wesley*, vol. 10, p. 329, emphasis in original.

9 See his letter to the preachers of 4 August 1769, 'I am, under God, a centre of union to all our Travelling as well as Local Preachers': Minutes, 1769, in Rack, *The Works of John Wesley*, vol. 10, p. 377. Compare, for example, 'Be subject to the bishop and to one another as Jesus Christ was subject to the Father': Ignatius, Magnesians 13:2.

10 See *The Book of Discipline* (1988), p. 116, para. 112. While the specific analogy with covenant is missing from the abridged form of this paragraph in the 1996 *Book of Discipline* (p. 109, para. 109), the construal of connexion totally in terms of its horizontal dimension remains the same.

11 Costly Unity, para. 25, available in Thomas F. Best and Martin Robra (eds.), *Costly Obedience* (Geneva: WCC Publications, 1993).

12 Included with responses in Günther Gassmann and John A. Radano (eds.), *The Unity of the Church as Koinonia* (Geneva: WCC Publications, 1993).

13 *Fifth World Conference on Faith and Order: Message, Sector Reports and Discussion Paper* (Geneva: WCC Publications, 1993), Discussion Paper, p. 12.

14 *Fifth World Conference*, Report of Section I, pp. 6–8.

15 Rigg, *The Principles of Wesleyan Methodism*, p. 89.

16 Costly Unity, para. 31.

17 Letter to 'Our Brethren in America' (10 September 1784), § 6, in John Telford (ed.), *The Letters of John Wesley*, vol. 7, *March 23, 1780 to July 24, 1787* (London: Epworth Press, 1931), p. 239.

18 See Chapter 5, n. 32.

19 'Letter to a Roman Catholic', §§ 16–17, in Thomas Jackson (ed.), *The Works of John Wesley*, 3rd edn reprint, 14 vols. (London: Wesleyan Conference Office, 1872): vol. 10, pp. 85–6.

20 Sermon 39 [Catholic Spirit], in Albert C. Outler (ed.), *The Works of John Wesley*, vol. 2, *Sermons II: 34–70*, bicentennial edn (Nashville, TN: Abingdon Press, 1985), pp. 81–95.

7 The 'Large Minutes'

Ecclesiological implications[1]

The aim in this chapter is twofold: first, to tell an interesting story; and, second, to reflect on some issues that arise from it. If it comes to few firm conclusions that is because the issues are still up for debate.

Wesley's 'Large Minutes'

The annual conference seems to be universally a mark of Methodist polity. It has its origins in John Wesley's initiative in 1744 to gather a few friends for conversation. It became the first of a series. Wesley held the first Irish Conference in 1752, and from 1773 the idea was copied in what was to become the United States.

In Dublin in 1749 Wesley published two pamphlets, both entitled 'Minutes of Some Late Conversations between the Rev Mr Wesleys [i.e. John and Charles] and Others'.[2] They were different but complementary versions of the 'conversations' of the years 1744 to 1748, the one concentrating on doctrinal questions, the other on matters of discipline. He also published a pamphlet, undated, but covering the Conference of 1749. In 1753 (probably) he published again, 'Minutes of Several Conversations between the Rev Mr John and Charles Wesley and Others'. These were presented, somewhat artificially, as a digest of the conversations at the conferences of 1744, 1746 and 1749. For 1744 the material is arranged day by day, but the arrangement bears little relation to the dating of the material in the earlier publications, and not all the material under 1746 had appeared before. The result is a compendium of policy for the Methodist movement, presented in 'conversation' style, covering such matters as the conduct of the conference itself, where and when to preach, how to organise societies and classes, the duties of helpers and the more senior assistants, the need to maintain unity, circuit organisation and financial provision for the preachers.

Wesley revised this publication five times, in 1763, 1770, 1772, 1780 and 1789, mostly by expansion. In 1770 and again in 1780 there was extensive reorganisation and in 1780 some attempt also at abbreviation. A curious feature of the first two revisions is the fiction that the entire contents had been discussed in 1744, 1746 or 1749.

Comparing one edition with another and noting what is omitted or added, we glimpse the progress of the Methodist movement and the way in which issues came to the fore or receded. Some, such as persecution, became less urgent, others more so. Why was Methodism raised up? Should it separate from the Church of England? What was Wesley's authority? Doctrinal positions on perfection and predestination are defended. Yet much of the original text remained unchanged over the years.

It is couched in question–and–answer form. 'How can we farther assist those under our care?' A plan of house–to–house visitation, based on Richard Baxter, is introduced to encourage personal and family religion, including children. 'What general method of employing our time would you advise?' Rise at four, read, meditate and pray for an hour, with another hour in the evening, then five hours' serious reading, before setting out to visit. 'Why is it that the people under our care are no better?' 'Because we [i.e. the preachers] are not more *knowing* and more holy.' 'Why are we not more *knowing* [emphasis in original]?' 'Because we are idle.' 'Why are we not more holy?' 'Because we are enthusiasts, looking for the end without using the means.' 'Do we sufficiently watch over our helpers [i.e. the preachers]?' – a question that leads into an enumeration of the means of grace, including scripture, the Lord's Supper, fasting, Christian conference and personal discipline. 'What can be done in order to revive the work where it is decayed?' Practical arrangements are recommended. '[S]trongly and explicitly exhort all believers to go on to perfection.'

The answers are not, as in this summary, one–liners, but developed in great detail. We see Wesley's iron discipline, his emphasis on fasting, his concern with practical detail (no late night suppers, which lead to 'nervous disorders', and make sure your horse is rubbed down, fed and bedded), his genius for good order. The *Twelve Rules of a Helper* are here, and, from 1763, the classic statement of Methodism's purpose: 'To reform the nation and in particular the church; to spread scriptural holiness over the land.' Above all, we see his pastoral and evangelical passion: 'O brethren, if we could but set this work on foot in all our societies, and pursue it zealously, what glory would redound to God! If the common ignorance were banished, and every shop and every house busied in speaking of the word and works of God, surely God would dwell in our habitations and make us his delight.'

Although these 'Minutes' were published they are essentially conversations between John Wesley and the preachers. When they deal with members – admission to societies, personal conduct, money–raising and the like – they do so by directing the preachers how to manage such matters. They do not address the members directly. The 'Rules of the United Societies' (1743) are not included, nor are the 'Band Rules' of 1738 and 1744. The conversation is exclusively about the preachers, their work and self–discipline; it is pastoral advice and instruction.

Moreover, the advice is Wesley's own, not a committee product. He always regarded the conferences as advisory. The decisions, and therefore the text, were his. They are the directions of the chief shepherd of the Methodist movement, caring for a growing population of converts in the societies and classes, served and 'managed' by the army of itinerant preachers, the helpers and assistants, that he stationed to the circuits.

But there is a hard edge to the advice: not 'Take it or leave it' but 'Take it or leave us'! When a preacher is accepted on trial he is to be given a copy of the 'Minutes' to look over, and when he is finally received he is to be given one inscribed 'So long as you freely consent to, and earnestly endeavour, to walk by these rules, we shall rejoice to acknowledge you as a fellow-labourer'. While the form may be advice and opinion, it sets out the standards by which the preachers are to discipline themselves and to which they will be called to account. Published as 'Minutes of Conversations', and referred to colloquially (and later officially) as the 'Large Minutes' – to distinguish them from the smaller, annual minutes that were published from 1765 on – they became, when handed to the preachers, the 'Rules'.

There is nothing here about general doctrine. That was taken for granted; it was the doctrine of the Church of England, as set out in the *Book of Common Prayer*, the *Thirty-Nine Articles* and the *Homilies*. Only points of controversy are dealt with: perfection, predestination, antinomianism and good works.

Some of the questions quoted above, introduced in 1770, point to evidence of decline, or at least of the movement settling down with the passing of the years. They continue to be asked, and the same answers are given in each subsequent revision: the preachers are urged to greater discipline, greater zeal, more vigilance. To modern eyes, seeing the same remedies reappear, they look more and more tired. One cannot escape the sense that Wesley is to some extent Canute trying to hold back the tide. The fact is that times were changing; so were the Methodist people and the preachers. What we see in the successive editions of the 'Large Minutes' in Wesley's lifetime continues to be observable after his death: a changing situation but a static time-honoured response.

Britain after Wesley

The subsequent history of this text is interesting because it is significantly different on the two sides of the Atlantic. John Wesley's death in 1791 left British Methodism with a number of very difficult problems. Who would succeed him? What would be the relation to the Church of England? What provision was to be made for the sacraments? What was to be the status of the (mainly lay) preachers? What voice were the really lay members to have? There was much controversy. A compromise of sorts was reached in the Plan of Pacification of 1795, but in 1797 Methodism's first major secession, of the Methodist New Connexion, took place. All this preoccupied the Conference in its first years, and it was not until 1797 that they revised the 'Large Minutes'. What emerged was a rather different document. Much of the content was retained from Wesley's 1789 edition, but it was completely reorganised. Inserted at different points was new material – for example, about the new organisational structure of districts, which had first been introduced in 1791 – and the modified text of various documents, including Wesley's posthumous letter to the Conference, the Plan of Pacification, letters of the Conference to the connexion in 1794 and 1797 on matters in dispute, and sundry resolutions adopted by the Conference between 1791 and 1797, collected in a separate chapter. It was a real hotch-potch. Nevertheless, in form it was still a document for pastoral managers, and, although it was issued in the name of the Conference, much of it was still Wesley's text, his pastoral advice to the preachers.

What happened after this borders on farce. All the preachers in the Conference signed a declaration, which was printed in the published 'Minutes' for 1797, in which they stated that they had carefully revised Wesley's 'Large Minutes' and pledged themselves to abide by them. They published the revised text, like its predecessors, as a separate booklet, but in doing so managed an error on the title page, giving the date of publication as 1779 instead of 1797. As it set out the discipline by which the preachers were to be bound,[3] this ought to have been the copy that was handed to each preacher on reception into full connexion. Instead, they went on distributing the 'Large Minutes' of 1789, with the 1795 Plan of Pacification and the 1797 Address to the Societies attached, and the traditional inscription 'so long as you freely consent to…walk by these rules…'. Alongside it, from 1798 onwards, other publications, official or semi-official, were produced that collected together regulations of the Conference made from year to year.

Matters came to a head in 1835, 40 years on, when Samuel Warren challenged in the Court of Chancery his suspension by the Manchester District Meeting over the Theological Institution controversy. He argued that the laws of the connexion were contained in the 1789 'Large Minutes' and other documents given to him when he was received, none of which gave power to the District Meeting to suspend him.[4] The matter went before the Lord Chancellor, who, fortunately for the Conference, ruled that the 1797 'Minutes and Form of Discipline' were the Conference's code of laws and that the documents handed to the preachers were only a guide to their conduct. As a result, from 1835 it was the 1797 'Minutes' that were handed to the preachers and regarded as the discipline by which they were bound, and this continued to be the case until 1895. No amendments were made to it except the addition of a few footnotes drawing attention to some changes adopted since 1797. After 1820 the 'Resolutions on Pastoral Work' were attached. It was an absurd situation, for the book was soon patently out of date.

Not until 1895 did the Conference authorise a new publication, first issued in 1896 and periodically revised thereafter. This included, in an 800-page volume entitled *A Summary of Methodist Law and Discipline*, some elements of Wesley's text scattered here and there, still in question–answer form, combined with, and overshadowed by, much material of later date, and new explanatory paragraphs, all arranged on different principles and with notes as to the source and date of the material quoted. In 1905 this volume was officially declared to have taken the place of the 'Large Minutes' and, with the traditional inscription, was handed to the preachers on ordination. The change of title is revealing. The new book was as much for lay use as for ministerial, and most of what it contained was resolutions of the Conference regulating the conduct of affairs in the church. Both in content and in intention there had been a change.

It was all swept away by Methodist Union in 1932. A new legal framework was established and the main part of the discipline is now in the Standing Orders of the Conference, which are open to revision every year and are published annually in the second volume of the two-volume *Constitutional Practice and Discipline of the Methodist Church*. Wesley's texts have not survived, though the Rules of the Societies and the Twelve Rules of a Helper are printed as historic texts in volume 1, along with various legal documents, which hardly anyone reads and most ministers do not seem to realise they possess.

The United States

The situation was very different in the United States. One of the actions of the Christmas Conference in 1784 was to revise the 1780 version of the 'Large Minutes'. Actually, Francis Asbury and Thomas Coke as the bishops (in consultation with others) followed Wesley's precedent and edited the text themselves, and continued to do so until the 1804 General Conference resolved itself to revise the *Discipline* line by line.

The first revision, published in 1785, was a relatively modest affair. Naturally, there were new things to include: a statement about the new church's relation to Wesley, a declaration that they were forming themselves into an episcopal church with bishops, elders and deacons, provisions for the election of and statements of the duties of such persons, and various adjustments to life in the newly independent United States. Much of Wesley's text was abbreviated, but it remained Wesley's text, with the important difference that now it spoke not in the name of Wesley but in the name of the Conference. The title remained traditional, at least in its opening: 'Minutes of Several Conversations between the Rev Thomas Coke, LL.D., the Rev Francis Asbury and Others at a Conference begun in Baltimore in the State of Maryland on Monday the 27th of December in the year 1784, composing a Form of Discipline for the Ministers, Preachers and Other Members of the Methodist Episcopal Church in America'. But note the wider scope; this is a discipline for the whole church – ministers, preachers and members alike.

The Conference met annually from 1784 until 1792 and every four years as the General Conference thereafter, and each time the *Discipline* was revised and reissued. What had been a continuous text in 1785 was broken up into sections and chapters and, in 1804, into two parts, the 'Spiritual Part' and the 'Temporal Economy'. Other documents came to be added, the 1743 Rules of the Societies, the Articles of Religion, a clutch of tracts on predestination, Christian perfection and baptism, and the sacramental services and ordinal. Changes in the title of the volume over these years reflect the changes in content. The early volumes until 1792, under various titles, purport to be the decisions of the Baltimore Conference in 1784, imitating the curious fiction of Wesley's early editions. By

1792 the title becomes, and thereafter remains, *The Doctrines and Discipline of the Methodist Episcopal Church in America*, with reference to the Conference of the year in question. Apart from the structure and title the most obvious change as the years passed was the introduction of new legislation. The book expanded and the older material inevitably came to occupy less space in proportion. Standing by itself in this sequence is the edition of 1798. It is basically the edition of 1796 copiously furnished with explanatory notes by Coke and Asbury.

What we witness, therefore, is a process of evolution. The *Discipline*, revised at first annually, and then from 1792 onwards every four years, did not become static, almost a fossil, as it did in Britain. What is extraordinary, therefore, is the persistence of the specifically Wesley texts from 1780. Even the appeal for the American General Fund was backed by his words, adopted from the parallel fund in Britain, including the paragraph 'Men and brethren help! Was there ever a call like this, since you first heard the gospel sound?', which survived until 1860. What persisted longest was his material on the duties and disciplines of the ministry. Even the recommendation to rise at four or five in the morning, and the reference, by name, to Baxter's plan of house visitation, is still to be found in the Methodist Episcopal Church *Discipline* of 1936. The same is even more the case with the other American Methodist bodies. The African Methodist Episcopal *Discipline* of 1992, for example, retains text from at least 17 paragraphs of the 'Large Minutes'. Somewhat less is discernible in the 1992 *Discipline* of the African Methodist Episcopal Zion Church.

It is extraordinary, because this was post-Independence America. In 1784 the Conference declared itself ready to obey Mr Wesley during his lifetime, yet it overruled his wishes in the key matter of the title of bishop, and in 1787 ignored his direction to elect Whatcoat as bishop and rescinded its earlier declaration of loyalty. This was a body of preachers, only four of whom had ever met Wesley, who nevertheless preserved his actual words, down to the exclamation marks in some cases, and whose successors, while in many cases probably unaware of their source, continued to do so as though they were holy writ.

It is very revealing about early American Methodism. Although there were some of whom it may not have been quite so true, this was generally a movement gripped not just by a personal experience of salvation, brought to them by the preached word and the Holy Spirit, but by a vision of common life in Christ and of missionary discipline that held them by the very words in which it was expressed, and that they clearly felt could not be improved upon. It was not simply, surely, that they lacked literary talent to restate matters for themselves (they had Thomas Coke among them, for one); nor simply that they were busy people who could not spare the time (Coke and Asbury found time to write the 1798 commentary). Somehow, it seems, these words of the movement's founder whom they had never met *were* Methodism for them.

Changes came, of course, with the various stages of Methodist union, in 1939 and again in 1968. Nowadays the *Discipline* incorporates doctrinal standards and historical and doctrinal statements, but is absolutely a book of rules for the church. No longer is it a book of pastoral counsel for those called to the care of the societies. Yet in one respect the United Methodist tradition remains more conservative than the British. Even now, in three paragraphs, there are questions to be asked about, and questions to be put to, candidates for the ordained ministry that go straight back to Wesley's 'Large Minutes', including 'Are you going on to perfection? Do you expect to be made perfect in love in this life?'.[5] In 1976 they were marked by an explanatory footnote. Now they are introduced as 'Wesley's questions' and 'historic examination', respectively.

Some reflections

The story of the 'Large Minutes' raises some interesting ecclesiological questions, and I offer them without in any way having come to a mind of my own about the answers.

Wesley's influence

First, the story illustrates yet again the abiding influence of John Wesley upon later Methodism. I am not thinking here primarily of his institutional legacy, Conference, circuits, itinerancy and the like, nor am I referring to what are now acknowledged to be historic texts (the Standard Sermons, or the Notes upon the New Testament, which are in the doctrinal standards of both the British Church and the United Methodist Church),[6] nor the Rules of the Society and his abridgement of the *Thirty-Nine Articles*, which also have authoritative status in the United Methodist Church. They can be referred to and interpreted. Rather, I am thinking of those more subtle aspects that one would have to refer to as ethos, of the paragraphs from the 'Large Minutes' that were incorporated into the *Discipline* on both sides of the Atlantic as though they were contemporary, but were in fact Wesley's words, his *ipsissima verba*, perpetuated as something to use and be governed by.

It is remarkable that so much of Wesley's actual prose was preserved for so long. It has been less noticeable in Britain than in the American forms of the tradition, but, as we have seen, even in the *Summary* of 1923, the last the Wesleyans published, there are paragraphs out of the 1789 'Large Minutes'.

Was that a good thing? No doubt for a long time these texts were retained and used because the preachers in the Conference identified with them. They took them in, interiorised them, as their own discipline. They do indeed contain much sound pastoral advice. But there must have come a time when that ceased to be the case, not all at once, nor at the same time for each individual. The up-and-coming generation may have found them less compelling than their seniors, and some individuals may have found their appeal fading with the passage of years. There must have come a time when these texts became not the expression of personal spirituality or an ideal to be looked up to but more a badge of identity, a distinguishing mark of Methodism. To retain them was a sign of loyalty. To strike them out would have seemed like rejecting one's parents – even though everyone knows we don't do things their way any more.

Eventually, it seems, even that was felt to be an embarrassment, and the traditional material was dropped.

Had its retention for so long been a good thing? It clearly failed to keep Methodism orthodox, as the story of theological waverings on both sides of the Atlantic shows. Yet I suspect that it did tend to hold Methodism back. Keeping eighteenth-century texts as though they were contemporary contributed to a backward-looking stance and discouraged Methodism from moving forward into new patterns of ministry and new expressions of faith and spirituality that changing times demanded. It also encouraged a romanticism about the past that ignored some of the sterner eighteenth-century realities. At Methodist Union in Britain in 1932 one of the complaints made by the Primitive and United Methodists was that the Wesleyans (who had retained the Wesley texts for so long) were too traditional and too obsessed with Wesley. They had become entangled in their own roots.

But the question all this raises is: how is tradition best preserved in the church so as to be creative and constructive, not limiting and ossifying? Is the distinction I hinted at earlier, between reference documents, acknowledged to be ancient and subject to interpretation, and performative and regulatory documents such as the liturgy and the discipline, a useful one?

Discipline and rules

I draw attention to the distinction that needs to be drawn between discipline and rules. The two words are often used interchangeably, even by Wesley. In Britain we call the book including the Standing Orders of the Conference (which are indisputably rules) *Constitutional Practice and Discipline.* In the United Methodist Church the word 'Discipline' has been used as the title for the rule book, as we have seen, since 1787. But we can also see how the rule aspect, the regulations, have expanded and taken over from the more pastoral discussion, and how those traditional paragraphs about personal discipline and lifestyle, the Wesley texts, though they survived for a very long time, eventually disappeared almost entirely. Today it is not the devotional life of individuals but the communal life of the community that we seek to regulate.

Rules and discipline are not the same, however. Discipline may be codified in rules, but need not be. It can be imposed by social convention, custom, habit. Our behaviour in church – not eating crisps during prayers, for example – is not codified by rules, but it is a discipline we observe. Moreover, discipline is most importantly an interior thing. It is how we control ourselves. Without that the rules have no heart. Every community needs to retain, or recover, a discipline, if the rules are to be sustained. That is as true of wider society as it is of the church.

Every church needs a discipline, an inner coherence to which members give assent and by which, if need be, they are judged. Some of it, for extrinsic legal reasons, requires to be codified. But our historic tendency, perhaps today abating a little, is to codify everything. Some people in other denominations used to identify us by 'the Black Book'. What are the ecclesiological implications of such connexional control? What is the relationship between organisation and order? How else is communal discipline to be sustained?

The place of tradition

Last, there is the broader question of the place of special denominational traditions in a body of people who claim to be a church. There has been a revival of interest in the Wesleyan traditions in recent decades and what they offer for today, and I can only touch on the issues here. Of course, other denominations have their foundation documents, and there are differences of theological emphasis between the churches that are the subject of ecumenical dialogue. There are not many parallels in other church traditions, however, to the dominant place held by the person of John Wesley in Methodist identity. Moreover, in Methodism the distinctive element in the tradition, in so far as it covers doctrinal matters, relates to a pattern of devotional life, an entire way of being Christian, a progress from awakening, through justification, to sanctification – strictly, being made perfect *in this life*. This is the heart of the Wesley texts in the *Disciplines*. What is the proper place of such a tradition in the life of a community that claims be a church, bearing the marks of the church's unity, holiness and apostolicity, and especially of its catholicity, its wholeness? If we hold the Wesley way of being Christian and a Christian minister to be one among many patterns of discipleship and devotion, ancient and modern, that God offers for the enrichment of the church, and yet at the same time we make that way the discipline of our church, a test of being authentically Methodist, are we not abandoning the claim to be an expression of the church's wholeness? If, on the other hand, we say that Wesley's way is the only true way to God in Christ, are we not 'un-churching' denominations that offer other patterns of discipleship? Even in the eighteenth century many people were left untouched by the Wesley way but were led by other paths into faith in Christ and godly living; that would still be true today. Can one have both catholicity and exclusiveness?

There are, as I see it, two clear ways out of this dilemma. One would be to emphasise the Wesley way for Methodists, and require adoption of it as a condition of Methodist church membership, but look for wholeness – the catholicity of the church – in the wider family of churches of which Methodism is a part. Methodism would then be a valid but partial expression of what Christianity in totality may be. In such a case, ecumenical relations would become paramount, for the implication would be that every denomination is but one piece in the jigsaw that makes up the one holy catholic and apostolic church, and our catholicity will be recovered only when we are united. In such a view we would be free to go back to the old Wesley ways and make them mandatory, so far as we can; reintroduce the Wesley texts or some modern equivalent into our books of discipline and accept them as a condition of continued belonging as Methodists. Methodism would become more emphatically Wesleyan. There are pleas for that in some quarters in the United States and elsewhere.

The other way out of the dilemma would be to affirm that Methodism does now claim to be more than a movement within a wider church with special doctrines and lifestyle; it is a church in the full sense of that term, witnessing to the catholicity, the holiness and the apostolicity of the church of Christ of which the Creed speaks. In that case Methodism would need to broaden itself, to embrace other ways of being Christian, to adopt other patterns of ministry alongside our traditional ones, to abandon talk along the lines of 'We don't do that sort of thing in our church because we are Methodists'. In that case we could no longer impose Wesleyan standards of piety and ministry upon all. We would have to eliminate the reference to the Standard Sermons and the Notes upon the New Testament from the doctrinal standards in the Deed of Union. They could remain with us as inspirational material, alongside the writings of many other historic Christian teachers, men and women, and other Methodist texts, such as the 'Liverpool Minutes' of 1820 and 1885. Individuals could adopt them as a personal covenant, but they would no longer be normative. We could feed on them but not include them in our discipline. Traditions are one thing, disciplines are another.

I suspect that, in its history over the last hundred or so years, Methodism on both sides of the Atlantic has been drifting towards the second option. Indeed, I am not sure the first is practical politics any more. We now think of ourselves as a church. It remains an important question, however, as to which is the better way forward for the glory of God and the good of the universal church.

Notes

1 A version of this chapter was published in *Heritage*, the bulletin of the Virginia Conference Historical Society of the United Methodist Church, vol. 26, no. 1, 2000, pp. 1–10. Reprinted by permission.

2 For a detailed study of the Minutes and the history of the publications, see Rack, *The Works of John Wesley*, vol. 10.

3 It was entitled 'Minutes of Several Conversations between the Rev John Wesley A.M. and the Preachers in Connexion with Him, Containing the Form of Discipline Established among the Preachers and People in the Methodist Societies'.

4 What documents Warren actually relied on is not fully clear. See the debate between Wesley Swift and John Bowmer in *Proceedings of the Wesley Historical Society*: vol. 31, no. 7, 1958, pp. 158–9; and vol. 39, no. 6, 1974, pp.187–8. Neither view is conclusive or covers all the evidence. Only reference to the original court papers would clinch the issue but these have apparently not survived.

5 *The Book of Discipline* (1996), paras. 305, 321, 327.

6 In the British tradition the sermons in question are 'the first four volumes', amounting to 44.

8 Conference *episcope*

History and theology[1]

The claim has often been made over the last few decades, in ecumenical discussions of episcopacy and more generally in Methodist ecclesiological writing, that, while British Methodism lacks the office of bishop, it does possess *episcope*, exercised by the governing Conference and by individuals and groups under the Conference's authority. Although the claim is justified it conceals significant variations both in practice and in understanding. In current understanding Conference *episcope* represents corporate oversight of the church by a representative body, shared collaboratively by ordained and lay. It has not always been so. Of course oversight has always been exercised in Methodism since the days of John Wesley, but when it has been exercised corporately it has not always been shared, and in so far as it has been shared it has not always been seen as oversight in the fullest sense.

The use of the anglicised Greek word *episcope* for the English 'oversight' is relatively recent and is intended to distinguish between the exercise of personal oversight in the office of bishop, 'episcopacy', and the ministry or function of oversight in itself, however exercised. At the same time it gives the notion of oversight a theological undergirding, protecting it from misrepresentation in purely secular managerial terms. The earliest use of it I have discovered in Methodist writing is in an exchange of articles in the *Proceedings of the Wesley Historical Society* beginning in December 1956, when it was evidently already a familiar term. But the English alternatives, 'oversight', 'superintendence' and 'watching over', are much older in Methodist use.

It is, understandably, in ecumenical dialogues, between British Methodism and the Church of England and internationally between the World Methodist Council and the Roman Catholic Church, that *episcope* came to be employed, from 1963 in the one case and from 1976 in the other. But it is important to note a shift in emphasis in successive reports, from functions of *episcope* exercised in some respects by individuals and in others by the Conference in the earlier dialogues, to its overall exercise by the Conference, which authorises individuals to act on its behalf in the later ones, and from a concentration on collective ministerial oversight to a recognition of oversight as a gift to the whole church, shared by lay and ordained alike, which came to full expression only in the Methodist/Roman Catholic document *Speaking the Truth in Love* in 2001.

Two recent Conference reports set out what British Methodism currently understands by *episcope: Episkopé and Episcopacy* (2000) and *The Nature of Oversight: Leadership, Management and Governance in the Methodist Church in Great Britain* (2005). It is comprehensively defined as 'the function of ensuring that the church remains true to its calling'. It includes governance, management and leadership, and involves pastoral care, the discernment of God's will, leadership in mission, interpretation of doctrine, the admission, ordination, appointment and oversight of presbyters and deacons, general ordering of the church's constitution, concern for its unity, and the exercise of authority and discipline. It is exercised primarily by the Conference, but also – under its authority – by presbyters and deacons, by district synods and a range of circuit and local church bodies and by lay individuals throughout the church. It is only in the collaboration of ordained and lay that oversight is fully exercised. Such a definition easily bears comparison with ecumenical statements.[2]

Certain features of it are important for our discussion. While presbyters have a significant part in the oversight of the church, it is not their exclusive province. Oversight is shared between ordained and lay leaders throughout the church, and by ordained and lay in more or less equal numbers in the Conference. It is also a holistic concept. All aspects of the church's life and mission come within the Conference's purview and are embraced in *episcope*, including finance, property, publishing and general organisation.

The Methodist Conference

There is no doubt that John Wesley functioned, in effect, as Methodism's bishop, even though he eschewed the term and was furious when the title was adopted by the Methodists in the United States. It is also undisputed that after his death in 1791 the British Conference assumed the authority that once had been his. The more interesting questions are whether this was what he intended, and whether the authority his successors exercised over the Methodist Societies was as securely grounded as they claimed. In time they grounded their claim theologically in the doctrine of the pastoral office, to which I shall return shortly, but they also assumed that it had a legal basis in the Deed of Declaration that Wesley executed in 1784.

Forty years earlier, in 1744, Wesley had gathered a group of five sympathetic clergymen and four lay preachers to confer with him about doctrine, discipline and practice. It was the first of an unbroken and continuing succession of Methodist Conferences. Two aspects of it are important. It was a mixed gathering in which ordained and lay shared, though not in equal numbers or influence, and it was advisory. Whether in later years its members all considered it so we may doubt. In practice it was a barometer for Wesley of opinion among the preachers and from time to time a means by which internal disagreements could be resolved, but he always insisted on its advisory status. It was an instance of what might now be called 'bishop in council'. It is also significant that its minutes were published. Its conversations were, in effect, a set of directives for the preachers and for the wider Methodist membership.

Wesley's hope in 1769, in a letter to the preachers of 4 August, was that after his death the preachers would elect a committee of between three and seven, each of whom would be moderator in turn, and who together would take over Wesley's functions of proposing preachers for trial, admitting and excluding them, stationing them and fixing the date of the next Conference. What is interesting is that these duties were to be carried out by a committee, not by the preachers in Conference, reflecting his view of the Conference as no more than advisory.

But what was his intention in 1784? In that year, in the vacuum created by the absence of ecclesiastical authority after American independence, he conducted his first ordinations, of Richard Whatcoat and Thomas Vasey, for the Methodist societies there. He gave the Americans 'full liberty simply to follow the Scriptures and the Primitive Church', but he did not delegate any specific powers to their Conference. He also laid hands on Thomas Coke, who was already ordained, and appointed him and Francis Asbury joint superintendents in America. The best interpretation of this is that he was delegating his own supervisory authority to Coke, to be shared in turn with Asbury. The conclusion must be that he expected the American Conference, like the British, to be advisory. In the event, however, Asbury refused to accept appointment as superintendent until it had been ratified by the vote of the preachers in the Conference, and thereby significantly shifted the balance of authority, although in subsequent decades it became apparent that there were conflicting interpretations as to whether the 'general superintendency' exercised by the bishops was subordinate to the General Conference that elected them or co-ordinate with it and not subject to its control.[3]

Subsequently, when Wesley began to ordain preachers, first for service in Scotland and later for England, he ordained Alexander Mather, as he had Coke, as superintendent. This suggests that he anticipated a similar arrangement in Britain after his death as had obtained before it: a superintendent in his place and an advisory Conference. It was certainly the fear of this that led to the often quoted decision taken in 1791 that they would not have another 'king in Israel' but an annual president instead. One reason cited for their decision was that it would be in conflict with the 1784 Deed. Careful attention to the terms of the Deed, however, suggests that in that respect they misunderstood its scope, supporting the view that Wesley intended that his place should be taken by an individual.

As the opening recitals make clear, the explicit purpose of the Deed was to secure the chapels for the use of Methodist preachers. The standard form of trust deed for the chapels specified that they were for the use of preachers appointed by John Wesley and after his death by the Conference, with a proviso about the doctrine to be preached. Wesley had been advised that the reference to the Conference was insecure, and the 1784 Deed therefore gives the Conference a legal identity, empowers it to enrol and deploy the travelling preachers and provides for its continuation in perpetuity. There is no suggestion in the recitals that the Deed was intended in any wider sense to provide for the future governance of the Methodist people.

The main part of the Deed begins by referring to the situation obtaining in 1784 when it was drawn up. The Conference is declared at that date to be advisory. The only functions attributed to it are the admission of preachers on trial and into full connexion, their expulsion and their stationing. These functions are then assigned to the future Conference. They are precisely the functions mentioned by Wesley in 1769, and are those necessary for identifying which preachers might occupy the chapels. Apart from that there is nothing in the Deed to suggest that the Conference was to cease to be advisory. No mention was made of the wider oversight of the Methodist societies or the formulation of rules for them. By no means all the societies had chapels, so the powers the Deed provided were of limited scope. Nor was there any mention of the local, as distinct from the itinerant, preachers, or of the funds that by this date featured in the annual minutes. The Deed achieved what it set out to do: establish the Conference and guarantee its powers over the trustees to decide who should preach in the chapels.

During Wesley's lifetime affairs in the local societies were regulated in part by the various sets of rules that he published, and in part by the periodic visitations conducted by himself or the itinerant preachers appointed, notionally by the Conference, in reality by Wesley himself. It was the preachers, and in particular the 'assistants' (later called 'superintendents'), who on Wesley's behalf determined who should be admitted as members, continued in membership or struck off. It was in keeping with this that the annual published minutes, and the periodic summaries of them known as the 'Large Minutes', were cast in the form of instructions to the travelling preachers about the exercise of their ministry. This national extra-parochial system of pastoral oversight was only possible, however, because in every local society Wesley entrusted the day-to-day care of society members and the management of their financial affairs to lay class leaders and stewards. Although they were accountable to him, and were appointed or removed from office by him or the itinerant preacher, they represent a sharing of oversight by laypeople that has remained an important feature of Methodism.

After Wesley's death all this continued, but now the preachers no longer acted in his name but their own. And with the change came subtle differences. They were mostly laymen, but, because of the role they played in the oversight of the societies, they had all along had a quasi-ministerial relationship to the members of the societies, and now they began to see themselves in ministerial terms. The custom began of an annual letter from the Conference to the societies. The annual minutes began to lose their character as a record of conversations between preachers about the conduct of their ministry and take on the tone of legislative pronouncements for the general membership, a process driven by the need in the years following Wesley's death to resolve disputes about worship and relations with the Established Church. The notion quickly took hold that the 1784 Deed gave a legal foundation for all the powers that the Conference exercised.

The basis of it was established custom, however, not legal entitlement – custom and consent. The Methodist connexion was a voluntary association, as Wesley himself and subsequent writers were fond of stressing, and it would hold only so long as its members consented to its arrangements. That custom was soon to be challenged and the consent, by some at least, withdrawn. It is worth underlining the fact that some of those who did so, in 1797 and subsequently, argued that the 1784 Deed gave the Conference authority only over the preachers and not over the societies and circuits. On the face of it they were right. Later Wesleyans were in the habit of quoting the statement of the vice-chancellor in his judgment in the Court of Chancery on the Warren case in 1835 – 'The Conference has been the supreme legislative and executive Body since the death of Mr Wesley' – but that was an observation based on what was admitted by both sides in the dispute, not a ruling; in legal terms the remark was *obiter*. The scope of the Conference's powers over the whole connexion was never tested in the courts.

The Conference identified by the 1784 Deed was a conference of 100 of the travelling preachers, and although, in respect for Wesley's wishes, other preachers attended and joined in the debates, there was no provision for participation by representatives of society members. In an age of rising democratic aspirations that was bound to be questioned. The Methodist New Connexion separated in 1797, in part over the issue of relations with the Established Church, and in part over the composition of the Conference. Their constitution provided for an equal number of travelling preachers, in later terminology 'ministers',[4] and lay representatives in the membership of the Conference, and for lay members also to share in government at district and more local levels.

Other breakaway movements in the period from 1800 to 1850 went further. The Bible Christians ensured that every five years at least there would be an equal number of ministers and lay members. The Primitive Methodist Conference consisted of two lay persons to every minister, while the United Methodist Free Churches instituted their Assembly with fewer powers over the local churches, constituted by free election, ordained or lay, from the quarterly meetings of the various circuits. The details of these arrangements matter little for the present discussion; what is important to note, however, is that these Conferences, however constituted, and whatever the extent of their authority, exercised a supervisory role in which no distinction was made between 'spiritual' and 'temporal' affairs.

Meanwhile, the Wesleyan Methodists began to develop a theological rationale to underpin the exclusively ministerial membership of their Conference and the manner in which it exercised its authority, the doctrine of the pastoral office. Shepherds, according to their reading of the New Testament, were divinely appointed to preach, to teach and to rule, and in consequence to relinquish the power of government to others in the church would be a betrayal of a sacred duty. Laypeople might be consulted on various matters, locally on the admission or exclusion of members, or in district and Conference committees on 'temporal affairs' (specifically money), but the final decision on such matters continued to be reserved to the ministers. It was central to the Wesleyan position that one could not be held accountable (to God or to one's peers) for oversight that one could not enforce; but this was to take an excessively disciplinary view of *episcope*, to the detriment of the aspects of encouragement and nurture.

The modern reader is struck by the emphasis on rules and discipline in the literature of the period. In essence it goes back to Wesley's conception of a network of religious societies dedicated to the pursuit of holiness. 'Ruling' the flock meant ensuring that each member's manner of life conformed to the faith he or she professed, and that he or she observed the rules requiring regular attendance at weekday class meeting and Sunday worship. Otherwise he or she would be removed from membership, and the final decision on that was jealously reserved to the ministers.

It is not surprising that in the early decades of the nineteenth century this authoritarian and inflexible stance caused widespread resentment and was the cause of major schisms, culminating in the loss of one-third of the Wesleyan membership in the 1850s. It is more surprising today that so many lay Wesleyans supported it for so long. Even so, it could not survive. Change had begun with the appointment of 'mixed committees' of ministers and laypeople (not strictly representatives, but chosen by the ministers) reporting to the Conference, the earliest being in 1803. From 1819 district meetings of ministers included lay officials from the circuits to discuss financial matters. Gradually a series of national committees were set up to deal with the various connexional funds and business related to them. Most of these met on the eve of the Conference itself and reported to it, so that the same business would be discussed within the space of a few of days by two overlapping groups. It was largely for reasons of economy, therefore, that in 1878 the Conference was opened up to lay representatives, no longer chosen by the ministers but elected by the lay members of the district committees or by the mixed session of the Conference itself.[5]

Ministerial authority remained entrenched, however, in two respects. The 'Legal Hundred', identified as the Conference in John Wesley's 1784 Deed, continued to operate and had to confirm all decisions taken by the larger gathering. Moreover, the business of the representative session, comprising ministers and laypeople, was restricted to what were considered to be 'temporal' affairs. All matters relating to the selection, admission, oversight and discipline of the ministers, the discipline of lay members on appeal, the supervision of publications and the conduct of public worship (effectively, therefore, all doctrinal matters) and pastoral supervision generally were reserved to the pastoral session comprising ministers only. The developments of 1878 do not represent *episcope* shared by ordained and lay alike.

Throughout the second half of the nineteenth century attempts were made to reintegrate divided Methodism, and the first fruit of it was the union of the Methodist New Connexion, the Bible Christians and the United Methodist Free Churches in 1907 to form the United Methodist Church. Its annual Conference was composed of equal numbers of ministers and laypersons, continuing the tradition of the New Connexion, and its authority over all aspects of the church was given legal basis by Act of Parliament in the same year.

The union of this body with the Wesleyan and Primitive Methodists in 1932 was the subject of protracted negotiations because of the differences involved. There is no need here to go into the details, but it is important to note the outcome. As in 1907, the Conference was given legal foundation by the Methodist Church Union Act 1929 (now superseded by an Act of 1976). The Wesleyan tradition was continued: a representative session, with elected ministers (presbyters) and lay representatives in equal numbers, and a ministerial session, with additional ministers. To the ministerial session were reserved all matters relating to the selection, oversight and discipline of ministers and the final decision as to their stationing, the annual pastoral address to the churches, pastoral consideration of the state of the church and pastoral efficiency and 'all ministerial and pastoral subjects of like nature'. No definition was offered of the word 'pastoral'. Reception of ministers into full connexion with the Conference (effectively their licensing) was reserved to the representative session, but the decision to ordain, and the ordination service itself, were acts of the ministerial session. In practice this arrangement meant that a number of issues were brought to both sessions, particularly matters of doctrine and ecumenical relations. In many respects the distinction between temporal and spiritual was retained, and there was no mechanism by which conflicting decisions by the two sessions on the same issue could be reconciled. This could, and did, lead to difficulty, and – effectively – to a ministerial veto.

As a result a major revision of the Conference was adopted in 1988–9. This now clearly locates the authority of the Conference in its representative session, at least one-half of whom must be lay. Apart from oversight of those in training for the ordained (presbyteral) ministry and acting as a final court of appeal in the discipline of ministers, all the decisions of the ministerial session are recommendations reported to the representative session, although in relation to ministerial candidature, ordination and retirement that session cannot act without such a recommendation. The ministerial session now meets essentially as a professional gathering, concerned not only with the maintenance of professional standards but also with the general life of the church, about which it can express its views to the representative session. Similar provisions were introduced in 1998 for the order of deacons, whose representatives now meet as a committee of the Conference.

Thus, although the Wesleyan tradition continues in the existence of a separate gathering of presbyters for the discussion of Conference business, it is true to say that as at present configured the Conference, comprising ordained and lay in more or less equal numbers, exercises oversight over the whole life, 'temporal' and 'spiritual', of the Methodist Church. But it has been a long journey to reach this point, and earlier statements, prior to 1990, about Conference *episcope* have to be understood in the light of the distinction then obtaining between the authority of ordained presbyters and that of lay members.

Theological rationale

What theology or theologies can be said to underlie these attitudes to the Conference? The answer is not always apparent. Because the Conference in the 1790s was driven by circumstances into a legislative role it is the language of government rather than pastoral oversight that dominates all sides in the polemical literature, even though in practice all the Conferences of divided Methodism would continue to comment on the spiritual state of their societies. But when the Wesleyan ministers came to defend their exclusive jurisdiction it was to theology, and specifically to scripture, that they turned.

We have seen the understanding of the pastoral office upon which they grounded their practice. Following the line taken by John Wesley himself, they held that the New Testament made no distinction between presbyters and bishops and that consequently all powers of oversight resided in the travelling preachers, who were responsible for the welfare and progress of the connexion, including authority to select and admit (ordain) new members to their ranks.

As we have seen, the changes in 1878 were not driven by a change in theological conviction. If they had been, negotiations for the 1932 Union would have been less difficult. The theology of the pastoral office, though now restricted in scope, remained. Ministers retained their own session and held half the seats in the other.

What of the non-Wesleyan bodies? Considering the political atmosphere of the period from 1790 to 1850, it is not surprising that there was much talk of 'liberty' and the right to self-government. There were ecclesiastical precedents to hand, too, in congregationalism. But it would be a mistake to think those were the only influences. Apologists appealed to the New Testament to show the involvement of the whole church in its government. Government, however, as for the Wesleyans, was the key concept. The wider, pastoral, language of oversight is hard to find in their writing about the Conference.

Surprisingly, little use seems to have been made by them, in print at least, of 'the priesthood of all believers'. They regarded the Wesleyans as exercising 'priestly domination' and 'popery' comparable to what had obtained at the Reformation, and asserted against it the freedom and right of every member of the church to exercise whatever ministry God might from time to time call them to, and to take an equal share in decisions about the church's governance, but they do not seem to have expressed this in the theological language of universal priesthood.

By the twentieth century, however, it was certainly being discussed, and at the Union of 1932 it was incorporated into the statement of doctrinal standards of the united church and was instrumental in meeting non-Wesleyan fears about the status of the ministry:

> Christ's ministers in the church are stewards in the household of God and shepherds of his flock. Some are called and ordained to this sole occupation and have a principal and directing part in these great duties but they

hold no priesthood differing in kind from that which is common to all the Lord's people and have no exclusive title to the preaching of the gospel or the care of souls. These ministries are shared with them by others to whom also the Spirit divides his gifts severally as he wills.

The Methodist Church holds the doctrine of the priesthood of all believers and consequently believes that no priesthood exists which belongs exclusively to a particular order or class of men [*sic*] but in the exercise of its corporate life and worship special qualifications for the discharge of special duties are required and thus the principle of representative selection is recognised.

Significantly, the first of these paragraphs was lifted almost verbatim from a statement adopted by the Wesleyan Conference in 1908, and shows how far that body had come by that time. Earlier, Wesleyan writers such as W. B. Pope had acknowledged universal priesthood as a Reformation doctrine, but made little application of it. There is still in these paragraphs a reference to the 'principal and directing part' taken by ordained presbyters, however, which was the theological undergirding for the reserved powers still assigned to the ministerial session of the Conference in 1932.

What of the changes in 1988–9? Both practical and theological factors were involved. The exclusive authority of the ministers over their own ranks was gradually being eroded. Laypeople were becoming involved in the selection of candidates and in various committees dealing with their oversight. Slowly the conviction was taking hold that laypeople had insights and experience that were relevant in such cases. There was also the difficulty of conflicting decisions taken by the two sessions, to which I have referred.

Perhaps more important, however, is the fact that in 1932 the uniting church had included a significant proportion, about 40 per cent, of members and ministers who had been steeped in the non-Wesleyan traditions, and who might as a matter of practice accord ministers a 'principal and directing part' but would continue to appeal to the priesthood of all believers to insist that, in principle, the exercise of all forms of ministry is open to those whom God calls and equips, whether ordained or lay. Often that appeal was in negative terms, about individual 'rights', and lacked the rich corporate and liturgical content of the New Testament references and the classic expositions of Reformation writers. But that non-Wesleyan tradition persists and was for many a driving force behind the changes to the Conference introduced in 1988–9.

The principal factor in 1988–9, however, was a wider ecumenical shift in theological understanding placing greater emphasis on the 'people of God'. It is no coincidence that another report presented to the 1988 Conference was entitled *The Ministry of the People of God*. Greater stress was being placed on the calling of every Christian individually, and of all Christians collectively, to take responsibility for the life and mission of the church. It came to be recognised that all Christians are 'lay' in that they belong to the one *laos* of God, and that the differentiation between ordained and unordained is a differentiation between different specific callings and gifts. One stimulus to this had been the structure of the 1964 Dogmatic Constitution on the Church of the Second Vatican Council (*Lumen Gentium*), which discusses church and ministry in the context of the calling of the People of God. A similar emphasis can be seen in World Council of Churches (WCC) publications of the period. This was more than a reaffirmation of the priesthood of all believers as understood earlier. That had tended to concentrate on rights. Now the stress could be on gifts. Every member, as a member of the Body of Christ, had a contribution to make towards its well-being and a share of responsibility for the quality of its life. The implication was that oversight, *episcope*, is a responsibility in which all share.

Such an emphasis resonates well with Methodist experience. Ever since John Wesley had instituted the office of class leader laypeople have exercised oversight in their local situation. Underneath the conflicts over governance in Methodism's history lies a frustration that laypeople, called to and entrusted with oversight, were entrusted only so far. For most people, the exercise of that responsibility will be in the local church of which they are members; for some, in the wider sphere of the circuit or district. Those who are office holders will have particular perspectives and exercise specific responsibilities, but none in principle can abdicate. In the governing Conference, in which oversight responsibility for the faith and order, worship and mission, spiritual well-being and material maintenance of the church ultimately resides, *episcope* is shared by ordained and lay on terms that acknowledge that, while some are particularly called and ordained to a ministry of oversight, and are consequently more strongly represented proportionately to their overall numbers than laypeople, they have no exclusive voice, and no overriding veto, in the process of discerning and executing God's will for his church.[6]

Personal, collegial, communal

Recent ecumenical discussion of *episcope* has distinguished three ways in which it may – indeed, should – be exercised: personally, collegially and communally. The personal aspect may be exercised not only by those designated bishops but by others, ordained or lay, who have leadership responsibilities. 'Collegial' refers to the collective action of those having personal oversight who consult together, agree on common policies and so act in concert. The communal dimension refers to the involvement of the whole body of believers in consultation.[7] These definitions leave unclear the precise relation between the first two and the third. Are those with personal oversight subject to the communal authority, or is the communal gathering simply advisory? Of course, the problem may be resolved by assigning separate spheres of authority to each, but the often used phrase 'bishop in council' fails to provide for the situation when the two disagree.

Personal *episcope* is exercised in Methodism in many ways: by the President of the Conference, district chairs, circuit superintendents and other presbyters in their various appointments and by lay officers and pastoral assistants. But all are accountable, through the appropriate oversight bodies, ultimately to the

Conference, from which all exercise of *episcope* is delegated, by ordination or appointment. There are various contexts in which collegial oversight is exercised, such as in circuit staff meetings, which may often include presbyters, deacons and lay officers.

But what of the Conference? For John Wesley, as we have seen, the Conference was advisory. Oversight resided in him and those to whom he delegated it, including not only the travelling preachers but also local stewards and class leaders. For the New Connexion and Bible Christians, authority lay with the Conference; for the Primitive Methodists in the early days, partly with the Conference and partly with the district synods, later with the Conference; and, for the United Methodist Free Churches, with the Conference for connexional (nationwide) matters, such as the deployment of ministers, and with the relevant society and circuit meetings for all local matters. Representative ministers and laypersons were involved in all of these; there were no special powers reserved to individuals, and so oversight in these traditions was truly communal.

The case with the Wesleyans and with Methodism after 1932 is more complex. We have already seen that in the early nineteenth century the Wesleyans developed a doctrine of the pastoral office. The logic of this position was that oversight resided not in the Conference per se but in its members, and was derived from their divine calling and consequent recognition as pastors (after 1836 by formal ordination with the laying on of hands). The Conference represented their 'united counsels', ensured consistency of oversight throughout the connexion and reinforced the authority of each minister. The Conference did not delegate authority to the ministers; they imparted their own authority to it. In 1828 Richard Watson could write, 'The sum of [the Conference's] power is nothing more than the power which is essentially vested in each Minister, by the very duties which he is under scriptural obligation to perform.' Each was 'received' by the Conference into connexion with it on condition of observing its rules. All ministers were accountable to each other and were regularly interrogated in the annual Conference and district meetings. The outcome was collegial episcopacy in all but name.

The adjustments made in 1878 when laypeople were included alongside ministers in a representative session introduced a communal element but dealt with the tension between personal-collegial and communal by splitting the responsibilities. The communal body essentially dealt with 'temporal' matters while the collegial body of ministers retained oversight over the 'spiritual' (and, legally, authority still lay with the collegial 'Legal Hundred' established by the 1784 Deed, who had to ratify all decisions). This arrangement was essentially carried over at Methodist Union in 1932 without the potential veto of the Legal Hundred. The ministerial session retained a collegial responsibility for its own membership and to some extent for the wider church. It is only with the changes of 1988–9 that Conference *episcope* became truly communal. Such collegial presbyteral oversight as remains, in the sense of retaining a final decision, is confined to recruitment and final appeals over discipline. For the rest it processes business for final ratification elsewhere and acts as a gathering for mutual support. The same may be said of the order of deacons, with the exception that, being also a religious order, there is collegiality in the annual Convocation.

Thus a Conference exercising *episcope* over the church has been a feature of Methodism since John Wesley. Its composition and powers, so far as Britain is concerned, and its theological rationale have changed over the years. The language of *episcope*, introduced by ecumenical discussion, is recent, but the exercise of oversight, collectively and individually, has always been present. It is ironic that what now obtains – oversight over the whole life of the church shared by lay and ordained on equal terms – was first introduced by the Methodist New Connexion in 1797, without any separate ministerial gathering. It has taken a long time to return to that point. But it now rests on broader theological foundations.

Notes

1 First published in Mervyn Davies (ed.), *A Thankful Heart and a Discerning Mind: Essays in Honour of John Newton* (Dursley: Lonely Scribe, 2010), pp. 110–26. Reprinted by permission.

2 For example, *The Nature and Mission of the Church*, Faith and Order Paper no. 198 (Geneva: WCC Publications, 2005), paras. 90–8.

3 The story is set out in James E. Kirby, *The Episcopacy in American Methodism* (Nashville, TN: Kingswood Books, 2000).

4 In 2012, after this chapter was originally published, official terminology was changed again, from 'minister' to 'presbyter', when referring to those ordained to the ministry of word and sacraments. 'Minister' is now used only to include ordained deacons as well as presbyters. In this chapter, however, 'minister' is generally used in its earlier sense.

5 See, for example, Thomas Percival Bunting, *Laymen in Conference?* (London: Elliot Stock, 1871).

6 More recently the attempt has been made to link shared oversight to the relational aspects of the doctrine of the Trinity, but it has not been very fully developed. See *The Nature of Oversight*, § 4.7.

7 See *The Nature and Mission of the Church*, para. 96; and, earlier, *Baptism, Eucharist and Ministry*, Faith and Order Paper no. 111 (Geneva: WCC Publications, 1982), p. 26, para. 26.

9 Richard Matthews

A layman overlooked[1]

The Methodist church in the village of Histon, just north of Cambridge, that was opened in 1896 is named 'the Matthews Memorial Church' after Richard Matthews, a native of the village. Displayed inside is a late nineteenth-century framed photo, given by the family, of an 1820s drawing of a fresh-faced, earnest young man, and a notice preserved from the opening, giving brief details about him. But in historical writing he is barely mentioned and his very considerable service to his church and to the anti-slavery movement is largely unknown. This chapter seeks to give him some of the recognition he deserves.

The Matthews family were farmers in Histon in the eighteenth and early nineteenth centuries with considerable land holdings. Richard himself was born in April 1796, the son of Richard and Frances Matthews, who already had a daughter, Elizabeth, born in 1794. There were no other children. Methodism arrived in Histon at the end of the eighteenth century[2] and Richard senior and his wife were involved in its coming. By 1816 Methodists were worshipping in the now widowed Frances' home. Three years later the young Richard took out a licence for a chapel, opened in 1822. By then he was already a local preacher, and circuit records from 1823 to 1825 show him as a class leader and circuit steward and involved in support for the Wesleyan Methodist Missionary Society. Those local commitments soon ended, however, for in 1823 he was admitted to the Middle Temple to study for the bar, and by 1825 he had moved to London, to be joined by 1828 by his mother and sister. On 25 April 1828 he was called to the bar and began in earnest his life's work as a lawyer in the courts, with chambers in London but practising on the Northern Circuit, which embraced Lancashire, Yorkshire, County Durham and all points north. It is an indicator of his parents' relative affluence and status that he was able, with some supplement (of which more later), to meet the costs of his studies, and to be listed officially as the son of a gentleman.[3]

On 29 September 1835 Richard married Hannah Day from Histon, and the couple set up home in the recently developed area of Barnsbury Park, worshipping in the newly opened Liverpool Road Wesleyan church. The marriage was clearly a happy one, but ended sadly with Hannah's premature and painful death five years later, on 27 November 1840. Richard published a memoir of her[4] that gives a moving insight into the piety of the period, with their routine of daily prayers, her determination in spite of crippling pain to maintain her attendance at chapel, twice on Sunday and once in the week, and her refusal of drugs at the end, saying: 'I want my head quite clear.' On 29 September 1843 Richard married again, to Lucy Maria, daughter of George and Mary Heald, of Garston, near Liverpool. Her father was a calico printer and very probably the older brother of James Heald, the philanthropist, Member of Parliament for Stockport and benefactor of Didsbury College. Over the next ten and a half years Richard and Lucy had six children, four girls and two boys.[5]

The memoir of Hannah was not Richard's only publication. Nine other titles carry his name and three more can be safely attributed to him, one of which is a collection of hymns and moral poems primarily by his sister Elizabeth, who set up a school for young ladies just round the corner from him.[6] Most of the others were legal handbooks, digesting and giving advice on criminal law, the execution of wills and the newly introduced legislation of 1836 for the civil registration of marriages and the registration of births and deaths. There were also pamphlets, including an open letter in 1830 to the Lord Chancellor advocating the civil registration of births, and a lecture given in a series attacking socialism, *Is Marriage Worth Perpetuating?*.[7] His interest in marriage law and registration was to serve the churches well, as we shall see.[8]

It is his work for the Wesleyan Methodist Connexion and the Anti-Slavery Society that most concerns us here. The record in Histon Chapel outlines the details, almost certainly derived from his two surviving daughters, who returned to Histon for the latter part of their lives, but scrutiny of original records reveals much more, and shows the extent to which the Methodism of his day, and in a crucial period the anti-slavery movement, depended on his services. From 1828, when he was called to the bar, until 1851 he was a member of the Conference Committee of Privileges, and from its formation in 1843 of its subcommittee; he was a member of the Wesleyan Methodist Missionary Society Committee over the same period, from 1828 to1850,[9] and from 1842 to 1851 was a member of the Education Committee. Of his contribution to the last of these there appears to be no record, but of the first two more can be said. There is no reason to think that his service to education was any different from other committees: frequent attendance at meetings, membership of ad hoc subcommittees, giving formal opinions and acting professionally for the committee. It is a pity that, although committee minutes record requests for opinions, and one can sometimes gather from other sources what his views were, for the most part the content of these opinions is lost.

The Committee of Privileges was set up by the Conference in 1803 as a 'mixed' committee of ministers and professional laymen to 'guard our religious privileges' in an age when those privileges were few and precarious and non-Anglican communities subject to considerable legal disabilities. There are long gaps in the surviving minutes of the committee but they do exist for the 11 years 1835 to 1845 and are revealing for the activities they embraced. They show that two laymen – Richard Reece, a solicitor, and Richard Matthews, the barrister – were the principal advisors and agents of the committee throughout the period.

To read through these minutes is to gain an insight into the problems the Wesleyans, along with others, had to contend with: local magistrates (often Anglican clergy) finding various petty excuses to put legal obstacles in their way. In one example a circuit preaching plan submitted in evidence that a preacher was travelling to an appointment and therefore exempt from road toll charges was rejected because it was not signed – but no direction was given by the magistrate as to who should do so! There were disputes as to whether preachers, either itinerant or local, were exempt from toll charges at all – and, if so, whether the exemption extended to mid-week appointments – and as to what precise procedure had to be followed to secure a licence for a chapel for public worship.

Some court cases involved issues of great principle. A particularly distressing one in 1840 involved the vicar of Gedney, in Lincolnshire, who refused to bury a child in the churchyard on the ground that baptism by a Wesleyan minister was not valid. His was not the first instance, nor the last, but, in spite of existing legal opinion that such baptisms were valid and general support by the bishops, he insisted – egged on by others – on taking his case to the Judicial Committee of the Privy Council, which ruled against him. Matthews gave a formal opinion and later, with others, appeared as counsel for the church.

Equally momentous was a challenge earlier, in 1838, to the Wesleyan model deed. In 1832 the Wesleyan Conference had adopted the device of a model deed stating the trusts upon which church property was held, to be referred to in all subsequent deeds without the necessity and cost of spelling out the trusts afresh each time. The Conference had adopted the policy with care, seeking the opinion of four counsel, including the Solicitor General, before doing so. All were favourable, and the Solicitor General's opinion was co-signed by Richard Matthews as junior counsel. Richard also addressed the Conference on the matter.[10] In 1838 there was a serious challenge, however. In the village of Llanbister in what is now Powys, central Wales, a clergyman sold houses and land to the local Wesleyans, which they settled on the model deed, and then gave them a larger sum with which to build a chapel. On his death his son challenged the transaction on a number of grounds, including the claim that the model deed had not been properly enrolled in Chancery, that it did not cover land and houses as well as chapels and that the deed of sale ought to have specified the trusts in detail and not by reference to the model deed. Had he succeeded, not only would the local trustees have lost both their land and their chapel but the whole concept of a model deed would have been invalidated at a stroke. The case dragged on through two hearings and two appeals over two years, Richard Matthews appearing for the church, but in the end the church won its case. It is not surprising that two years running, in 1839 and 1840, the Conference recorded a vote of thanks to him and Richard Reece by name.[11]

Much of the attention of the Committee of Privileges had to be given to proposed legislation, and involved Matthews in subcommittees, the giving of opinions and, from time to time, deputations. It is striking how easy it appears to have been for the Wesleyans to secure interviews with quite senior government ministers in an effort to get them to change their mind, and ministers' readiness on occasion to accept and incorporate amendments. It is evidence of the growing social standing and political importance of the connexion. Two such instances involved educational matters, and to modern eyes do not show the Wesleyans in a particularly attractive light. In both the Committee of Privileges met jointly with the Conference's Education Committee. In 1839 the government proposed a system of national education, which was to involve an establishment, publicly funded, for teacher training along with a model school. It was bitterly opposed, not only by the Wesleyans, principally on the grounds that it would allow religious instruction for Roman Catholic pupils to be based on the Douai version of the Bible. A more general objection, to which Jabez Bunting and Richard Matthews put their names in the committee, was that 'any attempt to instruct, in the same school, the children of the poorer classes (whose parents, in the exercise of their undoubted rights as men and Britons, belong to various Christian denominations) by teaching adapted to every prevailing variety of religious belief or opinion will…be found impracticable; and even if practicable…would, in many instances, produce among the children so incongruously mingled together, a dangerous spirit of scepticism and unbelief'.[12] The proposed legislation was dropped.

A second instance of protecting denominational educational turf arose in 1843 over a proposed Factories Bill, designed to regulate the employment of children and provide for their education. Here the objections, voiced by Nonconformists generally, focused on the dominant role given to Anglican clergy in the provision and control of schools, objections made sharper by reaction to the growing influence of the Anglo-Catholic movement. After intense lobbying, in which Matthews was involved, the educational clauses of the bill were dropped. What is sad in these episodes is how little interest the churches appear to show in the social needs the government were seeking to address, though the Wesleyans did create their Education Committee and expand their day schools after 1839.

Two other examples of legislative issues are worth mentioning. Consternation was caused in 1844 by a bill to give Unitarians legal title retrospectively to chapels built before the Unitarians were legally recognised. Matthews attacked it in print as unnecessary and potentially subversive of the existing law of equity.[13] A major weakness was that the bill provided that, when there was no explicit doctrinal statement in a chapel trust deed (there was no more than a reference to Wesley's sermons and New Testament explanatory notes in the Wesleyan model deed), an oral affirmation of what had been the teaching in the chapel over the past 25 years would determine its denominational allegiance. In the event, negotiations between the committee and the government led to acceptable amendments. It was a particularly sensitive issue for the Presbyterians, many of whose congregations had turned Unitarian over the years and stood to gain a chapel as well.

The second example occurred a year later, when the government attempted to introduce a bill to regulate and supervise charities. In today's regulatory environment it seems a timid affair, and we would regard trustee accountability as highly important, but it was an innovation that the Wesleyans strongly opposed, Matthews again being involved in subcommittees and giving a formal opinion. The bill was defeated.

His support for the Wesleyan Missionary Society can be traced, as we have seen, to his early days at Histon, and in later years there is evidence that he was in demand to chair public meetings.[14] A far from exhaustive survey of the extensive minutes of the General Committee and its subcommittees reveals a similar pattern of involvement to that of the Committee of Privileges: attendance at about half the meetings (absences no doubt attributable to professional duties) and his services called upon periodically for advice and action. Of particular note is his participation in the search for a permanent Mission House for the society following the success of the Centenary Fund appeal of 1839. He was a member of the search committee that finally secured the City of London Tavern at the end of that year and he advised on (but did not draft) the trust deed upon which it was settled in 1841. He was also drawn into a dispute in 1839 concerning allegations against Isaac Whitehouse, a Wesleyan missionary in Jamaica, who had been accused by a Baptist missionary, John Clark, and a Quaker, Joseph Sturge, of possessing and ill-treating slaves. The allegations were vigorously denied, and Whitehouse was officially cleared, but the accusers persisted and Matthews volunteered to mediate, only to have his offer rejected by them on the grounds that he was a Wesleyan and committee member.[15] Jamaica in fact occupied a good deal of the committee's attention in this period. In 1832 the mission there suffered considerable damage to its property from riots and was unable to get redress from the courts, the magistrates, like the planters generally, persistently showing hostility to the missionaries. Jamaica was a chartered colony, responsible to some extent for its own laws, so the legal situation was unclear, and the committee, with Matthews' assistance, pressed the British government for clarification, and for a declaration that the Toleration Act of 1812, which lifted some of the restrictions earlier imposed upon non-Anglican Protestants, extended to all the colonies.

But without question his contribution of greatest importance was in connection with the abolition of slavery, and on this his various professional interests in property questions, the legal status of Nonconformist churches, marriage and registration came together in the service of the Missionary Committee and the Anti-Slavery Society. There is no doubt about his commitment. His earliest known publication, produced in 1824, possibly even before he left Histon, was a pamphlet under the pseudonym 'Anthropos', *The Rights of Man (not the Paines) but the Rights of Man in the West Indies*.[16] It is a vigorous attack on slavery. Bodily freedom is a right, given by God, that is beyond all law. Its exercise has to be kept within bounds by law so as not to interfere with the rights of others, but it cannot be taken away. If, therefore, the slave is denied by the law the protection it ought to give him he has a right to rebel, and no moral guilt can be attached to resort to violence. Appeals to history to justify slavery and arguments for merely ameliorating the condition, for delay and for compensation for the planters are swept aside in a call for immediate emancipation, and for a boycott of (subsidised) West Indian sugar and the use of East Indian instead, so as to undermine the planters' resistance. Reading it one is reminded of the debates in Britain after World War II about decolonisation, and cannot help wondering what Matthews would have made of the timid response of the British churches to the World Council of Churches' call for support for African liberation movements in the 1970s and 1980s.

It is intriguing to speculate what might have kindled his commitment to the abolitionist cause, which, judging by her published poems, his sister Elizabeth shared. Missionary Society and other publications were no doubt influential, and there were prominent abolitionists in Cambridge. But it is also to be noted that, around the time Richard and his sister were born, the ex-slave and campaigner Olaudah Equiano (Gustavus Vassa) married a woman from Soham, 12 miles from Histon as the crow flies, and one of their daughters who died in infancy is buried at Chesterton, only three miles away.

So it comes as no surprise to find Matthews applying in 1825 for the vacant post of (employed) secretary of the Anti-Slavery Society[17] or that, when he resigned because of the pressure of professional duties, he was immediately voted onto the committee as a member because of 'their sense of his zeal'. The committee was a large one, some 40 members, though its meetings rarely involved more than a handful, of which Matthews was frequently one. He must be considered one of the more active, though never prominent, supporters of the movement. But it was not until the cause was effectively won that he came into his own.

In the period after emancipation in 1833 the Anti-Slavery Society, along with the missionary societies, began to monitor the effect of the various laws in force and their effect on freed slaves. The matter was complicated by the distinction, already mentioned, between the Crown Colonies, legislated for by the Westminster Parliament, and the Chartered Colonies, which had their own legislatures. Surveys were made, in which Matthews was involved, of the situation in the various jurisdictions. A particular issue concerned marital status. Prior to emancipation, although it was legally possible for slaves to be married in the Established Church with the permission of the owners, it was rare, and many were married informally by missionaries of the various non-Anglican churches, which required cohabiting couples to be married before admitting them to Holy Communion. Once they became free persons, however, their status and entitlement to legal protection, inheritance and property rights were thrown into doubt, and, if they had resorted to the Established Church for (re)marriage, their existing children would have been rendered illegitimate.[18] Pressure was put on the British government to address the problem and various remedies were contemplated. It has to be remembered that, until 1836, it was not possible in English law for people (apart from Jews and Quakers) to be legally married except in the Established Church, and one remedy suggested was to attach a clause to one of the two 1836 Acts that introduced civil marriage in England and Wales and the registration of births, marriages and deaths; another was to attach the clause to one of the Emancipation Amendment Acts that were found necessary after 1833, but neither of these came to anything. Eventually it was agreed with the government that separate legislation would be required.

Richard Matthews was not the only lawyer involved,[19] but he does seem to have taken the lead. In his capacity as a member of both the Anti-Slavery Society Committee and the Wesleyan Missionary Committee he appeared before a Parliamentary Select Committee in May 1836, and submitted written evidence in July that led the committee in its report to recommend that the issue be addressed. He was able to assure the committee that he was acquainted with the legislation of every one of the West Indian colonies. It was not until 1838, however, that a bill was finally drawn up. The Anti-Slavery Society Committee minutes show that it was Matthews, at the request of the colonial secretary, who drafted it. It passed into law by Order in Council in September 1838. It is a remarkable document. Not only does it provide retrospectively for the legal recognition of the existing marriages of former slaves, including partnerships when no religious ceremony of any kind had taken place, it also makes provision for the future that goes far beyond what would be the case in England and Wales until nearly the end of the century, in that it authorises non-Anglican ministers both to officiate at weddings and to act as registrars for them. The status of 'authorised person', obviating the need for the presence of a civil registrar, was not introduced in England until 1898. The Act must be regarded as Richard Matthews' most significant legacy to posterity.

But the battle was not yet over. Matthews' Act applied only to the Crown Colonies, for which the Westminster Parliament legislated directly. The Chartered Colonies, which had their own legislatures, had to be persuaded to come into line. Whether through reluctance or careless drafting it took some time for them to do so. The British government's trump card was that their legislation could be denied the royal assent. An Act passed by the legislature in Nevis was disallowed after representations, with Matthews' aid, were made to the colonial secretary. The Bahamas also provoked objections, as did Jamaica, but in 1840 the latter finally passed an Act of which Matthews, having noted some minor faults, observed, 'The measure surpasses my most sanguine expectations of Jamaica Legislation and I think we ought to be thankful and content.'[20]

It was the West Indies that captured Matthews' devotion. After the Anti-Slavery Society was wound down in 1839 he did not apparently associate himself with the British and Foreign Anti-Slavery Society, concerned with worldwide slavery, but he was involved (one of only two who were not officers of the society) in the subcommittee of the Missionary Society dealing with Negro schools in the West Indies.

In 1852 there came a public dispute between Matthews and his church. The context was the massive defections and expulsions in consequence of the Fly-Sheets dispute of 1849–50, which cost the Wesleyan connexion over

100,000 members. In a pamphlet addressed to the president of the Conference,[21] Matthews held that the expulsions were in contravention of the Conference's own published rules. In this he was relying on the text of a version of the *General Rules of the Methodist Societies* published in 1798, rather than, as the Conference did, on the revision of the 'Large Minutes' published the previous year. At the heart of the dispute was the question whether the power of the Leaders' Meeting in expulsions was limited to determination of guilt, the sentence being decided by the itinerant preacher, or extended also to sentencing. Matthews held the latter to be the rule stated in the 1798 publication and the one under which his father and family had first come into Methodism. It was not a new question; the issue dogged all the disputes from 1800 to 1850. It was complicated by the fact that the 1797 Conference had promised a publication of its rules, but included the letter containing that promise within the compilation of documents that formed the 1797 'Large Minutes', leading to the supposition that the rules were to be found elsewhere. Discussion was made intractable by the development of the doctrine of the Pastoral Office, according to which the church's pastors had the divine right and duty to rule the flock, a doctrine Matthews dismissed as a 'new-fangled notion'.

The result was a somewhat indignant and condescending reply by William Arthur,[22] who nevertheless had little difficulty in showing that the 1798 booklet on which Matthews relied could not, by its contents, be the comprehensive collection of rules promised the year beforehand. It is difficult to know what effect this dispute had on Matthews' relations with the church. In 1852 his name disappeared from all Conference committees, but whether for this reason or because of increased professional duties we cannot now know. It is reassuring, however, to note that the *Wesleyan Methodist Magazine* published an obituary in 1854, limited, as was common, to his Christian character, and included a more informative reference to him in conjunction with his sister's obituary in 1870.[23] Still more significant is the warm tribute paid to him in the Missionary Committee minutes a few days after his death, even though he had not been a member of the committee for nearly three years.

One other service Richard Matthews performed for his church deserves mention. In 1847 he published, anonymously, *A Companion to the Wesleyan Hymn-Book*, a collection of 228 tunes for use with the words-only 1780 *Collection of Hymns for the Use of the People Called Methodists* and its 1831 supplement, together with 18 psalm chants.[24] It was published by the Conference Office. According to James Lightwood,[25] it was 'perhaps the most highly esteemed of all…and long remained a favourite both in church and home', but despite being often reprinted it is surprisingly rare today. The music is set out unusually, alto–tenor–soprano–bass, and there are explanatory introductions, one (added in a second edition) explaining the layout of the music, another on the singing of chants, beside a more general preface that reveals Matthews' tastes. He laments the fact that many good hymns are falling out of use for want of a tune, and the 'highly inconvenient practice of requiring from the preacher before he enters the pulpit a list of the hymns he intends to use, by which he is intruded upon at a time when undisturbed composure is most desirable, and is prevented the use of any other hymn, however appropriate, which may afterwards strike his mind'. He urges singers to avoid 'gurgling' and drawling, and insists that the organ must lead and not drown. 'It is a mistake to suppose that congregational singing is improved by the performer always having his hands full of notes.' He says he began the compilation in manuscript for his small village congregation 30 years previously (i.e. about 1817, before the first Histon chapel was opened, when he was about 20). It would be interesting to know whether at that stage it included the psalm chants.

In July 1852 Matthews was made a serjeant-at-law, and was widely expected to be made a judge.[26] Tradition preserved at the Histon church claims that he was offered two colonial judgeships, which he declined.[27] But time was running out. In September 1853 he made his will, and on 24 February 1854 he died. He is buried, with his wife and sister and four of his children, in Highgate Cemetery.

Sadly, no biography will ever be written, as no personal papers or letters appear to have survived. Apart from what he reveals of himself in the memoir to his first wife we can only guess at the sort of man he was. He was not particularly wealthy: he does not feature in the subscription lists for the 1839 Centenary Fund as a major donor.[28] He seems to have been a modest man, if that is the reason for his anonymous publications. But he was devoted to his church, to the cause of overseas missions and particularly to the abolition of slavery,[29] and as a preacher, musician and – above all – a lawyer he brought his gifts (and a lot of his time) to the service of those causes and to his Lord. He was one who, in Charles Wesley's words,[30] 'engaged all his powers' to 'serve the present age, his calling to fulfil', and he deserves to be honoured.

Notes

1 Originally a paper presented at the Oxford Institute of Methodist Theological Studies in August 2007, published in the *Epworth Review*, vol. 35, no. 3, 2008, pp. 52–63. Copyright Trustees for Methodist Church Purposes, reprinted by permission.

2 The exact date is uncertain. Frank Tice in *The History of Methodism in Cambridge* (London: Epworth Press, 1966) gives it as 1798, but the preacher involved, Thomas Pinder, was not stationed in the area until the following year.

3 Social status rather than education was the primary consideration in admission to the Inns of Court in those days, but it is evident that both Richard and his sister were well educated, though it is not known by what means.

4 Richard Matthews, *The Last Days and Hours of Mrs. Hannah Matthews* (London: John Mason, 1841).

5 The Bible he gave Lucy before their marriage still survives. Into it he inserted some collects and a table of daily readings through the year, three chapters in the morning, one at night, similar to the one he and Hannah had previously used.

6 *Original Hymns and Moral Poems for Children and Young Persons, by Elizabeth Matthews and R*, 2nd edn (London, 1835).

7 Richard Matthews, *Is Marriage Worth Perpetuating? The Ninth of a Series of Lectures against Socialism* (London, 1840) – a reply to a published series of lectures by the

social reformer Richard Owen (1771–1858) arguing against the institution of marriage. Regrettably, Matthews does not show up well, relying heavily on sarcasm and not, one would now think, addressing the underlying issues.

8   There is also extant a printed calendar, 'An Almanac for Two Centuries', constructed by him, enabling dates to be calculated from 1800 to 2000. Whether it was formally published – and, if so, what circulation it enjoyed – is not known.

9   There are three gaps, 1832, 1837, 1846, because the committee operated a system by which members retired in rotation, to be renominated after a year.

10   Benjamin Gregory, *Side Lights on the Conflicts of Methodism* (London: Cassell, 1899), p. 93. His reference to 'Mr C Matthews' in that context must be a mistake.

11   It was a rare honour. There are only ten such tributes in the 25 years to 1850. Another was to Matthews in 1842 over the Gedney case.

12   *Wesleyan Methodist Magazine*, 1839, pp. 582f.

13   Richard Matthews, *Strictures on the Dissenters' Chapels Bill* (London: Hatchard, 1844).

14   See, for example, *Wesleyan Methodist Magazine*, 1847, p. 137, where his remarks are reported.

15   See George Smith, *History of Wesleyan Methodism*, vol. 3, *Modern Methodism*, 4th edn (London: Carlton and Porter, 1864), pp. 357f.; and *The Watchman*, 1839, p. 242.

16   The attribution is secure. The British Library copy contains a manuscript inscription '1824 by Mr Matthews of Histon Cambridgeshire' and the *Histon Parish Magazine* for June 1902 (when his daughter lived in the village) ascribes it to him.

17   It no doubt also helped to finance his studies.

18   See Henrice Altink, '"To Wed or Not to Wed?": The Struggle to Define Afro-Jamaican Relationships, 1834–1838', *Journal of Social History*, vol. 38, no. 1, 2004, pp. 81ff.

19   Joseph Beldam and John Jeremie are also named.

20   Wesleyan Methodist Missionary Society minutes, 1 September 1841.

21   Richard Matthews, *A Reprint of the Rules of the Methodist Societies…to which is added a Letter to the Rev John Hannah DD* (London: Simpkin, Marshall, 1852).

22   William Arthur, *Has the Conference Broken Covenant? A Protest and a Disproof* (London: John Mason, 1852).

23   *Wesleyan Methodist Magazine*, 1854, p. 671; 1870, p. 1053.

24   There can be no doubt about the authorship: (i) it is mentioned in the notice preserved at Histon, dating from the time when one of his daughters lived in the village; (ii) Arthur, in the pamphlet mentioned above, refers to 'the excellent *Companion* [emphasis in original]' in a way that implies that Matthews compiled it; (iii) Francis B. Westbrook, in an apparently unpublished paper in the Methodist Church Musical Society archives, refers to papers in the possession of a Miss Foster that include a letter to Matthews authorising publication of the copyright tune 'Judaea'. The letter, incidentally, makes it clear that the first publication was in 1847, not, as Lightwood believed, 1846. Also among Miss Foster's papers was a manuscript copy of part of the *Companion* bearing the signature of A. J. Moxley, organist of St Paul's Covent Garden, whose assistance in the compilation is acknowledged in the preface.

25   James T. Lightwood, *The Music of the Methodist Hymn-Book* (London: Epworth Press, 1935), p. xx; see also the introduction to the 'Tunes' edition of the 1933 *Methodist Hymn Book*, para. 5.

26   The serjeants were the most senior rank of advocates in the courts, with exclusive rights until 1846 to plead in the Court of Common Pleas, but in time their prestige

was eclipsed by that of Queen's Counsel. There were no appointments after 1875 and the order died out.

27 Judges were appointed at the time from the ranks of the serjeants. Family tradition regarded him as a judge, but official records fail to confirm it. It is probable that, as a serjeant, he presided over trials on circuit, as was often the case.

28 10 guineas from himself and 5 guineas each from his wife, mother and sister. Some donors gave £1,000.

29 He named his second son George Granville Sharpe.

30 *Hymns and Psalms*, 785, verse 2. The quotation picks up the theme of the Oxford Institute at which the paper was originally given: 'To Serve the Present Age, Our Calling to Fulfil'.

Part II

Identity

Introduction to Part II

This part considers various aspects of identity. What is Methodism? What holds it together? Is the bond strong enough to prevent it, as in the past, from pulling apart? How is Methodism to be distinguished from other Christian traditions? And what is the role and what are the obligations of theological education in preserving its identity?

Methodism has always been obliged to define itself. In its earliest days the need was to explain itself to puzzled observers, later to take a stance as an Arminian movement in distinction from those holding to a Calvinist theology. By the end of John Wesley's life there were questions to be resolved about its relation to the Established Church, one of the issues over which the Methodist New Connexion separated from the Wesleyans in 1797. Throughout the nineteenth century, while some Wesleyans retained sympathy for the Church of England, attitudes generally hardened, especially after the rise of the Oxford Movement in the 1830s, and by the end of the century all branches of Methodism counted themselves among the Free Churches. The tone of apologetic writing of the period is defensive and critical. Methodism is defined by (or perhaps in) contrast to other traditions, Anglican, Presbyterian, Congregational. With the rise of the ecumenical movement, however, effectively from the 1950s onwards, the mood has begun to change. The requirement now is to define what may distinctively be offered to partner churches, as the emphasis shifts from amalgamation, with the implied threat of the imposition of alien traditions or the loss of valued ones, to the mutual sharing of treasures.

It does not make the task of self-definition any easier. One of the features of the later twentieth century was the erosion of older hallmarks. In British Methodism, for example, more choice is now left to local churches to determine appropriate administrative structures. Worship styles are more diverse than at any time in Methodism's history. Each new hymn book contains fewer Charles Wesley hymns than its predecessor. Fewer members are cradle Methodists. Many are members, or just fellow worshippers, because the Methodist Church is conveniently accessible. If they move home they may well connect to a church of a different tradition without sense of loss. In some urban areas churches are enriched by the presence of Methodists from overseas, bringing with them their own interpretation of the tradition. It is now harder to say what Methodism is than it has ever been. To say what Methodism is globally is harder still. Some of the chapters that follow explore these issues.

Other chapters address more directly the causes of division and issues of reconciliation. Today they are often ethical and cultural rather than overtly theological. How is the church to respond to changing attitudes in a multicultural, multi-religious, widely atheistic society? Such questions affect, and threaten to divide, all Christian denominations. The chapters in this part do not answer all such questions but consider how the church may hold together under such pressures.

Meanwhile, progress in ecumenical reconciliation continues, albeit slowly. In 1965 the reciprocal anathemas of the Roman Catholic and Orthodox churches were revoked after 900 years. In 1973 European Lutherans and Reformed churches signed the Leuenberg Concordat, which British and other European Methodist churches have subsequently joined. The Methodist Church in Britain and the Church of England signed a covenant in 2003, after a long and troubled search since Archbishop Fisher invited the Free Churches to 'take episcopacy into their system' in 1946. At the time of writing new attempts are being made to address the difficult issue of episcopacy. Other developments in rapprochement could be mentioned, in Wales and Scotland, and in the wide spread of local ecumenical partnerships. Meanwhile, Anglicans and Lutherans in parts of Europe have achieved a breakthrough in the Porvoo Common Statement, and also in the United States, as discussed later in this part.

The final chapters in the book address the question of identity in other ways. In an age in which management theory has become an academic discipline in its own right, how is the church to organise itself? How are traditional practices to be matched to the everyday expectations of church members and the requirements of government legislation? How is identity preserved under such constraints? Finally, in chapter 12 it is noted that an international gathering of theologians in the broadly Wesleyan tradition rejected the idea of any constraints upon what constituted Methodist teaching. The final chapter, therefore, asks what a Methodist theological institution is for. Originally a beginning-of-the-year address to the Vanderbilt Divinity School in the United States, it examines the role of theological educators in relation to the church's traditions. How far is it their task to preserve and communicate the tradition, how far to question it? Although the chapter presupposes an American context, its relevance is much wider. The future leadership of the church depends on the answer to such questions.

10 Who are we?

The elusive Methodist identity[1]

Why ask the question? People ask 'Who am I?' when they are in some sort of crisis: memory loss, collapse of a familiar world, failure of long-established projects, indecision. What prompts the question in today's Methodism? Worry about numerical decline? Is it the result of the ecumenical and liturgical movements, which have tended to assimilate the denominations to each other in some respects, and led to an emphasis on what we have in common rather than those things on which we differ? Is it caused by social mobility, which is producing fewer lifelong, 'conviction' Methodists and more who choose for the time being to be Methodists for reasons of neighbourhood and convenience? Is it Methodism's growing diversity? At one time the attraction of an English market town was the diversity of its shops and the reassuring certainty that, on Sunday, a visitor would know what to expect in the Methodist church. Today the opposite is the case. Are such developments good or bad?

More important, what are we going to do with the answer (supposing we can find it)? What does a distinctive identity imply? That we wish to remain separate? Would that make us sectarian? Is whatever is distinctive about Methodism an element of the catholicity of the Church of Christ, held in trust for the whole, or a tolerable variant from the mainstream for those to whom it appeals? There are still Methodists and Anglicans who would see the future of Methodism where it began, as a society or order within a wider church. Are we cherishing the family silver to be admired by a coterie, or as a dowry for a future marriage?

There is perhaps an ecumenical answer to all this. If we wish to be taken seriously by other traditions in any conversation about the recovery of the church's visible unity, they are entitled to know who they are talking to. What are we to say to them? Part of our offering will be the ecclesiological statement *Called to Love and Praise*[2] and comparable documents, but I guess that behind the question lies the fear that there may be a growing distance between such normative documents and the reality of things in the local church.

Who are the 'we'? There are, in fact, many Methodisms. The view of the Conference (rarely truly unanimous anyway) is not always shared by the proverbial person in the pew, or even the person in the pulpit. The local Network secretary or Junior Church leader may each see things differently. The lifelong member of a rural chapel might well not agree with the relative newcomer to a large suburban church as to what Methodism is. How do we arrive at an answer that commands broad, even if not universal, assent?

Moreover, we in Britain are widely regarded as the 'Mother Church of Methodism', but our perception of the Methodist tradition is not universally shared, and would not be seen as definitive. To itinerate between Rochdale, Hamburg, Buenos Aires, Lagos and Franklin, Tennessee, would produce some ecclesiastical culture shocks. The United Methodist tradition generally is much more tenacious of John Wesley's legacy than we are in Britain. This chapter deals with British Methodism, but it is important to remember the wider context.

For an answer, it would seem logical to turn to clause 4 of the Deed of Union, the church's official doctrinal standards. Churches are often defined by their doctrinal statements. Unfortunately, Methodism is not well served. Clause 4 sets out standards of doctrine rather than expounding the doctrines themselves. It indulges freely in generalisations. The 'doctrines of the evangelical faith', for example, are nowhere defined; we are merely told where to look for them ('based upon the divine revelation recorded in the Holy Scriptures'). Because it was the product between 1920 and 1932 of compromise over contentious issues, it makes a meal of some topics and ignores others. Nevertheless, some things are affirmed and others excluded. Methodism is part of the Holy Catholic Church, affirms the historic creeds (or at least their 'fundamental principles', whatever they may be), bases its doctrines on the Bible, has a mission to spread scriptural holiness, attaches to itself key words such as 'evangelical' and 'Christian experience', holds the doctrine of the priesthood of all believers, ordains its presbyters (who are also preachers), believes in lay as well as ordained pastoral and preaching ministry, holds baptism and eucharist to be of divine appointment and perpetual obligation, and repudiates any doctrine of an exclusively presbyteral priesthood. But many things can be made of such statements and much is left out. In any case, much of it merely classifies Methodism as a species of the genus 'British Protestantism'.

John Wesley would have had little doubt how to define Methodism. God's 'grand design' in raising up the Methodist preachers was 'to reform the Nation, and in particular the Church; to spread scriptural holiness over the land'.[3] For Eric Baker, the doctrine of perfection was the essential distinguishing mark of Methodism,[4] but it is important to remember that, for Wesley, sanctification was not only a point of doctrine. It was also the deliberate focus of spiritual formation, for the sake of which societies, classes and bands were organised and the disciplines of early rising, diary-keeping, prayer, worship and fasting were self-imposed. The doctrine remains in Charles Wesley's hymns, but the formative framework, and even, I suspect, the spiritual intention, have largely gone. One wonders how British ordinands would react to the questions still asked of their American counterparts: 'Have you faith in Christ? Are you going on to perfection? Do you expect to be made perfect in love in this life? Are you earnestly striving after it?'[5]

Others would pinpoint a broader range of identifiers, the 'Four Alls': all need salvation, all can be saved, all can know they are saved, all can be saved to the uttermost.[6] Certainly, the legacy of John Wesley's Arminianism is very strong. One meets few Calvinists in British Methodism.[7] It is true too that Methodists generally are driven by what Gordon Rupp used to call 'the optimism of grace': God can do anything. Here, then, are two markers. Yet I doubt whether this formulation does justice to Methodism's commitment to education or to its strong tradition of social concern, most evident since the 1880s but traceable to Wesley.

Certainly, reference would have to be made to the sense of being a church in mission. Structurally, the marks of it are retained in the circuit and the itinerancy, though nowadays these serve other purposes and are not primarily missionary. But in self-definition in ecumenical debate attention has often been drawn to this characteristic of Methodism's understanding of the church,[8] and mission is often spoken of as the constituent of the church almost to the exclusion of worship.[9]

Many would want to press the point further, and speak more specifically of evangelism. Historically, this note has been very strongly sounded, and Methodism has traditionally looked for an experience of conversion on the part of every member. Experience in fact features very prominently in Methodist-speak. John Wesley added it to the established tools, tradition and reason, for the interpretation of scripture. In 1919 John Scott Lidgett, in an attempt to identify what the three Methodist denominations then held in common, pointed to a common spiritual experience and ethos as the unifying factor.[10] It would probably be fair to say that now, at least in some quarters, the traditional emphasis on conversion is being modified. If that is true the reasons may be a recognition that some may grow into faith rather than burst into it, a weakening sense of sin as guilt and burden, and the broadening of 'conversion' to include commitment to social justice. Correspondingly, though these things are difficult to judge, I doubt whether we can still be confident that Methodists share a common spiritual experience.

However that may be, the church (at least in official statements) has consciously set its face against limiting 'mission' to 'evangelism'. Wesley-like, we have combined seeming incompatibles: evangelism, social caring and the struggle for justice.[11] Our social responsibility tradition is very strong, as noted above, and resists marginalisation.

In fact, it may put us off the scent to look too closely for a theological answer. Tom Langford has observed that, in Britain, current Methodist theological interest is not in the distinctive Methodist themes but in general Christian issues.[12] One might detect in that a loss of any sense of theological distinctiveness. Certainly, there is a contrast with the United Methodist Church here. British identity is less apparent in theological reflection and more in spirituality and church life.

What, then, of Methodism's spirituality? Its primary vehicle has always been hymnody. It remains significant that there is a core of hymns by the Wesleys and Watts that are known only to Methodists, and that very many of these deal with assurance and the aspiration after holiness. Perhaps the most serious threat to Methodism's traditional identity lies precisely in the neglect in some quarters of what is left of that corpus of hymnody and its replacement by occasional verses of varying quality, some very good and deserving to endure, some crying out for an early and merciful neglect, few embodying anything distinctively Methodist. But, as a check to righteous indignation, it is worth remembering how much even 100 years ago had already been lost of the hymnodic legacy, not merely so many of the hymns that were the substance of Wesley's 1780 hymn book but the organising principle that framed it: the assumption of a spiritual pilgrimage from awakening to sanctification, with provision, so sensibly, for recovery after backsliding.

There are other carriers of spirituality. The excellent *Methodist Worship Book* is less a book of Methodist worship and more an ecumenical worship book produced by Methodists, but its origins show through in various omissions and inclusions, and particularly there is the Covenant Service, which is now liturgically and theologically more satisfying and has recovered its late 1920s glory after the over-severe pruning of 1975. Here one can find an emphasis on intense personal religion, on an experience of God known as unlimited grace and unconditional demand, and on the church as a fellowship, an experienced community of mutual support.

'Fellowship' is an overworked word in Methodism, and at its worst may represent little more than jollity over the teacups. But at its best it is an understanding of the church in which shared baptism is translated into reciprocal ministry of prayer, friendship and pastoral support to which every member contributes. What is left of the system of class meetings, class leaders, pastoral visitors and membership tickets is a framework for this, but it operates even in the absence of these supports. Some, indeed, would stress lay ministry, both preaching and pastoral, as one of the distinctive characteristics, but sometimes we congratulate ourselves overmuch on such things. Theory and practice do not always coincide.

One could of course look to structural particularities: to the connexional system, and the conviction of interrelatedness that lies behind it; to circuit and district, itinerancy and stationing, to connexional recognition of circuit or local action in admitting local preachers and members, to the long, but limited, reach of Conference, to the constraints imposed by the Model Trusts, to the authority of the Doctrinal Standards and the existence of officially sanctioned hymn and service books. Even so, such things are not what they were for the Wesleyans of the eighteenth century, nor even for Methodists in the 1950s. Many of the connexional bonds that held Methodism together have been loosened, either by Conference decisions modifying local church, circuit and district constitutions or by local initiatives, such as the adoption of alternative hymn books, or by ventures of ecumenical partnership. The principle of connexionalism remains – belonging together – but this can take many forms, and as a principle distinguishes Methodism only from churches of a congregational polity. Nineteenth-century Methodists readily saw Anglicans and Presbyterians as belonging to connexional churches.

My own instinct is not to look for a single defining characteristic but for a combination of things. Any individual is identified by a particular combination of, and variations on, features common to the whole population. I doubt whether there is any one feature of Methodism that cannot be found elsewhere in the family of churches that make up the Church Catholic. If there were, it would call into question the claim to catholicity. It is often said of John Wesley, plagiarist and epitomiser par excellence, that his genius lay in the combination of things usually held apart: the Catholic emphasis on holy living with the Protestant stress on salvation by grace alone, the mystic and pietist emphasis on personal communion with God together with a stress on societal religion (fellowship in the church and commitment to social reform outside it), evangelism with social action, experiential religion with reliance on reason, 'knowledge and vital piety'.[13] Similarly, today I would argue that what Methodism brings to the ecumenical table is not some peculiar confection of its own but a distinctive blend of common (or widely shared) ingredients.

A proposal

Here, then, is my attempt at an answer. It is always possible to fault an ideal by quoting bad practice that negates it, but at its best and most authentic British Methodism.

- Is Arminian in theology and aspires to be an inclusive church. Although Calvinism in the twenty-first century is not what it was in the eighteenth, we are suspicious of it.
- Lays stress on personal experience of God in Christ through the operation of the Holy Spirit, whether that includes a 'conversion moment' or not, and looks for continual growth in discipleship, aspiring to perfect love.
- Is connexional in its understanding of membership and in its expectations both of churches and of presbyters and deacons, expecting strong churches to help the weak and seeing the ordained ministry as a common resource to be deployed, not a workforce to be drawn on.
- Acknowledges the sacraments of baptism and eucharist, often being hazy about the significance of the former, and valuing the latter as an act of communion rather more than as a sacrifice.
- Lays great emphasis on preaching and expresses devotion by singing.
- Expects the local church to be a close-knit and supportive fellowship in which faith is shared.
- Looks for collaborative ministry and resists any notions of a distinctive ministerial priesthood or 'hierarchy'.
- Believes the church to be called to mission, not only in the conversion of individuals but also in engagement with society, and considers the exigencies of mission to take priority over the maintenance of traditional structures.

Is that a description or a prescription, what Methodism happens to be or what it must strive to remain? If it sounds a little more optimistic than the preceding paragraphs it is because I have erred on the side of prescription. When one has found one's identity, there is a question of remaining true to oneself.

How is tradition sustained? Of course churches change – even the most traditional. Some so far lose their grip on the convictions that originally brought them into being as almost to fade away; arguably, the eighteenth-century slide of English Presbyterianism into Unitarianism illustrates the danger. Yet without adaptation to changing environment churches die. Methodism is with us today because of evolution.

Will that process eventually lead to Methodism's disappearance, or to its assimilation into a wider, perhaps blander, Christian community? Will it lead to disintegration into a series of smaller networks, evangelical, charismatic, radical, traditional, held together (or maybe not) by ties it is easier to keep than to get rid of (such as the Model Trusts)? Will 'our discipline' finally disintegrate because there are no ideological sinews to sustain loyalty to it? Whether we view such possibilities with equanimity or see them as a danger to be resisted depends on the view we take of Methodism's current identity. It is at least worth reflecting on the process by which that identity has been sustained so far.

It would not surprise me if a random survey of Methodists threw up a large number who had little or no idea as to what Methodism stands for. It would not even surprise me that some of these might be holding office. In any organisation there will be a core of members who have intense commitment to its ideals, and surrounding them a larger number whose loyalty, for various reasons, is not in question but whose ideological commitment shades off to nil at the circumference. What does sometimes amaze me is the grasp of the essentials to be found where one might, condescendingly, least expect to find it. How do people without formal theological education or intellectual pretensions acquire such a deep and firm grasp of the faith and of the Methodist tradition?

The answer is, of course, that tradition depends for its transmission first and foremost on the corporate life of the church, the shared faith of its members, communicated by casual conversation and lived example; second, on its provision for corporate worship, its scriptures, creeds, liturgies and hymnody; and, third, on the ministry of those who are specifically charged with the care and transmission of the tradition, its preachers and teachers, ordained and lay, and such official bodies as may be put in place (the Faith and Order Committee in Methodism, elsewhere the Sacred Congregation and the like). Every church has its equivalent, if only informally, of the *magisterium*, responsible for guarding the faith, always effective only if it is in tune with the wider *sensus fidelium*.

If, then, there is nurturing of the tradition to be done in Methodism's stewardship for the future, the ultimate aim must be to make all Methodists aware of their heritage. But the immediate target, if that aim is to be achieved, will be in the formation of those who shape opinion in the church; presbyters, deacons, local preachers, worship leaders and – as important as any – those who teach in youth groups and (by whatever name) junior church. We sometimes deplore the way (as in ecumenical votes) the ordained ministry can be a drag on pro-gress,[14] but what is amiss there is the unresponsive exercise of a ministry that is properly theirs. It is the vocation of all who are appointed to leadership in the church to be, in the proper sense of the word, conservative.

Notes

1 Adapted from a paper written at the request of the Methodist Church's Faith and Order Committee as a contribution to discussions on Methodist identity and pub-lished in the *Epworth Review*, vol. 27, no. 4, 2000, pp. 22–30. Copyright Trustees for Methodist Church Purposes, reprinted by permission.
2 *Statements and Reports*, vol. 2, pt 1, pp. 1ff.
3 Large Minutes, 1763, Q. [4], in Rack, *The Works of John Wesley*, vol. 10, p. 845.
4 Eric Baker, *The Faith of a Methodist* (London: Epworth Press, 1958).
5 *The Book of Discipline* (1996), para. 327.
6 John Munsey Turner has traced this formulation to William B. Fitzgerald in 1903: see his *Modern Methodism in England 1932–1998* (Peterborough: Methodist Publishing House, 1998), p. 39.
7 Calvinistic Methodism, fully entitled to the name, was never part of Wesley's con-nexion, and is not within the purview of this discussion.
8 See the Methodist statement in *Reflections*, pp. 44–51.
9 Compare the recently introduced definition 'A discipleship movement shaped for mission' and the debate it provoked as to its adequacy.
10 William J. Townsend, Herbert B. Workman and George Eayrs (eds.), *A New History of Methodism*, 2 vols. (London: Hodder & Stoughton, 1919): vol. 2, p. 422. The entire chapter makes interesting reading. Identity seems as elusive then as now.
11 Donald English, *Sharing in God's Mission: A Programme for a Living Church* (London: Methodist Church Home Mission, 1985).
12 *Methodist Theology* (Peterborough: Methodist Publishing House, 1998), p. 85.
13 The phrase is Charles Wesley's: 'Collection of Hymns (1780)', no. 461, verse 5, in Hildebrandt and Beckerlegge, *The Works of John Wesley*, vol. 7.
14 Witness the comment in an ecumenical house group: "All went well until the minister joined us." *Views from the Pews* (London: British Council of Churches & Catholic Truth Society, 1986), p. 85.

11 A Methodist theological system?[1]

Is there a distinctive system that can legitimately be termed 'Methodist theology' and is it especially useful? I was asked the question once. The questioner sounded doubtful. So what should we be looking for? We need to unpack the question.

First, the term 'Methodist'. Anyone who has attended the quinquennial World Methodist Conference will have realised how diverse Methodism is worldwide. At the Oxford Institute of Methodist Theological Studies in 1987, when theologians from around the Methodist world addressed the question 'What should Methodists teach?', the only conclusion they could reach was that there was no consensus.[2] The differences were not only geographical and cultural, nor only due to the way separate denominations had developed the traditions they had inherited from Wesley. For many of those present the starting point was not inherited tradition but their current context of economic, racial or gender oppression. No one in that gathering was permitted to claim a definitive version of Methodism to be imposed on others. Yet all acknowledged some common bond in the fact that they shared one historical origin in John Wesley's movement and were addressing the question together. The international dialogues between the World Methodist Council and the Roman Catholic and other churches represent more of a consensus, but even they acknowledge differences.

So I limit myself to British Methodism. Even here, however, we need caution. British Methodism is changing. In 2004 the Church's Faith and Order Committee sponsored a study project on Methodist theology since union in 1932.[3] One of the points made by a contributor is the fact that Methodists of African and Afro-Caribbean origin bring to the British church a distinct history and church tradition (we should also refer to communities from Asia and the Pacific).[4] Our inheritance is no longer a compound of 'ex-Wesleyan', 'ex-Primitive' or 'ex-United', as it was in the 1940s or 1950s. The twentieth century witnessed a steady departure in Britain from traditional Methodist theological emphases. As an example, compare the contents pages of *Hymns and Psalms* or *Singing the Faith* with Wesley's 1780 hymn book or even the *Methodist Hymn Book* of 1933. There are (and will be in the foreseeable future) fewer cradle Methodists in the churches. We need to be aware too of the increasing influence of ecumenical sharing on Methodist ways of thought. The annual Prayer Manual is widening the horizons of Methodist spirituality. To that must be added the fact that, in Britain as on the wider scene, some will begin not from Methodist tradition but from the experience of racial or other discrimination. On the other hand, under the influence especially of American scholarship, there has been an awakening of interest in John Wesley as a theologian.

So what counts as Methodist theology? There are publications by Methodist authors, including articles in the pages of the *Epworth Review.* The Faith and Order Committee project approached the question by looking at a variety of sources – letters to the *Methodist Recorder*, memorials to Conference, as well as training manuals for members and preachers, worship books, even *Constitutional Practice and Discipline* – to try to get a grip on the theology by which Methodists actually operate. Then there is the argument that Methodism expresses its theology not in words but in action, as Clive Marsh noted in an article in the *Epworth Review*.[5] So, to quote the 2003 Conference report on Holy Communion, 'In order to know what Methodists believe it is necessary to look at what they do.'[6] On the other hand, according to the Methodist Church Act 1976 and the Deed of Union, the Conference is the final authority in regard to all questions concerning the interpretation of Methodist doctrine.[7] Accordingly, there are volumes of Faith and Order reports adopted by the Conference since 1932 and other official statements, such as those on social responsibility.

Is Methodist theology what Methodists generally think (or do) or what the Conference officially declares? There must surely be official doctrinal criteria by which all else is measured, to avoid a collective drift into heresy, syncretism or plain shallowness. History offers many cautionary tales. But it is plain that what Methodists think and do sometimes conflicts with Conference pronouncements. The never-ending stream of memorials to Conference about extending lay eucharistic presidency indicates a sizeable number of Methodists who are not convinced by the official position, and I guess most presbyters practise an 'open table' at communion, even if they subscribe to the official doctrine that a communicant is expected to have been baptised.

Official and popular theology are not linked by a one-way street. When Conference pronounces, it may in time influence popular views, as ideas percolate through publications and the pulpit. On the other hand, Conference pronouncements, when wisely made, draw on what is seen to be general consensus. The refusal to arbitrate in *A Lamp to My Feet and a Light to My Path* between competing views of biblical authority actually held within the church[8] and the survey approach taken by the report on Holy Communion mentioned above illustrate the point. In any event, the Conference does not pronounce on everything. It is important, therefore, to take a broader view.

British Methodism is less well equipped in this respect than the United Methodist Church, which has inherited as doctrinal standards Wesley's adaptation of the 39 Articles and his Rules for the Societies as well as the Standard Sermons and Notes upon the New Testament, and includes in its *Book of*

Discipline both a doctrinal statement, noting what is held in common with the wider church and what is distinctively Methodist, and a social creed. In Britain we refer to 'our doctrines', defined as 'those truths of salvation which are set forth in the Methodist doctrinal standards',[9] but they are not formally listed or expounded, and the definition does not unambiguously embrace the wider theological framework of the creeds or the Articles. We leave much to unexpressed consensus.

All that makes a specific Methodist theology difficult to identify.[10] If we were dealing with a single author there would be a defined body of material to analyse. With Methodism the material is unlimited and undefined, and we have to rely to some extent on impressions. Yet, as I argue in Chapter 10, there are a clutch of theological reactions that one would expect to find in Methodist speaking and writing, and others that would be absent. That list could be extended. More weight is laid on the cross than on the incarnation as the redemptive act. There is stress both on divine grace and on human responsibility (see the Covenant Service). Despite the changes in hymn book arrangement, a survey of hymns actually in use would surely still highlight many unknown outside Methodism, focusing on personal forgiveness, assurance and a longing for holiness. A historian would no doubt point to the influence of social factors in some of those features, but we must resist easy reductionism. They reflect what Methodists believe.

Is all that 'distinctive' (to return to the question put to me) and does it add up to a 'system'? Such doctrinal positions are clearly not *exclusive* to Methodism, in the sense that Methodists alone hold them. Taken one by one they can be found in many Christian traditions. Even taken together they may be found elsewhere. They are not even *distinctive*, in the sense that without embracing the entire package one cannot be counted a Methodist. But they are *characteristic*, both in what they include and what they do not, and they are characteristic as a cluster, not just item by item.

Does such a cluster comprise a system? Plainly not, if by 'system' we mean an articulated scheme in which all the elements are consciously interrelated and shown to be derived from some primary principle. Methodist theology does not represent a constructed system in that sense. It is forever being said that John Wesley did not write a systematic theology. Moreover, he did not intend to be an innovator, and recent studies have underlined his indebtedness to a number of sources, notably the Eastern Fathers. His primary interest lay in the doctrine of salvation, that teaching that would 'show the way to heaven'.[11] It can be shown that his various references to 'our doctrines' identify a number of topics that he considered fundamental. The list is not always identical but commonly includes original sin, justification by faith, the new birth and inward and outward holiness. In other contexts, however, he simply insisted that the doctrines he and his colleagues preached are those of the Church of England as exhibited in the Prayer Book, Articles and Homilies. Neither the narrower nor the broader definition of 'our doctrines' amounts to a systematic exposition of doctrine in the style of Calvin's *Institutes*.

Moreover, the doctrinal clause of the Deed of Union makes it quite clear that Wesley's *Notes upon the New Testament* and the *Forty-Four Sermons* 'are not intended to impose a system of formal or speculative theology on Methodist preachers, but to set up standards of preaching and belief' that are related to the gospel of redemption and the experience of salvation.[12]

But theology can be systematic without being a system. Charles M. Wood in an article in the American *Quarterly Review*, drawing on H. Richard Niebuhr, refers to the 'grammar' of Methodist theology – that is, the underlying principles that give it coherence, the rules by which, like a language, it 'works'. One does not have to know the rules of grammar to speak grammatically, but the rules spell out the reasons why one's speech is grammatical.[13] Similarly, Randy Maddox, in a major work on John Wesley's theology, invokes the notion of an 'organising principle' that holds doctrines together, rather than a central idea from which they are logically deduced.[14] Is there such an organising principle behind current British Methodist theology, or is it no more than a series of knee-jerk reactions or rationalisations of pragmatic choices that have no intrinsic relation to each other? As with grammar, one does not need necessarily to be aware of the principles; the question is: are we theologically more coherent than we think we are?

A number of studies have recently argued for such an organising principle within Wesley's writing. In addition to Maddox's work, reference should be made to Theodore Runyon's *The New Creation*.[15] But Wesley does not represent contemporary Methodism. The case has been argued for the contemporary United Methodist tradition by Walter Klaiber and Manfred Marquardt.[16] British readers, however, are likely to feel that, for all its merits, their work bears the marks not only of the subtly different United Methodist tradition but also of the continental European context in which it was originally written – evidence of the difficulty of writing for a global denomination out of any one particular context.

So is there an organising principle, a connecting thread, behind current British Methodist theology? It would take more than a brief chapter to explore in detail. All that can be done here is suggest a possibility. For fuller treatment a doctoral project awaits some enterprising mind.

If one surveys what is characteristic of Methodist theology it is difficult to get away from the fact that its focus is still, as it was in the eighteenth century and again in the doctrinal clause of the 1932 Deed of Union, on God's gracious work of salvation, experienced as personal and corporate, unlimited in its reach and possibilities. It is the unlimited character of God's grace that drives both the sense of mission and the emphasis on an inclusive church. All have worth, for Christ died for all; all share in ministry, for the Spirit is given to all; all are called to renewal of life, for there is no limit to the possibilities of transforming grace. Salvation is neither simply done for us nor simply achieved by us, but is a work of grace eliciting the response that makes transformation possible. The transformation is corporate because we are restored to one another as well as to God. That is not to say that other doctrines (the Trinity, for example) are of no concern. We hold them in common with the wider church, but we are likely to approach them from that salvation perspective.

If this is an accurate analysis it is apparent how much of John Wesley's theological legacy is still with us, not in its precise formulation but in its shape and thrust. Is there a phrase that will capture the essence of these convictions, their connecting thread? In their more precisely focused work on John Wesley, Maddox offers 'responsible grace' (emphasising the means, God's initiative and human response) and Runyon 'new creation' (emphasising the end, the product of God's transforming power). Neither quite highlights the universal scope of what is on offer. 'Unlimited grace in reconciliation and renewal' perhaps sums it up.

What use is all this (the second question put to me)? Several answers suggest themselves. From Socrates to modern psychology, self-awareness has been recognised to be a good thing. We should know what drives us, theologically as much as emotionally. It contributes to consistency of character and self-confidence, and enables us to address new issues from a recognised common basis.

Of course, it has dangers. Preoccupation with 'our tradition' may make us inward- and backward-looking, resistant to what needs to be learned from other traditions. Encounter with the riches on offer in the ecumenical marketplace brings home how limited we all are. But the converse of that is the fact that our heritage also is on offer, not buried in embarrassment nor lost by neglect. To be able to articulate what characterises us and how it holds together will in fact assist ecumenical partners to understand who they are dealing with.

Is such a unifying theological principle prescriptive? Must one subscribe to it to be counted as Methodist? Plainly, one cannot guarantee that the views of every Methodist will fall within the pattern. Moreover, as we have noted, Methodism in Britain as elsewhere has always been in a process of evolution, and one cannot prescribe the future of every item of doctrine. My intention so far has been to describe rather than prescribe. Nevertheless, if the organising principle of our beliefs were to change, the change would be radical indeed, for (to use computer-speak) the principle operates as virus protection, resisting the easy assimilation of other ideas.

Two examples may illustrate the point. In Methodism we do not go in for devotion to Mary or invocation of the saints (not even on 24 May). One could easily attribute that to historical accident, a legacy of our birth in eighteenth-century Protestantism. More important is the fact that we lack the theological framework for such a spirituality. Will Methodism ever adopt the practice? Only if it comes to be seen as consistent with the organising principle I have tried to identify.

Second, in 1946 Archbishop Geoffrey Fisher invited the English Free Churches to 'take episcopacy into their systems'. It was, and is, a theological as well as a constitutional issue, and British Methodism is wrestling with it still. The question is not 'Do we like the idea?' but 'In what form, if at all, can the system, theologically as well as constitutionally, assimilate episcopacy without fracture?'. Methodism will one day decide that particular question and not continue to put it off. The general point illustrated by both examples is that systems, even in the limited sense used here of an organising principle, are not infinitely elastic. They exclude as well as include. That is why, to illustrate yet again, 'Calvinistic Methodist', for those in Wesley's tradition, is a contradiction in terms.

Notes

1 Originally published in the *Epworth Review*, vol. 31, no. 1, 2004, pp. 16–22. Copyright Trustees for Methodist Church Purposes, reprinted by permission.
2 See M. Douglas Meeks, *What Should Methodists Teach? Wesleyan Tradition and Modern Diversity* (Nashville, TN: Kingswood Books, 1990), especially pp. 131ff.
3 Clive Marsh, Brian Beck, Angela Shier-Jones and Helen Wareing (eds.), *Unmasking Methodist Theology* (London: Continuum, 2004); reissued as *Methodist Theology Today: A Way Forward* (n.d.).
4 See Valentin Dedji, 'Methodist Theology: Where Is It Heading? An African Perspective', in Marsh et al., *Unmasking Methodist Theology*, pp. 211ff.
5 Clive Marsh, 'The Practice of Theology in British Methodism', *Epworth Review*, vol. 28, no. 3, 2001, p. 38.
6 See *His Presence Makes the Feast: Holy Communion in the Methodist Church* in the Conference Agenda for 2003 (Peterborough: Methodist Publishing House, 2003), p. 185, B.14.
7 1976 Act, § 3 (2), Deed of Union, clause 5, in *The Constitutional Practice and Discipline of the Methodist Church*, vol. 1, p. 10; vol. 2, page varying with the year.
8 *Statements and Reports*, vol. 2, pt 2, pp. 644ff.
9 Standing Order 568 (2) (ii).
10 Some would invoke the 'Four Alls' (all need salvation, can be saved, know they are saved, be saved to the uttermost), but this twentieth-century formula lacks the crucial corporate dimension.
11 See the preface to the Standard Sermons, in Outler, *The Works of John Wesley*, vol. 1, p. 105.
12 Deed of Union, clause 4.
13 *Quarterly Review*, vol. 18, no. 2, 1998, pp. 167ff.
14 Randy L. Maddox, *Responsible Grace: John Wesley's Practical Theology* (Nashville, TN: Kingswood Books, 1994), p. 18.
15 Theodore Runyon, *The New Creation: John Wesley's Theology Today* (Nashville, TN: Abingdon Press, 1998).
16 Walter Klaiber and Manfred Marquardt, *Living Grace: An Outline of United Methodist Theology* (Nashville, TN: Abingdon Press, 2001), an English translation of a German original.

12 World Methodist theology?

The Oxford Institute of Methodist Theological Studies[1]

In 2007 the Oxford Institute of Methodist Theological Studies celebrated its jubilee. Its first meeting was the brainchild of the British minister Rex Kissack, by then stationed in Rome, and the American Dow Kirkpatrick, at the time minister of St Mark Methodist Church in Atlanta, Georgia. They had met in Oxford in 1946 when Kirkpatrick was a visiting scholar, and they had recognised the need for a forum in which Methodist scholars and pastors from around the world could exchange views. After protracted negotiations the Institute finally came to birth in 1958 in a ten-day residential meeting at Lincoln College, Oxford, of 100 men and eight women, mostly presbyters or probationers, predominantly from Britain and the United States, with 15 from continental Europe, four from Ireland and ten to represent between them the rest of the world. Since then the Institute has continued to meet under the auspices of the World Methodist Council every three or four years, since 1977 every five, and has expanded its membership to over 200, with a better, but still imperfect, balance of gender, country of origin and church affiliation within the broad world Methodist family, with more contributions from lay theologians.[2]

The early meetings can be characterised as 'Methodists discussing theology', with traditional theological topics − God, Christ, Spirit, Church − being addressed, and little sign of any serious search for a distinctive Methodist slant on such things, although one of the early aims had been to identify a Methodist contribution to the ecumenical movement. With 1977 came a significant change, as the contribution that Methodist tradition might make to the discussion of contemporary issues was seriously considered. Since then the Institute has always concerned itself with the exploration of the Methodist inheritance. It has become a gathering of Methodists discussing *Methodist* theology.

So it is natural to ask: is there, or has there developed from the approximately 163,000 person-hours of conferencing since 1958, a world Methodist theology? Is there a theological standpoint that all share or a body of doctrines to which all subscribe? The obvious place to look for an answer might seem to be the report of the1987 Institute meeting, entitled *What Should Methodists Teach?*, but a glance at the final chapter, in which Douglas Meeks sums up the preceding ten days' discussions, reveals an almost total lack of agreement: 'The final report must be: no earth shaking consensus, no false sense of unity on the question of Methodist doctrine.' The only 'ever so slight' consensus was this: 'Methodist teaching should be freed from domination, beginning with the teachers.'[3]

There were, and remain, a number of reasons for that negative outcome. Methodist churches throughout the world are extraordinarily diverse in size, historical origins and current contexts. Some owe their beginnings to a conscious separation from the parent body. The Oxford Institute meetings have embraced representatives of the Brethren in Christ, the Church of the Nazarene and other churches which look back to John Wesley but do not call themselves 'Methodist'. Many churches are the product of missionary and colonial expansion. Some are completely autonomous, but many others are bound together in the United Methodist Church, under the authority of the General Conference meeting in the United States. Since 1784, when the Methodist Episcopal Church was constituted at the Christmas Conference in Baltimore, there have been two main streams of Methodist tradition anyway, the British and the American, but all the churches have developed differently in interaction with their environment, and globally the environments are very diverse. For some minority churches the defining questions are ecumenical, as they seek to identify themselves in relation to other Christian traditions. For churches in the West the issues have often been those raised by a secular and scientific culture. In countries with dominant other-faith cultures dialogue has been the concern. In Latin America especially the overriding concern is with poverty and the abuse of power.

It is understandable, therefore, that there was strong resistance in 1987 to any suggestion that history, or the current official stance of the churches, should dictate the outcome of theological enquiry, and particularly strong objection to any assumption that the older-established churches in Britain and America should determine for everyone else either the theological agenda or the answers to the questions. Yet all had to acknowledge that they were only closeted together in the same room because they belonged to churches that owed their origin to John Wesley's eighteenth-century movement and they had come together to explore its theological significance.

In fact, there is more to be said. All the churches represented subscribe to the historic faith represented by the Scriptures and the Apostles' and Nicene Creeds. All consider themselves to be heirs of the Protestant Reformation. Most include in their authorised doctrinal standards and statements Wesley's Standard Sermons and Notes upon the New Testament. Those in the American tradition include the Twenty-Five Articles and the General Rules of the United Societies as well. Most are members of the World Methodist Council, which now includes in its *Handbook* a Social Affirmation, adopted in 1986, and a statement of 'Wesleyan Essentials of Christian Faith', adopted in 1996.

There is also the fact that the official ecumenical dialogues in which the World Methodist Council has been engaged, notably since 1966 with the Roman Catholic Church,[4] but also at various times with the Lutherans, the Reformed Churches, the Anglican Communion, the Orthodox, the Salvation Army and the Baptists, have apparently not found it difficult to outline a Methodist position on many issues, even if sometimes differences in the Methodist family have had to be noted.

Of course, none of this is evidence that an identical theology can be found among Methodists wherever one goes in the world. A survey of beliefs held by individual Methodist members in Britain, if undertaken, would reveal a considerable degree of variation from what the Faith and Order Committee and the Conference consider to be the norm. Worldwide, the variation will be even greater. In Britain and Ireland one of the structural supports of a shared theology is a common hymn book, on which a Methodist identity is stamped by the Wesley hymns. In other parts of the world these have largely fallen into disuse or have never been translated. Another factor in shaping the beliefs of church members is a common tradition of preaching, reinforced by connexional training and standards. These also vary across the world. Official doctrinal standards tend to be either historical texts, such as Wesley's Sermons and Notes, or compromise documents, such as the British Deed of Union and the doctrinal statements in the United Methodist *Book of Discipline*, which may be appealed to when contention arises but ignored from day to day. They do represent, at the point of their adoption, some sort of general consensus, and tend to support the continuation of that consensus thereafter, but they are no guarantee of it. How far do Wesley's views of Christian perfection and its attainability, as expressed in the Sermons and Notes, represent the beliefs of British Methodists today? Reports of ecumenical dialogues represent what Methodist participants believe they can with integrity subscribe to on behalf of the churches they represent, but, as the comments of the British Faith and Order Committee on the World Methodist/Roman Catholic dialogues indicate, they cannot guarantee to carry their churches with them, and certainly do not reflect the views of all individual Methodists.[5] Generalisations about what Methodists in the pew believe worldwide are hazardous, therefore, not to say impossible.

A better place to look would be the authorised expositions of theology put out from time to time by the relevant authorities of each church in the Methodist tradition. A comprehensive and detailed analysis of such material has yet to be undertaken, however. The nearest thing we have is the reports of ecumenical dialogues. Nevertheless, in the absence of such research it is possible to attempt some generalisations. If one attends not only to the content of ecumenical dialogues but also to the discourse of Methodists from diverse contexts around the world when they meet in the Institute or other forums, and particularly those accredited as representatives of their churches whose views may therefore be taken as characteristic, I believe one can detect a broad profile, which explains the sense of family when Methodists from different countries meet.

A broad profile

There is, first, the fact already alluded to: that all the churches concerned come within the broad spectrum of Trinitarian Protestant orthodoxy. In the Oxford

Institute there have been vigorous debates about the contemporary relevance of some traditional doctrines over against more pressing issues of liberation and justice, and questions about the patriarchal character of the biblical and later Christian tradition. By 1987 all members of the Institute had been made sharply aware of the issues raised by liberation theology in its various forms and were beginning to recognise that global poverty was a context that, in different ways, embraced them all. But there has been no serious attempt to disown those traditions. It is here especially that the absences are telling. Key features of Roman Catholicism and Orthodoxy, such as the veneration of Mary, the adoration of the consecrated Host or the monastic tradition, are missing. Methodism is in the Protestant fold.

Second, there is the presence of John Wesley in the collective memory. He has been regarded by some as a sort of collective mascot, by others as an evangelistic benchmark from which all subsequent generations have declined, by others again as an embarrassment to ecumenical progress, by yet others simply as an irrelevance. Whatever the view taken of him, he is there. I think it can be shown that one of the contributions of the Institute since 1982 has been to encourage consideration of his theological contribution. His capacity to blend the traditions of east and west, Catholic and Protestant, and particularly his commitment to the poor have sparked interest among theologians in very diverse contexts and generated some first-rate theological writing. A second feature of my attempted profile, then, would be an awareness of John Wesley and the question of his contemporary relevance.

Third, churches in the Methodist tradition would consider themselves to be mission churches, for which evangelism in some form is an imperative. The response to the World Methodist Council's initiatives over the years for global evangelism is evidence of the powerful attraction of the idea, even if, for some, questions about method and objectives abound. Notoriously, many churches in the global south are growing while many in the north are struggling. Even where there is no discernible overall growth, however, as in Britain, its absence causes concern, not just because no one likes to belong to a shrinking organisation but because of a deep sense that it is contrary to Methodism's identity. We were born as a movement of mission, the genes remain with us and we feel frustrated.

Allied with this is the fact that Methodist churches are Arminian in their theology. The formal eighteenth-century controversies with Calvinism have died away, but it would be a mistake to assume that no differences of nuance remain, or that all those in the Reformed tradition hold the same mediating position as was expressed in the World Methodist/World Alliance of Reformed Churches dialogue from 1985 to 1987.[6] There are no signs of any Methodist change of heart on the issue, however. For Methodists, Christ died for all, and they do not have much room in their thinking for notions of election.

Another common feature is the stress on what Wesley referred to as experimental religion – the religion of the heart, conversion, personal piety and growth in grace. This has received criticism, particularly from Latin American theologians, who have argued that it distracts the believer from engagement in social action and reflection on the social and political dimensions of life. The criticism is often valid, but it is essentially a call for a redefinition of what it means to be converted and personally committed, not a move away from conversion and personal commitment as such. It is hard to say where holiness fits into this spirituality. In some churches in the world Methodist family it is a major emphasis, in some others possibly a dead letter. In some the stress is on the pursuit of national and international justice rather than personal improvement. Where the holiness tradition continues it is variously interpreted.

One last common feature may be noted. Methodist churches stand in the connexional tradition and adhere to a more or less centralised polity involving conference, both as an authority within the church and as a method of coming to decisions. Of course, the structures and the interpretations put upon them vary from church to church (as, for example, in the absence or presence of bishops, and, when they are present, in their authority and relation to other elements in the structure), but 'connexion' (even if spelled differently) and 'conference' are common parlance. This is ecclesiologically significant and an element of a shared theology.

In future?

In the last few paragraphs I have attempted a profile, and I acknowledge its subjectivity. It would be nonsense to claim that any one of these features, excepting the reference to Wesley, is exclusive to Methodism, but – taken together – I believe they are typical of the family worldwide. The various components are given different weight and interpreted in different ways in different places, but I suspect they are all to be found. But does it all add up to a common theology? Yes, in the sense that all the items (including conference and connexion) have theological significance; no, in the sense that they do not represent a coherently integrated theological package consciously held as such. The various member churches of world Methodism hold to them because they have inherited them, but they have not spent a great deal of time working out their interrelations.[7]

It is here that the work of the Oxford Institute has potential. Over the years it has addressed a variety of contemporary issues from the perspective of John Wesley's life and thought: liberation and sanctification, evangelism, global poverty, community and power, the old creation and the new. Other historical periods beside the eighteenth century have been studied in specialist groups, but it is the eighteenth that provides the common ground between the various traditions, because the nineteenth and twentieth witnessed the separation and diversification that now account for the complexity of world Methodism. As already mentioned, a significant contribution of the Institute has been an awakening of interest in Wesley as a theologian, and as a result of the work that has been done, inside and outside the Institute meetings, it is now easier to see how the various elements in his thought hold together and what they may offer for contemporary thought. Aspects of his thought, such as his deep commitment to the poor and his concern for social and economic conditions, hitherto often neglected because of concentration on his experience at Aldersgate in 1738, have been brought to the fore. Of course, there can be no question of imposing an eighteenth-century framework or limiting theological enquiry to the lines he initiated. The twenty-first-century world is immeasurably different from his. But the more a coherence is seen in the various elements of his thought, the easier it will be for the contemporary churches to recognise the coherence of those theological emphases they have inherited from him.

Does it matter? The question is not just whether there is a 'world Methodist theology' but whether there needs to be one. A single, clearly defined Methodist position on all topics would undoubtedly be convenient for ecumenical dialogue, but an authentic response by all church and local communities to the context in which they are called to serve God is surely more important, even if it leads to greater diversification. Yet one of the dangers of diversity is that we get trapped in our contexts. One of the services the Oxford Institute has rendered over the years has been to enable, even compel, Methodists from diverse traditions and different parts of the world to listen to each other and to recognise the limited nature of the perspective each has on the world. Within its meetings, representatives from the affluent and dominant West have had to listen to those who represent the world's poor and oppressed. Those who have pressed the case for liberation theology have had to hear those for whom interfaith dialogue is an even greater priority. The Institute has witnessed many confrontations, yet participants return, particularly, I believe, because of the sense of a shared inheritance to be explored. The take-up of the published proceedings after each Institute has not been high, and without committed and indulgent publishers they would not have seen the light of day. But the influence of the Institute has not been confined to its published proceedings. Its members have been presbyters (preachers, therefore) and theological teachers, ordained and lay. Many have held positions of leadership in their respective churches. Having been influenced by the encounters in the Institute they have, in turn, exercised an influence within their own spheres. While they may have been critical of some of what they have heard, they have also been shaped by it, and so wider perspectives on the world and on the Methodist tradition in its various forms have been disseminated. These are small seeds, but they perhaps hold the possibility for the future of a more developed and more clearly articulated Methodist theological position worldwide.

Notes

1 Originally published as 'World Methodist Theology?' in the *Epworth Review*, vol. 32, no. 3, 2005, pp. 17–24. Copyright Trustees for Methodist Church Purposes, reprinted by permission.

2 For a history of the Institute, see my *Exploring Methodism's Heritage: The Story of the Oxford Institute of Methodist Theological Studies* (Nashville, TN: General Board of Higher Education and Ministry, United Methodist Church, 2004).

3 Meeks, *What Should Methodists Teach?*, p. 132.

4 For a survey of these, see the Faith and Order Committee's report to the 2003 British Conference, *His Presence Makes the Feast*, pp. 161–80.

5 See the report cited in note 4 and compare the treatment given to the first phase of meetings arranged by the Anglican–Roman Catholic International Commission ('ARCIC I') by the Vatican. The generous attitude to the possibility in the future of an 'effective leadership and primacy in the bishop of Rome' ('Towards a Statement on the Church': Pontifical Council for Promoting Christian Unity and World Methodist Council, 1986, para. 62) would not find an echo among many Methodists in the pew.

6 'Distorted teaching on these points still adversely and directly affects the lives of people in some parts of the world... We believe the key...must be the doctrine of Christ as God's Elect One in whom we receive our standing.' 'London Colney Report' (Lake Junaluska, NC: World Methodist Council, 1985).

7 In saying this, I am not ignoring the work of particular writers, but they have written as individuals; there has been, so far as I am aware, no inter-church articulation of a shared theological position. The Wesleyan Essentials of Christian Faith adopted by the World Methodist Council in 1996 do not go beyond a series of bullet points. Interestingly, they do not refer to 'connexion'.

13 The idea of a national church[1]

This is a subject upon which, so far as I am aware, the Methodist Church has not officially pronounced. What follows is therefore a personal view, though I hope it is not unrepresentative.[2]

There is a history, of course. Methodism's beginnings were in the Church of England of the eighteenth century, but it will not do just to point to John Wesley's pro-establishment views, or his rather less pro-establishment practice, as though he represented Methodism past and present. Eighteenth-century Methodism was in fact divided in its attitude to the Established Church, and the nineteenth century saw a steady drift apart, with the rise of the Oxford Movement in the earlier part and the emergence of the Free Church alliance in the closing decades. Methodism's experience of being on the receiving end of establishment attitudes, particularly in the rural areas, did not encourage the view that establishment was a good thing. The negative reaction was compounded by the emergence in the first half of the century of other Methodist groups, including the New Connexion, the Primitive Methodists and the Bible Christians, that had no Anglican roots nor any inherited sympathy for the Church of England. All that flowed into the now united Methodist Church of today and remains in the collective consciousness, albeit tempered by the more recent experience of ecumenism. A referendum is too simplistic a measure, but if one were to be taken of contemporary Methodists, for or against the establishment of the church, I have no doubt that the vast majority would be against it. That begs a lot of questions, however.

First, I want to distinguish between a national church and an established one. One can aspire to being national without the privileges of establishment. Consider names: the Church in Wales, the Church of Scotland, the Church of England, the Church of Ireland. Only two are established by law, each in a different way, and the reality is that each of the four is but one among many, even if the most numerous, in the country concerned, and that fact is acknowledged in practice. Those names are of course the product of history, and perhaps we have to live with what we have inherited, but the implication of such a name is that those other churches are somehow peripheral, awaiting their gathering in to the body that claims the historical high ground. That is sometimes reflected in attitudes; it is certainly assumed to be the case by the media.

Second, I address the question 'What nation are we talking about?', a question that we might not have bothered with 30 years ago. In Ireland all the main churches span the north–south border. In Britain the Methodist Church (which does not include Ireland) is one church in what we now increasingly call three nations. That puts Methodism at a disadvantage in some Welsh and Scottish quarters, but it also bears witness to an important truth, or at least questions glib assumptions. I will not resolve that dilemma – political developments will no doubt do it for us – but I return to the issue later.

Third, I suggest that every church is in one sense, to a greater or less degree, a national church. The Methodist Church in Britain is not identical in ethos to its sister church in Ireland, nor to those in the United States or South Africa. All churches, even those that are seemingly most globally uniform, bear the marks of the cultures in which they are set. In some cases, indeed, they may be significant bearers of the culture. The Orthodox Church in Russia is an example, as are the Nonconformist Churches in Wales. Indeed, a church may be the focal point of cultural identity for expatriates in a foreign land: there is a Tamil-speaking Methodist congregation in Hammersmith in west London that draws its members from halfway across the country. It is not the only language-based gathered congregation. Punjabi, Korean, Chinese and Welsh come to mind. There is no such thing as a global brand of Christianity, and if there were it would be rootless. But I am assuming that that is not the sense in which we are discussing the notion of a national church.

The longer I reflect on the subject, the clearer I become that it resolves itself into two principal questions: does the nation need a national church, and is a national church a legitimate theological concept?

Does the nation need a national church?

First, does the nation, however we delimit it, need a national church? Taking an overall view of history, one can readily see that communal religious observances have more often than not been the glue that has held society together. Evidence could be drawn from large societies and small, in many parts of the world, and is not confined by any means to the Christian religion. Religious practice has bound populations together by the expression of shared values, and made the state answerable (in theory at least) to higher authority. It has also invested the state with higher authority in relation to its subjects. One could devote an entire semester to illustrating that fact, and seventeenth-century England would as good a period and place as any for illustrating its pros and cons. The alternatives are an atheist state that seeks to restrict or suppress religious groups, or a neutral one that tolerates them. But the presupposition of a national religious expression that functions in that way is a common religious viewpoint shared by the population.

Historically, it could once be said that Britain had one. Even in 1953 Britain could still reasonably be described as a Christian nation; not only were there then, as now still, many residues of Christian tradition in the culture but

14 Unity and conscience[1]

Recent Methodist debate on human sexuality has highlighted an issue that periodically becomes acute in the life of the churches, the tension between the claims of Christian unity and the claims of Christian conscience, and it may be useful at this stage to reflect on it.

We can begin from the fact of the constant movement in the life of the church towards and away from unity. Contrary to the way in which it is sometimes depicted, the goal of unity is essentially unattainable. Unity is a dynamic process, not a state that we shall one day reach. Only in the age to come do we finally arrive. In this age there is a constant tension between movements that are centripetal and those that are centrifugal. The ecumenical movement of the last hundred years or so is witness to the centripetal process, the drawing close together and the healing of divisions. But more recently we have become conscious again of the centrifugal pressures on the churches, as divisions have occurred or been threatened, for example over the charismatic movement and house churches, the ordination of women or the place of homosexuals in the life of the church.

In reflecting on this tension and the issues it raises, a simple – perhaps simplistic – analysis of the causes of division is worth making.

Four causes of disunity

It is an ecumenical commonplace to speak of the sinfulness of our divisions. There is a kind of consensus that, if only our ancestors at the time of the Great Schism, or the Reformation, had been as wise, or as clever with language or as charitable as we are, it could all have been avoided. They fell into the sin of division, and we remain in the sin of perpetuating it.

I believe this to be a dangerous oversimplification, and the experience of the problems of unity and division in the present day helps to correct the misapprehensions of hindsight. In reality, there are at least four causes of disunity in the life of the church. Only some can be directly branded as sinful. The others are so only in the sense that all the sons and daughters of Adam and Eve are under judgement as victims and perpetuators of the Fall. The more immediate causes of division, I suggest, are cussedness, culture, contradiction and conscience.

Cussedness

For cussedness, I suppose we do not need to look further than Philippians 4:2: 'Euodia and Syntyche I exhort to agree in the Lord.' They are the archetypes of many men and women we know in the life of our local churches. We know how often churches have split because of personal rivalries; we know too how often divisions that had other causes were made more intractable or wholly insoluble because of them. In so far as this is a factor we can truly speak of the sinfulness of our divisions.

Culture

But there are less personal factors. We are all of us trapped in the culture and history in which we live. Our histories, our language, our conceptualities, our whole way of living can distance us from one another, even in the life of the church. It makes sense to say that, even apart from the personalities involved, the disunity created by Chalcedon or the Council of Ephesus could not have been avoided at the time. It is a real miracle of grace when separate cultural worlds can be bridged, as in some cases they have been in recent times.

Contradiction

Then there is contradiction. This is perhaps the most common experience in the congregational life of many churches. Some practices and points of view are simply mutually exclusive. How can there be an accommodation between Quaker silence and charismatic choruses, between the ordered regularity of the daily office and the freedom to express worship in ever varied forms or between the eucharistic spirituality which stresses frequency of celebration, and that which sees the efficacy of the sacrament in part precisely in its rarity? What alternative can there be in such circumstances to separation? Whatever more tenuous bond may remain, the solution cannot be found in the one congregation gathered for worship. Of course, cussedness may enter in to complicate things, and so too may the fourth precipitating cause, conscience.

Conscience

I recall an address by the African-American theologian James Cone, to which I once had to respond. The title assigned to him was 'One Lord'. His treatment was to put a question mark against virtually all ecumenical endeavour.

> When Jesus asked his disciples, 'Who do men say that I am?', they gave different answers... As this same question is put to us today, we will undoubtedly give different answers. The rich will say one thing and the poor another. Rich European and North American Christians...will minimize the impact of their economic status by saying that the gospel is for

everyone, rich and poor alike. Poor Christians of the Third World…will not accept the European Jesus and his neutrality in their struggle for freedom… Without a unity in praxis that is based on the struggle to liberate the victims, then there can be no real unity in faith… It is not saying the same words about Christ in our creeds or sharing the same historical and theological traditions that makes us one. Rather we are made one by our engagement in the same praxis.[2]

Cone is a member of the African Methodist Episcopal Church, whose origins lie in the action of Richard Allen and others in walking out of St George's Church, Philadelphia, rather than accept segregated seating in church. How can there be unity without right practice?

I refer to this case because it is often the question of practice that sharpens the doctrinal difference to the point at which it becomes intolerable. We can disagree happily on the admissibility of so-called second baptism, until the point of decision is reached to permit or forbid it. Then conscience dictates whether we can tolerate what is decided. So too with the ordination of women. The phrase 'cost of conscience' touches the heart of it. The question of admitting avowedly practising homosexuals to ordination similarly sharpens the issue. Consciences are offended precisely because action is excluded or permitted. Then the question becomes: can I be true to my conscience and remain part of a church that permits (or does not permit) this?

When the causes of disunity are analysed like this, it becomes less clear that disunity is necessarily sinful. We are looking at the problems of the Reformation again, from the perspective of before rather than after. Is separation so clearly wrong in all circumstances? May it not sometimes rather be a matter of obedience to God?

So I try to address the specific question of unity and conscience: the dilemma of those who feel called to break ranks. It is a dilemma felt by those who recognise the call to unity, arising out of John 17, Ephesians 4, Philippians 2 and many other passages, as the call of God, and yet feel also that they are called by God to be loyal to the truth that, as they see it, the majority in the church (or in its policy-making bodies) has denied. It is a choice between two imperatives. In the balance between unity and conscience, on which side should the scale come down?

Addressing the dilemma

There are, of course, unacceptable ways of trying to resolve the dilemma.

Federalism

One is to assume that, as a matter of course, conscience must prevail. At the end of the day unity is not seen as the primary witness to the gospel. The primary witness is fidelity to scripture, or upholding the tradition, or the stand for justice or whatever the issue may be.

So true Christians must separate. Let those who are not prepared to stand for the purity of the truth go their own way. We will remain on friendly terms so far as we may, but beyond that we cannot go.

This is the federalist attitude to Christian unity, a view of churches in parallel. We do not deny their ecclesial character, but on the grounds of conscience we cannot unite. It is an approach exemplified most obviously by the Baptist churches, but in many ways it is where we all are in regard to some other members of the Christian family. At its worst it is the ecumenism of the clergy fraternal and the Week of Prayer for Christian Unity. It reminds me of Gordon Rupp's comparison[3] with 'the uneasy camaraderie of the waiting room at Bletchley station, where we all change trains and cannot wait to get back into our separate compartments again'.

The difficulty with this solution is precisely that it undervalues the imperative for unity. It ignores the ground of all unity in the unity-in-diversity of the Holy Trinity, and refuses to face the question of God's unifying purpose for the whole creation (to sum up all things in Christ), and the role of the church in this — that they may all be one that the world may believe. Moreover, as Geoffrey Wainwright says:[4] 'An ecclesiology which denies the gravity of disunity is docetist.'

Exclusivism

The second solution is a more hard-line version of the first. There is no problem of unity. Those who separate are alone the true church. Those from whom they separate have become apostate by virtue of the offending stance they have taken. Here is the position of the Ulster Orangeman, and the official position of the Roman Catholic Church before Vatican II. Historically, it is the Cyprianic view: outside the church (i.e. the church I am in) there is no salvation.

It is a solution that has the advantage of comfort. One does not need to trouble oneself about preserving the unity of the church, for it has not been fractured. The church has merely been cleansed. Purity of doctrine and praxis is paramount, and it has been preserved. The biblical motto is 2 Cor. 6:17: 'Come out from among them.'

It is a position beset by blindness, however. It assumes, what is demonstrably not so, that a clear and sharp line can be drawn between orthodoxy and orthopraxis, on the one side, and their opposites, on the other. Everyone knows that in practice, even in the most purist community, there are waverers and problems of definition. The logical consequence of the separatist position is the rigorous enforcement of internal discipline and repeated purges. To avoid this one has to turn a blind eye to the evidence of the very faults within the community on account of which the original separation occurred.

It is also a position that remains blind to the evidences of Christ in the 'apostate' body. The image of Christ in the rejected believers and the signs of the working of the Spirit among them have to be ignored or denied. It is difficult to see how this differs from blasphemy against the Holy Ghost.

Unity paramount?

If that solution exalts purity of doctrine and life above all else, a third option makes unity paramount. At all costs unity must be maintained. Whatever the tensions and contradictions, there must be no breaking of the fellowship.

The most damning thing to be said about this is that it trivialises matters of conscience. It makes unity an end in itself, rather than a concerted response to truth. It becomes a groupiness for its own sake rather than a gathering of the people of God for the world. It bears little relation to the strong negatives of the New Testament, which point to the narrowness of the gate, the need to make choices and the dangers of outer darkness.

Unity must have its outer boundaries. For all its openness, even the vision of the ultimate unity of humankind in the new Jerusalem at the end of the Book of Revelation excludes 'the cowardly, the faithless, the polluted, the murderers, the fornicators, the sorcerers, the idolaters and all liars' (21:8). Christian unity cannot mean that 'anything goes'.

If, then, these are unacceptable solutions to the dilemma, what theological and pastoral responses can there be? I offer seven.

(1) *Hierarchy of truths* We need a firm hold on the notion of the hierarchy of truths. We think of it as a Roman Catholic term, pointing to the different levels of importance of different doctrinal elements, and illuminating the way in which we are so often united in fundamentals and divided on issues lower down the scale of importance. But its essence is older. In his *Letter to a Roman Catholic* of 1749, for example, John Wesley sought to underline the fundamental articles of the creed and the vocation to love God and one's neighbour on which Protestants and Catholics were united. 'We ought, without this endless jangling about opinions, to provoke one another to love and to good works. Let the points wherein we differ stand aside: here are enough wherein we agree… If we cannot yet think alike in all things, at least we may love alike.'[5] The question remains a pertinent one. Just how important are our differences? What (to use the uncomfortable Reformation imagery) is it really worth going to the stake for? In the light of what we continue to share, the threshold to be crossed to achieve an exodus should surely be high.

(2) *Mission perspective* We need to keep firm hold upon a mission perspective. That may, of course, heighten the dilemma! One reason why some of our conflicts acquire such sharpness is the fear that in some way the gospel we present to the world will be compromised, weakened or made scandalous. Nevertheless, a mission perspective is essential.

I am not trying to imply that the 'world should write the agenda', in the pejorative sense of that phrase, or that 'the church should conform to the world'. But a clear awareness of the world and its needs might put some at least of our disputes into perspective and help us to perceive the hierarchy of truths to which I have just referred. If we had to justify our divisions to the beggar on the Calcutta street or the 16-year-old who brings her baby for baptism, while not making them the arbiters of the issues we might get a better sense of proportion.

(3) *No finality* We need to relearn the truth that there is no finality short of the coming of the Kingdom. In spite of what is claimed for the Roman Catholic *magisterium*, there are no irrevocable judgements. There can indeed be provisional judgements, and they can stand until they are seen to need amendment, but the only irreversible position is one of ever-renewed faithfulness to scripture and tradition.

That insight carries with it the point already made in criticising the exclusivist option noted earlier. There can be no such thing as a perfect church. The holiness of the church lies, and can only lie, not in its actuality but in its calling and in the justifying pronouncement of God. As the gospel of Matthew makes plain, while we are called to a righteousness that exceeds that of the scribes and Pharisees, we nevertheless have to live with the imperfection of the church until the Day of Judgement.

(4) *Enrichment of diversity* We need to recognise the enrichment of diversity. There was great diversity – contradiction, even – in the early church, and that fact is reflected not only within the New Testament texts but also in the diversity of the canon. Moreover, no one group or person can aspire to comprehend all the riches of God's creative and redemptive gifts. God the Holy Trinity is unity in diversity. What is more, without constant mutual interaction and internal criticism the church will become complacent. The prophetic voice and the discordant sounds it creates are essential to the church's health.

(5) *The God of change* We need to be open to the God of change as well as the God of the tradition. It is striking how often the crisis points for the unity of the church occur at times of great social or intellectual upheaval. One thinks of the Reformation, or the rise of Methodism, or the impact of science on Catholic Modernism or on Protestant Fundamentalism, or the influence of the shift in social attitudes and scientific understanding upon developments in the ministry of women or the place of homosexuals in the church. One side or another is in the position of resisting change, or protesting against change that is seen to have gone too far. But change cannot be eliminated. Unless one takes a purely deistic view of the doctrine of creation or abandons it altogether, one has to accept the possibility that God's will is revealed in present developments and is pointing the church towards change. A view of the church as totally immutable would be a denial of the reality of the historical process, which is essential for a proper doctrine of the incarnation.

(6) *Preserving the tension* We need to find ways of preserving the tension between unity and conscience. All the unacceptable ways resolved the tension in one direction or the other. This seems to me to be the fundamental mistake. We are called both to keep the unity of the Spirit in the bond of peace and to be obedient to the word of God and our conscience. The

tragedy of our historical divisions is that, whatever pain may have been felt by some at least at the outset, the awareness was soon lost, and the divided state of the church was accepted as right and inevitable.

(7) *Pastoral measures* So we need to develop pastoral measures to preserve the tension.

(i) We need to continue to pray for one another, as separated brothers and sisters in Christ, or even as lost, even apostate, members of the family. This is the ultimate ecumenical discipline.

(ii) We need to sustain the dialogue. If indeed there are issues of truth and conscience at stake, they must not be silenced by the erection of high walls. The issues must continue to be pressed and examined, until the rebellious conscience is enlightened or the unawakened are convinced. To stop talking is to ease the tension and betray the call to unity in truth.

(iii) We need to explore the possibilities of diminished communion. 'Communion' is a difficult word, for it covers so many forms of ecclesial relationship, none of which is perfect, but which vary in their degree of closeness. In our search for unity we have tried to identify stages on the way back, and there has been talk of intercommunion, communion *in sacris*, impaired communion, and so on. We are now beginning to explore stages, not on the way back but on the way to separation. Must the choice be between being one body and a total rupture? Can there be ways of affirming our continuing belonging even when we are separated by issues of conscience? We can observe the Anglican Communion struggling with this question.

(iv) Above all, we need to find ways to continue to worship together. This is what was so difficult for James Cone. Yet in my response to him at the time I was conscious of the eucharist in which we had all shared only days beforehand and its real capacity to override our many conflicts and differences worldwide. It was not hypocrisy to share together, because we were primarily affirming in one another's company our shared dependence upon the one Lord who is one, not because we have identical images of him but because, in the unity of the Holy Trinity, he is Lord from eternity. Worshipping together is not mutual affirmation, still less approval, but confession before one another that we are all sinners depending utterly on grace. In that there is the potential of a renewed discovery of Christ in one another and a new discovery of what the truth is. We turn to each other in worship as a result of first turning to the one Lord. Of course, for such worship both sides have to come together, and in the same spirit. So often dissident groups hive off and become a ghetto.

This chapter has not answered the question 'When does conscience have a higher claim upon us than ecclesial unity?'. Indeed, the question is unanswerable in theory, but only in practice as sharp issues arise. Existentially, individuals come to the crisis point in different ways, some not at all. In any case, the decision is hardly ever a matter of pure conscience. It is almost always complicated by the other factors that lead to disunity. One acts on impulse, or is carried along inexorably by the force of earlier decisions and public stances. Politicians, diplomats and industrial negotiators know about such things. But it is important to reflect on the issues, and this chapter has attempted to identify some pointers for us, as individuals and corporately in Methodism and the wider church.

Notes

1 Based on a paper read to a private ecumenical gathering in February 1993.
2 James H. Cone, 'One Lord', in Joe Hale (ed.), *Proceedings of the Fourteenth World Methodist Conference* (Lake Junaluska, NC: World Methodist Press, 1982), pp. 38–9.
3 At a public meeting in Cambridge in the early 1950s.
4 Geoffrey Wainwright, *The Ecumenical Moment: Crisis and Opportunity for the Church* (Grand Rapids, MI: William B. Eerdmans, 1983), p. 87.
5 Jackson, *The Works of John Wesley*, 3rd edn (1831), vol. 10, pp. 85–6.

15 'Until we all attain...'

Eschatology and the goal of unity[1]

A cynic might be tempted to say that ecumenical progress is made by waiting for the older generation to die. That is when obstinate blockages are removed, and fresh minds find new solutions to old problems. It is not difficult to give examples. The work of the Anglican–Roman Catholic International Commission (ARCIC) and the way in which Arminians and Calvinists are now able to address questions of predestination come to mind. On a smaller scale, one could cite cases of the reuniting of congregations that broke apart decades earlier over some local feud. The world moves on and perceptions change.

There is an inner dynamic and an outer dynamic to such a process. Within the Church every generation sees its life and its problems with fresh eyes. It brings to the resolution of those problems the advantage of experience denied to earlier ages. One day, for example, historians will assess the contribution that the opening of English universities to non-Anglicans made to the creation of a common theological discourse and the forging of relationships across confessional boundaries, which have enabled much progress to be made. Thus theological controversy became a dialogue among friends.

Outwardly, the churches, willingly or in spite of themselves, are affected by the world about them. Changes in the social structure of English society have diminished, if not entirely removed, the social distinctions between Anglicans and members of the Free Churches. Changing attitudes in the churches to the ministry of women have manifestly been influenced by the changing status of women in society, though it would be foolish to claim that as the only cause. The same could be said of the interaction between Marxism and the Church's 'option for the poor'. Changes in society and the Church's traditions cross-fertilise each other.

What this should alert us to is the danger of simplistic visions of the goal of unity and its attainment, for the process can move in the opposite direction. As in wider society, so in the Church, today's agreements and accommodations can become the seeds of tomorrow's discontent. 'Until we all attain the unity of the faith...the measure of the stature of the fullness of Christ' (Ephesians 4:13) must be seen as an eschatological vision, like all eschatological promises realised only fleetingly in the present, and in its finality and fullness only in the kingdom of God. The intention of this brief chapter is to reflect upon this truth.

One way of illustrating the point is to recall that the issues that have historically divided the Church have never been exclusively theological; if they were, there would be hope that in time they could all be resolved by rational argument. Nor are the theological issues confused only by personal and inherited misunderstanding, obstinacy and self-assertion. That such factors have operated in the past and still do operate is self-evident. It is right to speak, as prayers for unity regularly do, of the sin of our divisions. But our divisions are also the product of tensions that are present in any human community and that are essential to its well-being and renewal.

For example, there are temperamental differences – between the extrovert and the shy, the more predominantly rational and the more predominantly emotional, the doers and the thinkers (the antitheses can be described in different ways). Since Christian worship seeks to touch the depths of the human spirit and at the same time to be corporate in expression, there is an inherent pressure for diversification that is hard to satisfy within a single congregation or a uniform liturgical tradition. Denominational divisions have grown out of such pressures.

These differences are not merely the outcome of later Western individualism. We idealise the past if we imagine they are a feature only of the last 500 years of Christian history. Of course there is a cultural dimension, and the precise relationship between temperament and cultural conditioning is hard to specify, but the fact that world cultures differ so widely in this respect underlines the universality of the temperamental factor, whatever its precise origins.

This temperamental factor is but one example, however, of a wider tension, between the one and the many. It expresses itself in many forms: between uniformity and diversity, liturgical order and extemporisation, universality and local particularity, tradition and innovation, priesthood and prophecy, conformity and freedom. It has manifestations in congregationalism versus connexionalism, autocephalism versus universal primacy, the saying of the creeds versus the liberty of the inner light. Both poles of such a tension are necessary. History repeatedly illustrates the fact that any attempt to exclude either produces a reaction. The experience of England in the 1660s is a case in point. Achieving equilibrium between the two is no easy task, and the equilibrium, when attained, is easily disturbed. Old ecclesiastical divisions once resolved may resurface in new forms because they are only the presenting symptoms of a deeper problem. Many local ecumenical partnerships illustrate the point. Created to resolve denominational divisions and witness to the one Church in each place, they often accommodate the differences without reconciling them. Not only is their relationship to denominational parent bodies an uneasy one, but they may tend to an independent outlook that is in effect an option for one particular ecclesiology.

It is customary nowadays to try to accommodate this tension by speaking of unity in diversity. In principle, that must be right; but the phrase, reassuring as it is, masks two serious difficulties. One is that some of the polarities are mutually exclusive. Strict congregationalism, for example, excludes alternative ecclesiologies. The other is the fact that not only is there no hope of a resolution of our inter-church differences that does not take such polarities into account, but any resolution will be inherently unstable and will need constant vigilance.

I have referred to this instability as a non-theological factor; it is to be distinguished from the specifically doctrinal questions we try to resolve. But it has its own theological significance. It is not the product of human sin but of creatureliness. It is part of the givenness of creation, how we are constituted as human beings. It is therefore part of the task God sets us, not as an obstacle to be removed but a fact of our existence to be managed pastorally.

Contemporary pressures

Alongside all this we are conscious at the present time of new dangers. In a sense, they are further manifestations of the tensions just described, but their distinctive feature is that they cut right across old fissure-lines, threatening the life of each church from within and inviting people to make common cause across the denominations. Three examples will illustrate the point.

The role of women

In all churches there is a growing emphasis upon the role of women. The World Council of Churches' Decade of the Churches in Solidarity with Women did not achieve worldwide what its sponsors hoped for it. Nevertheless, churches are becoming more inclusively communities of women and men. In many world communions, but not in the two largest, this extends to the ordination of women to the presbyterate and, in churches that have bishops, to the episcopate. There is often a visual reminder of the changes that have taken place in a comparison of photographs of church assemblies 50 years ago and today.

But the issue is not just one of presence and participation but of influence. How far has the style of the conduct of affairs changed? To what extent has heightened awareness of the contribution of women led to sensitivity in the use of liturgical language, and how far should this go beyond quoting women as biblical role models or avoiding 'men' in prayers? What is to be done about our language of God? If men and women alike are created in the image of God, who must therefore be exclusively neither male nor female, is 'she' as acceptable (and as limited) a pronoun as 'he'?

Such questions are potentially a very serious source of schism, for they bear heavily upon the identity and distinctiveness of the Christian heritage. At present they are more openly pressed in some countries and some traditions than in others. They are pressed by men as well as women. They will not easily go away. Indeed, such is the nature of the global exchange of information, they are likely to become more widely asked and to present a serious test of the churches' capacity to hold together for many years to come.

Changes in moral attitudes

A second issue is presented by changes in sexual mores and the ethical questions that these raise. The impact of the general availability of contraception, especially in Western society, cannot be overestimated. It has led to quite radical changes in attitudes to marriage and the significance of the sexual act. There is now a widespread assumption that deep emotional commitment between two persons may appropriately, and will normally, find expression in sexual intercourse, regardless of whether there exists a contract of marriage between them. While the churches continue to uphold the institution of marriage and the lifelong monogamous ideal, it would be idle to pretend that thinking or practice among church members on such matters is untouched by attitudes in wider society.

Alongside this is the question of homosexuality, now openly discussed in the churches. There is a wide though by no means universal acceptance of homosexual orientation, and a willingness on the part of some (but still, one would judge, a minority) to see homosexual partnerships, including intimate sexual activity, as compatible with Christian obedience.

These are explosive issues, because they touch on deep emotions, and the likelihood is that they will continue to present a severe test of unity in diversity for all the churches. Already there is evidence that many leave the traditional churches, either for groups with a more explicit conservative stance or for communities more accepting of a gay or lesbian lifestyle.

Wider cultural change

A third example would focus on the more general impact of cultural change. It is difficult to overestimate the cultural shift in British society over the last half-century, although it is a more complex phenomenon than it is sometimes presented as being. To some extent it goes with a generational divide, but there are young and old on both sides of the line between traditional and contemporary. The gap between Church and society is widening in many ways and it is virtually impossible to rely upon a common currency of ideas and language between those who belong to the Church and those who do not. The importance of this for the churches lies in the proper desire to make formal acts of worship and the general culture of church life appeal not only to potential converts to Christian faith but to those within the Church whose sense of cultural alienation increases Sunday by Sunday and whose loyalty may be severely tested.

This is the gap that less traditional styles of worship and music seek to bridge. The most obvious instances would relate to music styles and experiments with 'rave' services, but more is involved than guitars and strobe lights. Underneath is often a shift of theological emphasis. Even where explicitly biblical language and imagery is retained there may be a shift away from tradition and sacramental life to the immediate experience of the Spirit, and from a more corporate to a more individual and private piety, even if it is expressed in large gatherings. That too is part of the impact of cultural change.

Alongside it must be set a further development. The greater mobility of the population and the emphasis upon choice and variety mean that fewer and fewer worshippers are deeply steeped in the traditions of the church they attend. What holds them to a particular congregation is more likely to be style and personal relationships than theological conviction. Even within one denomination there may be wide diversity and clearly differentiated congregational styles. Those who negotiate union schemes for the churches represent principles that many, perhaps the majority, of their churches do not deeply share.

In terms of cultural change, of course, we are speaking not merely of potential threats to the unity of the Church but of developments that have to some extent already taken place. The house church movement is already beginning to consolidate into a denomination as it shows the signs of institutionalisation that accompany the second generation of any movement.

Questions to be addressed

There are clear theological dimensions to all these contemporary problems, specific theological questions about particular issues – for example, about the nature of the image of God in its relation to human sexuality – but more general questions also, common to them all. Three may be mentioned.

(1) *Competing imperatives* How are we to weigh competing imperatives? Christians divide on issues of principle. Sometimes it is true that such principles are merely a cloak for human intransigence, but more often they are not. The prohibitions in scripture of homosexual activity or the ministry of women, or the obligation to keep faith with tradition over the threefold ministry or infant baptism, will for many people be matters of conscience that are not negotiable. For them, there can be no surrender. But to keep the unity of the Spirit in the bond of peace is also a scriptural imperative. Where do the claims of conscience drive us to break that bond, and where does the bond drive us to disregard principle in the acceptance of a brother or sister who disagrees?

(2) *'Legitimate diversity'* 'Legitimate diversity' has become a widely accepted description of a future united Church. What is the definition of 'legitimate', and how wide is the diversity to be? If the scriptural answer (as in I John 4:2) to the question 'How do we discern the Spirit of God?' is 'By confession of Jesus Christ', what in turn is the test of that confession? Is it by assent to credal formulae, or by recognition of the works of Jesus even where the name (or at least the formal credal doctrine) is not explicitly confessed? Is it even the case that to pose the question (as I have) in terms of theological criteria is a mistake, because discernment is not a matter of reference to criteria or the application of tests but something more directly intuitive? It is well known that a key factor in the 1987 Swanwick

Conference that led to the creation of the Council of Churches of Britain and Ireland and the national instruments for England, Scotland and Wales was the experience of worshipping together.

(3) *Integrity* There is also the issue of integrity. Continuity of some kind is essential to a sense of identity. Without a continuing thread, how can we say we are the same person? Whatever death and resurrection may mean for ecumenical relations (it is less commonly spoken of now, as the goal is less sharply defined in terms of the creation of new churches out of the death of old ones), it must imply, as for the death and resurrection of the individual (and of our Lord), a recognisable continuity through change. What, then, must be retained in order to keep faith with the past? What can be safely let go without betrayal?

The developments we have surveyed amply illustrate the fact that churches do not stand still. The idea, commonly assumed if not often explicitly expressed, that one day by prayer and dialogue we shall all reach the goal of unity is in fact an illusion. Even without the destructive effect of human frailty and sin, the goal would be unattainable in any final sense. That is not to denigrate the work done in international conversations and more local unity schemes nor to belittle the achievements of the many unions that have come about in the last hundred or so years. Such work must be continued, but it will never be complete. The goal lies in the *eschaton*. Like the horizon, it constantly beckons and constantly recedes. It is arrogant to suggest that the obstacles to progress lie only with the legacy of preceding generations. As we move forward we lay new blocks of our own.

The task is essentially pastoral. We have developed methods by which to address formal theological differences between church traditions. There are well-established patterns of dialogue and negotiation that produce clarifying statements and proposals for unity schemes. The methodology is less clear when the divisive issues cut across the churches, and there are no clearly delineated communities to negotiate with each other. But the same skills are called for: the willingness to listen and the ability to hear without distortion; the effort to enter into another's experience and see oneself through others' eyes; the willingness, with their help, to try to disentangle true and false, central and peripheral, in one's own position; the discernment of what must be retained and what must be let go; and the expectation that the partner in the dialogue will reciprocate with comparable seriousness. The responsibility lies on those who exercise pastoral ministry in the Church to ensure that there is an atmosphere in which potentially divisive issues can be addressed openly, with mutual acceptance and without fear. Ecumenical concern is one with pastoral concern and cannot be separated off as the preoccupation of a few enthusiasts.

We can reach the same point from a different direction by considering the concept of *koinonia*. One of the most important effects of the deployment of this concept in recent decades has been that it has encouraged us to approach the question of unity in a holistic way. Unity among the churches cannot be isolated from the unity of humankind, nor can the unity of humankind from the unity of the wider creation. Nor are these issues different in principle from questions about the quality of the common life within particular churches. Unity – *koinonia* – involves relationships in the context of sharing in the life of the Holy Trinity. It is never merely a matter of ecclesiastical joinery or finding formulae to bridge doctrinal differences. It requires persons to live in communion with God and each other in all their diversity. But such a definition of the ecumenical goal also means that the goal is never achieved. Indeed, it is not a goal at all, as something distant but coming nearer, but a description of a daily process.

This must be all the more evident once we set the unity of the Church in the wider context of the future of the human race and of the created order. If it is true that creation, redemption and sanctification are alike the work of the one undivided Trinity, then it must follow that God's purposes for and with the Church cannot be divorced from his purposes for and with the world as a whole, and the one cannot be complete without the other. But that wider context merely underlines the point: in the ever-shifting development of history there are no fixed points of achievement, no bridgeheads won that cannot as easily be lost. The quest for and nurturing of unity is the daily pastoral task of the Church.

The thrust of this chapter has been to emphasise the quest for Christian unity as a continuing and never completed feature of the Church's life this side of the *eschaton*. It is truly an eschatological vision, something promised in the coming kingdom. It is never a project that one day we shall put behind us, and the skills and disciplines for which it calls are not only those related to formal dialogues and the task of 'bringing the churches together'. It has an inherently pastoral dimension.

Consequences

What are the consequence of seeing the ecumenical vision in such eschatological terms? Clearly, it does not relieve ecumenical work of its urgency. The *eschaton* is not merely that for which the people of God wait; it is also that for which they work and pray and which they seek to bring into reality in the present. The urgency is not that the time is short, though in terms of the Church's missionary credibility it may be, but that those who look for the coming of the kingdom are bound by that commitment to live out its values here and now. In that way the future can be anticipated.

Allied to anticipation is foretaste. If the former term lays stress on human effort, the latter points to the gift of God. 'If I by the finger of God cast out demons, then the Kingdom of God has come upon you' (Luke 11:20). God grants in foretaste what he holds in promise for the future. Such foretastes are transitory, part of the changing scene of history to which we have called attention, but real nevertheless. It is right to regard 27 September 1947, when the

Church of South India came into being, as an eschatological moment, even though as we now look back we see that much was achieved but many hopes have remained unfulfilled.

So the ecumenical virtues we are called to learn and practise are essentially the eschatological ones: patience, watchfulness, forbearance and faithfulness. Patience is called for; not merely the patience of waiting for particular schemes to mature, or for the turning of the tide in the life of the churches that indicates 'now is the time' for decision, but the deeper *hypomone*, endurance, which bears the pain of the tension of belonging in the Body of Christ, and which takes up, again and again, the struggle to maintain the unity of the Spirit as new conflicts arise at the very moment when old ones seem to be resolved.

Watchfulness is needed, because the stress points that give rise to dispute and disharmony develop in small ways, often unnoticed, and grow, if left unchecked, into crises out of all proportion to their beginnings. The test, for example, of whether the churches will successfully cope with any of the issues I have illustrated above will be not in some grand response at national level but whether, in countless congregations, ministers and church members hold on to one another in love from day to day and week to week. 'Watch and pray that you enter not into temptation.'

Allied to it is forbearance. Relationships are essential to *koinonia*. The desire to see everyone else in all things like ourselves is very strong. But such uniformity or cloning is not given in the Body of Christ, which needs to learn to accept its own diversity, not just of functions and gifts but of personalities, cultures and histories. Cardinal Basil Hume, in a brief meditation at the 1997 Forum of Churches Together in England, spoke of the three dimensions of ecumenism: the spirit (prayer), the mind (theology) and the heart (friendship). All friendship is built upon forbearance, the tolerance of differences and hurts. Without it (and, where it has been lacking, without repentance and the healing of memories), there can be no true *koinonia*,

Within that context there is a job faithfully to be done. Ecumenical progress is painfully slow. Often schemes on which we set our hopes come to nothing, and it may be years before further steps can be taken. The 1960s and 1970s saw many such schemes fall, in Sri Lanka, in West and East Africa and here in Britain. The reaction of many is to abandon the journey. But, while such local schemes have failed, international dialogues have shown that progress can be made, perhaps because they are safely removed from the prospect of immediate implementation in a local scheme. Persistence and painstaking work do bear fruit.

Finally, an ecumenical perspective calls for the capacity to celebrate. The early Church kept alive its eschatological hope by affirmation, and particularly in worship: *Marana tha!* Come, Lord! But the affirmation included not only the future hope but the celebration of its foretaste in the Spirit-given events of the Church's life. 'As often as you eat the bread and drink from the cup you proclaim the Lord's death until he comes.' The ecumenical vision needs to be kept alive, by celebration of unity already given, by anticipation of what is achievable in the interim as particular issues are addressed and by affirmation of what is to come in the final gift of the kingdom.

Note

1 Originally published in Colin Podmore (ed.), *Community – Unity – Communion: Essays in Honour of Mary Tanner* (London: Church House Publishing, 1998), pp. 227–36. Reprinted by permission.

16 The Porvoo Common Statement
A Methodist response[1]

The Porvoo Common Statement, Together in Mission and Ministry, was published in 1993, as a result of which some 15 Anglican and Lutheran Churches in Britain and Ireland, Northern Europe, Portugal and Spain are now in communion, though not all can trace an unbroken succession of episcopal ordination from the Middle Ages.[2] I was invited to offer a Methodist comment.

Internationally, Methodism is very diverse. Not all Methodist churches are episcopally ordered. In those that are, episcopal ministry has evolved in different ways, sometimes in response to external political pressure. While in most such churches the episcopal office is held for life, in some it is for a limited term only. Behind this diversity, however, lie two main streams of tradition: one, episcopally ordered, derives from the formation in the United States of the Methodist Episcopal Church in 1784; the other, without personal episcopacy, has evolved in Britain directly from John Wesley's connexion of Methodist societies. It is impossible to reflect all this variety in this response. This chapter is written from a British perspective, although the implications of Porvoo for the United Methodist Church, the main representative of the American tradition, will also be briefly considered.

On several occasions the Methodist Church in Britain has declared itself willing to accept episcopacy in the historic succession, most recently in 2000. Previously it had done so in the context of unity proposals, the South and North India Schemes, the Anglican–Methodist Conversations of 1955–72 and the Covenant proposals a decade later. It needs to be remembered, however, that there were many who opposed those decisions, on the grounds that they required of Methodism a willingness to accept a condition for union that they saw as alien to their tradition and extraneous to the gospel, and who would have sympathy with the reservations of Danish and other Lutherans about the Porvoo agreement.[3] Communities that have laid great stress on justification by grace through faith do not easily accept an emphasis upon church order, which seems to them to limit the free availability of that grace. The theological basis offered for the emphasis upon historic episcopal succession is thus of paramount importance.

How, then, should one respond to the Porvoo Common Statement and its Declaration? First of all, naturally, to welcome any forward step taken on the long and painful road towards the unity that is God's calling and gift to the Church. That some of the impulse for this has come from the political and secularising situation in which the churches find themselves is only to say that the Spirit employs many means to make his voice heard. The fact remains that the Porvoo agreement and its acceptance is a step forward made possible by the grace of God.

The second response is to welcome the fact that unity and mission are held so firmly together. Ecumenists have often been accused of neglecting mission and diverting energies from it, and, indeed, ecumenical texts have sometimes done little to dispel the notion. That accusation cannot be made against Porvoo. By addressing the issues in the context of apostolicity, rather than, say, catholicity, the report has kept mission in the centre of the discussion.

Third, one must warmly welcome the clear recognition that apostolic continuity in the Church is carried along all streams of its life, in its theology, liturgy, spirituality, pastoral care, missionary outreach and witness, as well as in its order. That recognition is applied to achieve a breakthrough in establishing communion between Anglican and Lutheran Churches that had previously proved elusive. I shall return to this point later, but for the moment draw attention to its importance and the fact that it is a fruit of the widespread appreciation of the concept of *koinonia* as one that releases us from excessively static and structural approaches to church relations.

Welcome too is the recognition of diversity as the prerequisite of any significant unity. It is so often stated these days as to be almost an ecumenical commonplace, but it is often not wholly believed by those who are suspicious of where the ecumenical movement may lead. Equally welcome, especially to Methodists with their particular history, is the candid acknowledgement, following *Baptism, Eucharist and Ministry*, that the historic episcopal succession, though a sign, cannot be a guarantee of apostolicity. Given the part played by the shortcomings of eighteenth-century English bishops (for reasons, be it said, not wholly of their own making) in the separation of Methodism from the Church of England, Methodists cannot ask for less.

Important as the breakthrough is, it is not a union. The churches remain distinct and autonomous. They have much in common and will now be free to develop common structures and initiatives. To that extent the autonomy may begin to break down. Territorially, however, Anglicans and Lutherans overlap only in the presence of scattered expatriate chaplaincies. These will now be brought into canonical relationship with the host church, but in other respects the churches will coexist in communion. The comment of the House of Bishops of the Church of England is significant: 'The House can only imagine entering into a relationship of union with another church in England if that entailed a unity in faith, sacramental life, a single presbyteral ministry with a common episcopate in the historic succession and common structures: in short a single Church for the sake of strengthening a common mission and service to all.'[4]

Possibilities for Methodism

So, of course, Methodists will be asking: what is there in this for us? Does Porvoo offer a way forward that can fruitfully be followed in other contexts? That is the question this chapter seeks to explore, and, effectively, that means: does Porvoo offer a way to resolve the difficulties that confront Methodists and Anglicans? Numerically the Lutheran churches are not strongly represented in Britain, though they are active in ecumenical councils. Elsewhere in the world Methodists and Lutherans are to be found side by side, Lutherans often being the majority. The Methodist churches in Britain and Ireland and on the European continent have entered into agreement with the Churches of the Leuenberg Fellowship, which involves fellowship of word and sacrament including mutual recognition of ordination. The World Methodist–Lutheran dialogue has opened up bilateral agreements for pulpit and table fellowship in a number of places. Communion between Lutheran and Methodist churches, therefore, does not present insuperable problems. What, then, does Porvoo offer to Methodists and Anglicans, who in many parts of the world share the same territory but are still separated by the issue of the historic succession?

The detail of the Porvoo agreement needs to be noted carefully. The temptation on a superficial reading of concluding that historic episcopal succession is seen as but one sign of apostolicity among many so that, if the succession is broken, apostolicity can be carried by the others until it is restored, like a broken bone being supported by a splint, is one to be resisted. Each of the churches in the agreement claims to be the continuation of the medieval church in the country concerned. They are described as national churches (although the picture in Scotland in particular is rather more complex). Each is now episcopally ordered. Moreover, the justification offered for disregarding the interruptions in the episcopal succession is not simply that the churches are truly apostolic in other respects, but rests on a combination of factors: first, the interruptions were not deliberate or dogmatically based (there was no intention to embrace a presbyterian polity) but were forced upon the churches by political circumstances; second, when in 1536 consecrations in Denmark were performed, not by bishops but by Johannes Bugenhagen, a presbyter, they were performed nevertheless by one whose ministry can be regarded as episcopal in all but name; third, although there was not a succession in consecration, there was a succession in historic sees.[5] No Methodist church matches that combination of characteristics. Nevertheless, the movement beyond the simple insistence on continuity in episcopal consecration characteristic of earlier conversations is striking and welcome. Apostolicity is a multiple cord, not a single thread.

Equally striking are other allowances made. Episcopal ordination of presbyters is not invariably required practice in all the Lutheran churches concerned. In certain circumstances deans of cathedrals may ordain. But the Anglican churches have been willing to judge by the norm rather than the exception. Similarly striking is the degree of difference accepted in the interpretation of episcopacy. In the supporting essays published with the Common Statement it is made unambiguously clear that, for some at least in the Lutheran churches, the episcopate, though requiring a further act of consecration, is an extension of the presbyterate. The presbyterate is *jure divino*, the episcopate *jure humano*. The episcopate is not seen as a distinct order.[6] Moreover, the Lutheran churches remain free to be in communion with non-episcopal churches, thus taking a different view from Anglicans of the significance of episcopal succession. From a Methodist point of view these are hopeful signs.

Methodism cannot claim direct evolution from the medieval church. Its roots lie in the Church of England of the eighteenth century. Its development into a separate church was prolonged and messy. Many political and sociological factors were involved. In Britain it is impossible to name a date on which Wesley's Methodist societies became a church, though there are many landmarks along the way. In the United States it is clearer: at the Christmas Conference of 1784 they declared themselves to be the Methodist Episcopal Church in America and soon replaced Wesley's term 'superintendent' by 'bishop'. The critical point of no return for both sides of the Atlantic was Wesley's ordinations in September 1784.[7]

The precipitating factor was the situation created in America by the end of the War of Independence and the absence of any ordained clergy to minister to the Methodist societies there. It needs to be remembered that one reason for Wesley's action was to prevent the development of lay eucharistic presidency or the creation of a presbyterate *de novo* from the laity, for some of the lay preachers in America had already attempted to take matters into their own hands. It is also important that he took this step only after the Bishop of London and others had refused to act. He was thus attempting not only to provide pastoral oversight of the American Societies but to preserve some semblance of catholic order. He claimed theological justification in the thesis of Baron Peter King and Bishop Edward Stillingfleet that in the primitive church bishops and presbyters were of one order, and he therefore, as a presbyter, considered himself to be 'as real a Christian bishop as the Archbishop of Canterbury', though he vehemently refused the title.[8] That he had no canonical authority for this was, for him, set aside by the precedent of scripture and the primitive church and his sense that God had set him apart for the oversight of the developing revival.

Wesley not only ordained lay preachers as deacons and presbyters, he also ordained Thomas Coke, already a presbyter, as 'superintendent' for the American Methodist Church, with authority similarly to ordain Francis Asbury, who was already resident there. Although Wesley later fiercely resisted the conclusion, the Americans instantly recognised the implications of this action and the service book he sent them, which contained with few adaptations the threefold ordinal of the *Book of Common Prayer*. Coke and Asbury were bishops and the Church was episcopally ordered.

There has been much debate about Wesley's thinking on this issue, and it is difficult to excuse him from some element of inconsistency. One could reasonably argue, on the King–Stillingfleet principle, that Coke was already invested with the same episcopal authority as Wesley claimed for himself and needed no further ordination. On the other hand, in using the term 'superintendent' it seems that Wesley was recognising that Coke needed to receive from him a share for the American Church in the authority that he himself exercised over the whole connexion of Methodist societies and preachers. Wesley was an episcopal figure in all but name. To assert that bishops and presbyters were one order was not to deny the possibility of a wider ministry of oversight within it. To this day the United Methodist Church affirms only two orders of ministry, deacon and elder (presbyter), but consecrates elders to the (lifelong) office of bishop, to exercise collegially the 'general superintendency' of the whole Church.

The American Methodist situation thus bears resemblance in many respects to that of the Nordic and Baltic Lutheran Churches. The United Methodist Church is not a national church, nor is there a succession in historic sees (how could either be the case?), but it is an episcopally ordered church, whose orders were received by presbyteral ordination at the hands of a man who exercised (albeit not by formal appointment) an effectively episcopal ministry, at a time when external constraints (and the reluctance of the Established Church) made canonical observance impossible. That the episcopate is seen as an extension of presbyteral ministry is no different from the position of some Lutheran churches. There is substantial agreement on general matters of faith and doctrine, as the Anglican–Methodist International Commission has observed.[9] One asks: what more is required to bring Methodists and Anglicans together, not just in the United States but wherever the United Methodist Church and the Anglican Communion are represented?

The British situation is different. Although Wesley continued to ordain after 1784, most were for ministry outside the jurisdiction of the Church of England, in Scotland and overseas. Only at the very end of his life did he ordain men for England, apparently to provide for the situation after his death. In the event, these ordinations were ignored, and ordination by the imposition of hands was not generally introduced until 1836.[10] No attempt was made to continue the succession from those ordained by Wesley; rather, the reverse. The reasons were complex. There was still a strong desire after Wesley's death not to make a formal separation from the Church of England, and an equally strong desire not to perpetuate distinctions among the travelling preachers between ordained and unordained, all of whom in time came to exercise a ministry of Word and Sacraments. The result was that, when ordination by the imposition of hands was introduced, it was to a single presbyteral order.[11] Until then it was held that the formal act of reception into full connexion with the Conference was 'virtual ordination', and it has continued to be held that *episcope* over the whole church is exercised corporately by the annual Conference. British Methodism is not in any other sense episcopally ordered, though there are ministers (not least the president of the Conference) who exercise many episcopal functions.[12]

Methodists in the British tradition cannot therefore expect some sudden breakthrough as a result of Porvoo in the difficulties that have always beset formal relations with Anglicans. The most that could be asked is a generous recognition, in the spirit of Porvoo, that a *presbyteral* succession in ministry has been continued even though the accompanying *sign*, ordination by the imposition of hands, was lacking for some decades. It is unrealistic to expect that more should have been done in the circumstances of the 1790s and early 1800s.

The Quadrilateral

But that brings us to the heart of the matter: the long-standing stipulation, articulated in the Chicago–Lambeth Quadrilateral of 1886/88, that the historic episcopal succession must be a part of any reconciliation of the churches. If the goal is indeed, in the words of the House of Bishops, 'a single church', it is difficult to see how anything less could be required. If the succession is a valued sign of apostolicity and a gift that Anglicans bring, then clearly it should be preserved, unbroken, in any future united church. Provided that its acceptance does not imply an adverse judgement on the apostolic continuity (to use Porvoo's phrase) of the receiving church, there is no reason why Methodists should resist it. Indeed, there would be positive gain. The ministry of bishops whose consecration witnessed to the long continuity of the Church from apostolic times would help to rescue Methodism from its delusion that 'everything began with John Wesley'. There is little awareness in the corporate consciousness of Methodism (on either side of the Atlantic) of being heir to a living church tradition in the interval between the Bible and the eighteenth century.[13] British Methodism, as noted above, is already on record as being willing to receive the gift. The careful statement in Porvoo on apostolicity and its relation to the sign of historic episcopal succession, building as it does on earlier statements, is very helpful in this regard.

But a single church may not always be the goal. Geographical distance between churches or differences between them in inessential matters may make a structural union undesirable or not yet attainable. Yet each may recognise in the other elements of doctrine, order and spiritual life that it believes to be the essential marks of the Church of Jesus Christ, and on that basis a relationship of communion between autonomous churches may be declared to exist. Here the Anglican Communion does not appear to be speaking with a clear voice.

In August 1999 and July 2000, respectively, the Evangelical Lutheran Church and the Episcopal Church in the United States agreed a Concordat in which the two churches become interdependent but remain autonomous. The agreement provides that, from the date of adoption, the ministry of bishops in the historic succession will be the future pattern in both churches, seen as a sign, though not a guarantee, of the unity and apostolic continuity of the whole church. In the context of Lutheran commitment to receive this, the Episcopal Church has resolved to suspend its rules so as to permit 'the full interchangeability and reciprocity of all [Lutheran] pastors as priests or presbyters within the Episcopal Church, without any further ordination or re-ordination or supplemental ordination whatsoever'.[14] The contrast with Porvoo is striking. There the commitment is 'to welcome persons episcopally ordained in any of our churches to the office of bishop, priest or deacon to serve…in that ministry in the receiving church without re-ordination'.[15] Both agreements contain provisos about invitation and observance of regulations, but Porvoo is based on a recognition that all the churches already possess the historic succession, the American Concordat on a commitment by Lutherans to introduce it. Porvoo explicitly excludes presbyters who have not been episcopally ordained (as, for instance, those ordained by a cathedral dean, or, presumably, any received by transfer from another, non-episcopal, church); the Concordat does not.

One therefore has to ask: what does the phrase 'a sign of the apostolicity of the church' really mean? Paragraphs 52–53 of Porvoo are crucial:

> Faithfulness to the apostolic calling of the whole Church is carried by more than one means of continuity… The mutual acknowledgement of our churches and ministries is theologically prior to the use of the sign of the laying on of hands in the historic succession. Resumption of the use of the sign does not imply an adverse judgement on the ministries of those churches which did not previously make use of the sign. It is rather a means of making more visible the unity and continuity of the Church at all times and in all places.

I take it that 'sign' here means more than a mere emblem of something that is independently the case. The sign does not simply represent apostolicity; it contributes something to it.[16] Nevertheless, although it is one of the many elements that constitute apostolicity, it is not determinative. Churches that have not preserved the succession without interruption can be recognised as apostolic. One may think of other elements in the church's life whose presence enhances but whose absence does not deny its apostolic character.

When, therefore, one finds stipulations that presbyters are interchangeable between autonomous churches that are in communion with each other only if they are episcopally ordained, one is driven to ask whether the same understanding of 'sign' is operating. In this context it does not look like one among many signs whose presence makes apostolicity more visible but whose absence does not deny it. It begins to look like a *necessary* sign, whose absence is a serious impairment of apostolicity and an impediment to communion. It appears that it is not the apostolicity of churches that is at issue but the apostolicity of individual ministers. But, in dealing with the interrupted episcopal succession, that was precisely where Porvoo represented a breakthrough. Apostolicity is not carried by the individual but by the church that the individual represents. That is the view, evidently, that the Episcopal Church in the United States has taken.

One can understand the reluctance of British and Irish Anglicans.[17] The eucharist is at the centre of the Church's life. It represents visibly the continuity of the Church from the disciples at the Last Supper and the unity of all Christians in their dependence on the grace of the crucified and risen Jesus. As the sacrament is a sign of unity and catholicity, so also is the one who presides at it. But when two churches have reached the point of recognising each other as truly apostolic one has to ask whether a bar on the presidency by the minister of one Church at the eucharist of another endorses the fact that the eucharist is a sign of unity or denies it.

The logic is not entirely with the Concordat, however. Both parties to it are already episcopally ordered. A formal union is not contemplated. Yet full communion has been achieved only because the Lutherans have agreed to accept the sign of the historic succession. Here too the sign appears, not as a gift to be shared in common life but more as a condition of mutual recognition.[18]

This stance is all the harder to understand when one remembers that both in Porvoo and in the Concordat wide differences in the diaconate are set on one side. Historically, a formal diaconal ministry is at least as ancient a feature of the life of the Church as personal episcopacy. In the skein of apostolic continuity the absence of a diaconal thread might be considered a more serious, though still not fatal, deficiency than the absence of the sign of episcopal succession. Its contemporary forms and ordering are very diverse, but, while, clearly, a person ordained to one form of diaconate could not be appointed to serve in a diaconate of a different form, the lack of a common diaconate has not been seen as an impediment to communion.[19]

It seems, therefore, that, in addition to the ambiguity inherent in the word 'sign', there is an ambiguity or tension in the concept of apostolicity. Does the recognition of the apostolicity of a church really take us as far as we think and hope, or does it mask a reservation about ministerial orders still to be resolved – and, if that is the case, is 'recognition of apostolicity' appropriate language to use?

In making this point I do not wish to minimise the immense progress that has been make over the last half-century in Anglican–Methodist relations in many parts of the world. In England there is now canonical provision for non-Anglicans to receive communion in Anglican Churches, and for non-episcopal ministers to preside over the eucharist celebrated in their own tradition in an Anglican church building in an ecumenical partnership. Relationships in very many places are excellent. Over 100 ministers of the Church of England are officially authorised by the Methodist Church to minister to Methodist congregations. Formal conversations are taking place with the hope of further progress. At the time of writing the outcome is not known, though a proposal for a full union is unlikely.[20] In Wales and Scotland also conversations are proceeding. All this is real gain. But the less than full recognition of Methodist orders is already hard for many Methodists to understand, and would be even harder if there were a more formal recognition of communion between the two churches. Indeed, it is hard to see how Methodists could concur in a declaration of communion that excluded it.

As already noted, Methodist churches in the British tradition are not episcopally ordered, though they do exercise *episcope* in various forms in personal, collegial and communal ways. It would be appropriate for Methodism to accept episcopal ministry in the historic succession at the point of a union. Conceivably, as the outcome of present conversations or at some time in the future, there may be a proposal for an interim situation of parallel churches in communion, in which case there would be occasions when a Methodist minister is authorised to serve as vicar of an Anglican parish or is transferred permanently into the Anglican priesthood. Whether in a union or in an interim situation, the standing of Methodist ministers already ordained would need to be resolved. What one would look for would be some liturgical act that would receive them into the fellowship of those who stand in the historic succession and into the jurisdiction of a bishop, but fall short of a re-ordination or supplemental ordination implying that the minister's existing orders and previous ministry (or the apostolic character of the church to which he or she belongs) are somehow defective. But that is exactly what we have been looking for over the last 50 years, and so far the search has not borne fruit. Does Porvoo really represent, as the Concordat clearly does, a movement towards affirming the theological priority of church over ministry that would unlock the door?

Lay presidency?

There is a further question that might perhaps be added. It ought at least to be noted for the agenda of future discussions. As observed above, under the Porvoo Agreement Anglicans recognise the apostolic character of the Lutheran churches, even though they do not invariably practise episcopal ordination to the presbyterate. Exceptions to the norm are tolerated, even though ministry of the individuals concerned is not recognised. British Methodism has since 1932 affirmed the right of the Conference, exercising *episcope* over the Church, to authorise named laypersons to preside over the eucharist in specified places in cases of pastoral need. They are seen as exceptional, the norm being presbyteral presidency. The custom presents difficulties in formal unity conversations. Can Porvoo's attitude to non-episcopal ordinations be seen as a providing a precedent by which, without committing Anglicans to accepting the ministry of such a layperson, the practice could be accepted as not constituting an obstacle to communion? Such toleration might not be envisaged in a full union, but might offer a way forward if an interim stage of two parallel churches in communion were envisaged.[21]

Postscript

Since the above article was published the Anglican Church of Ireland and the Methodist Church in Ireland have gone much further. An agreement was enacted in 2014 that recognised all presidents of the Irish Conference, past and present, as 'episcopal ministers' and provided for the mutual involvement of both bishops and presidents in future consecrations of bishops and dedications of presidents. The agreement is fully retrospective, and, as a result, there is now full interchangeability of ministry. The first consecration of a bishop with the participation of Methodist presidents and ex-presidents took place in January 2016. It remains to be seen how this will be mirrored in negotiations elsewhere.

Notes

1 Originally published in Ola Tjørhom (ed.), *Apostolicity and Unity: Essays on the Porvoo Common Statement* (Grand Rapids, MI: William B. Eerdmans, 2002), pp. 245–57. Reprinted by permission of the publisher; all rights reserved.

2 See *Together in Mission and Ministry: The Porvoo Common Statement with Essays on Church and Ministry in Northern Europe* (London: Church House Publishing, 1993), especially pp. 30–3.

3 The Evangelical Lutheran Church in Denmark joined the Porvoo Communion in 2010, the Evangelical Lutheran Church of Latvia remains (in 2017) an Observer.

4 See *The Porvoo Agreement: A Report by the House of Bishops, June 1995*, House of Bishops Occasional Paper no. GS1156 (London: General Synod of the Church of England, 1995), p. 14.

5 See the chapter by John Halliburton, 'Orders and Ordination', in *Together in Mission and Ministry*, pp. 155ff.

6 See, for example, the statement on behalf of the Lutheran Church in Norway by Gunnar Lislerud, in *Together in Mission and Ministry*, p. 96.

7 For what follows, see especially the chapter by A. Raymond George, 'Ordination', in Rupert Davies, A. Raymond George and Gordon Rupp (eds.), *A History of the Methodist Church in Great Britain*, vol. 2 (London: Epworth Press, 1978), pp. 143ff.

8 Telford, *The Letters of John Wesley*, vol. 7, p. 262; vol. 8, p. 91. Wesley is sometimes quoted as dismissing the historic succession as a fable. His actual words were: 'The *uninterrupted succession* I know to be a fable, which no man ever did or can prove' (vol. 7, p. 284, emphasis in original).

9 See 'Sharing in the Apostolic Communion', a report of the Anglican–Methodist International Commission to the World Methodist Council and the Lambeth Conference (London: Anglican–Methodist International Commission, 1996) para. 68.

10 There had earlier been sporadic cases mostly for service overseas: see George, 'Ordination', in Davies, George and Rupp, *A History of the Methodist Church*, vol. 2, pp. 153ff.

11 A diaconate was not introduced until the last decade of the nineteenth century and not formally acknowledged to be an order of ministry until 1988.

12 None, however, has authority to ordain by virtue of office alone.

13 Official statements of course say otherwise; I am referring here to popular perceptions.

14 See 'Called to Common Mission: A Lutheran Proposal for a Revision of the Concordat of Agreement' (Chicago: Evangelical Lutheran Church in America, 1999), para. 16. This is effectively the approach adopted in the Church of South India, which encountered such difficulties elsewhere in the Anglican Communion.

15 Porvoo Common Statement, Declaration b (v).

16 See Porvoo Common Statement, para. 48.

17 But see the postscript, below.

18 A similar ambiguity lurks in the international Anglican–Methodist dialogue. It calls for 'Methodist and Anglican Churches everywhere…to recognise formally the apostolicity of each other's churches and our common intention to maintain the apostolic faith. Following this mutual recognition the churches together may institute a united ministry which includes the historic succession…' But it leaves

unclear whether agreement to the former will be conditional upon a declared intention to adopt the latter: ' Sharing in the Apostolic Communion', para. 85.

19 See 'Called to Common Mission', paras. 8–9.

20 In 2003 the Methodist Church and the Church of England signed a Covenant, as a result of which proposals are now (2017) before the two churches that would provide for the progressive introduction of episcopacy in the historic succession into the Methodist Church, beginning with the annually appointed president of the Conference.

21 It would mark an advance on the Anglican–Methodist Scheme, 1968, which recommended that the practice should cease as soon as possible.

17   A reflection on structural change[1]

In 1995 the Church of England published the report of an Archbishops' Commission, entitled 'Working As One Body', recommending ways to strengthen the effectiveness of the Church's central policy-making and 'resource direction machinery', generally referred to as 'the Turnbull Report' after its chairman, the Bishop of Durham. It led to the creation of the Archbishops' Council and the merging of several separate staff bodies into a single service. I was invited to contribute from a Methodist point of view to a volume published in 2000 discussing various aspects of the report.[2]

In 1996 the Methodist Church effected a major restructuring of its central (connexional) administration. Seven divisions, dealing respectively with overseas, home mission, social responsibility, education and youth, ministries, finance and property, each with its own board, staff, finances and committee system, were replaced, along with the Conference's General Purposes Committee and the President's Council, by a single connexional Team overseen by a Methodist Council of approximately 80 members and an executive of 13, with a single staffing structure and (so far as trust law allowed) unified finance. The express aim was to achieve an organisation that would avoid the appearance of competition between different interests, and secure coherence in policy-making and better oversight of ongoing work. Lurking in the wings was a widespread belief that the administrative machinery was too costly and, because of the duplication of divisional efforts, wasteful. There was also a suspicion that divisional boards, although answerable to the governing Conference each year, were in practice autonomous, too proactive and unresponsive to local needs. Interestingly, remarkably similar aims had been expressed in a previous reorganisation in the early 1970s, which had led to the creation of the divisions out of a multiplicity of large committees and departments, but this had been little more than a series of marriages between bodies with kindred interests. The 1996 reorganisation was a wholesale dismantling and reassembly.

   In preparation for 1996, in marked contrast to the proposals put forward 25 years earlier, which had lacked any theological rationale, two concise statements of theological principles were proposed to the Conference in successive years. The earlier, in 1992, reflecting current theological interest in *koinonia*, began from the communion of Persons in the Holy Trinity as the basis for understanding all relationships, personal, social and organisational. Without making the sequence of thought explicit the statement moved in the same paragraph to the Incarnation, which 'is expressed historically in the person of Jesus Christ and also in the institutions, procedures and structures of the church, the body of Christ'. This led to a description of the *koinonia* of the church, expressing both unity and diversity, with twin foci of worship and mission. A link was made between the idea of *koinonia* and the more traditional Methodist concept of connexion, a partnership in which resources are shared and the various elements in the overall structure of the church – Conference, divisions, districts, circuits, local churches – all work together. Hierarchical language was ruled out, the language of service and consent taking its place. 'All the work done connexionally is, in intention at least, sustaining the life of the people of God in the world, enabling the Church to be the Church for humanity.'

The 1993 statement arrived at the same point from a more traditionally Methodist starting point. Making the important observation that 'Methodists tend to do their theology on the move; they tell stories and have conversations on the work of God', the statement built on recent Conference reports and began from the creative and redemptive love of God for the world and the church's calling to become an agent of that love. The two foci of the church's life were restated as worship and mission – or, in other words, as discipleship and apostleship. Mission was defined holistically as including evangelism, social caring and the struggle for justice. 'The church is holy – turned towards God in worship and discipleship. It is apostolic – turned towards the world in mission and witness. It is catholic – it looks for the redemption of the whole world and therefore seeks to share a common life with all…' The church's structures and financial strategies should be directed to maintaining its orientation towards God and the world. The need to retain a sense of being a movement over against the tendency of institutions to become inflexible was stressed, and a penitential paragraph acknowledged that theological descriptions of the church and its calling are far removed from the historical reality that people often experience in their dealings with it.

The resonances of all this with the later Turnbull Report are clear.[3] There is the same derivation of proposals from the nature of God, leading from the Trinity via the notion of relationships and resource-sharing to structures that serve the worship and mission of the church. There is the same welcome affirmation that the church exists not for itself but for God and the world. There is the same emphasis on central structures serving the local church or parish, on the need for openness and trust, and on the need for more decisions to be taken 'from the bottom up'. There are similar problems to be addressed: too many over-large committees, a lack of coherence in policy-making, conflict between policy decisions and budgetary provisions, complaints about size, cost and relevance. Similar solutions are proposed: a single directing body with fewer subcommittees, a single staff structure, more responsibility taken at lower organisational levels. Naturally, the Turnbull Report lacks Methodist in-words such as 'connexion', but with one major exception either report could have provided the theological foundation for the other's constitutional proposals. The exception is the concept of 'the bishop-in-synod', for which, for wider ecclesiological reasons, there is no Methodist equivalent. More of that later.

Of course, there are parallels to be drawn in the case of both Anglican and Methodist proposals with current thinking about the management of secular organisations, much as there were between the divisionalisation of Methodist central structures in the early 1970s and the management theory then in vogue. Now contemporary emphases on 'flatter' organisational models, teamwork, the devolution of responsibility and multi-skilling all have their ecclesiastical echoes.

This is neither surprising nor to be deplored. If laypeople are truly to participate in the life of the church it is to be expected and encouraged that they should apply to issues of church government the experience and principles that derive from secular occupations. It might even be argued that the extent to which the management of church affairs does not reflect contemporary secular practice is an indicator of the extent to which the church is clerically dominated.

It is sometimes objected that 'the church is not a secular organisation', as though that implied secular organisational practices should not be imported into church life. The plain fact is that the church cannot escape. Churches are subject to the laws relating to charities and trusteeship, their accounting procedures must conform to official standards, their employment practices (with certain recognised exceptions) must accord with employment law, they must regulate their administration of property in ways that entitle them to retain ecclesiastical exemption from listed building and conservation area planning consent, and so on. The church is obliged to adopt secular practice in its administration.

That is not a matter of regret. If the Incarnation is the adoption by the divine of all the limitations, weaknesses and ambiguities of the human condition; if the glory of the Word is seen only because the Word was made flesh; and if, further, the church is in any sense a witness to, or even 'continuation' of, the Incarnation; then any view of the church that seeks to make it immune from contemporary culture (of which business practice is part) is ultimately docetist. It fails to take seriously that the church is truly the church only as it is part of the contemporary world. The question then is not whether common business organisation and practice should be adopted by the church, but how and to what extent? After all, the church's assets, nationally and locally, are considerable, and good stewardship of them is a moral and theological responsibility as well as a legal responsibility. But activity within and in the name of the church must be subject to theological and ethical constraints, even if there may be differences of view within the church on particular ethical and theological issues.

That leads to the central theological question in discussion of these matters: are there theological requirements for the ordering of the life of the church and do current arrangements accord with them? What is the relationship between organisational structures and church order?

A Methodist is likely to find this a difficult question to address. Part of the reason is historical. From the beginning Methodists have approached questions of organisation pragmatically. It was a standard line in inter-denominational polemics during the nineteenth century for Methodists to deny that any form of church order – episcopal, presbyterian or congregational – could claim exclusive scriptural sanction. The Methodist pattern was claimed, more modestly, to be not derived from scripture but consistent with it, though it has to be said that nothing so divided nineteenth-century Methodism as the role and powers of the pastors, which were seen (by the Wesleyan pastors particularly) as biblical and theological issues.

But there is a broader aspect to the difficulty. It was hard in nineteenth-century Methodism to address the specifically theological question of the nature of oversight in the church and who should exercise it because the issue kept transposing itself into other terms: democracy versus autocracy, laity versus 'priestcraft'. The social and political conditions of the times made this inevitable. This is nothing new. From the beginning the Christian Church has modelled itself on other patterns of social organisation, including the synagogue, the household and, later, the Roman Empire. Disentangling theological from other considerations has always been difficult.

Two criteria

It may help to suggest that two criteria need to be applied in assessing how the church is to be ordered. They are *necessary function* and *appropriate representation*. There will be some elements in the life of the church that define what it is. Several have surfaced in the summaries of reports given above. Foremost is the fact that explicitly theological questions have to be asked about it. The church is essentially a divine creation (albeit flawed by sin), poised between the fall and God's redemptive *eschaton*. Its character as *koinonia* is imparted by the fact that there is *koinonia* in God. Its catholicity, in all the world and for all the world, is given by the fact of God's outgoing love for all creation. It looks back to God's self-revelation in Christ; it looks forward to the kingdom to come, seeking to anticipate it in its contemporary life; and it engages with the living God in the present. It is set in the world as witness to God's redemptive activity, is itself evidence of that activity and is an agent (though not the sole agent) by which it is carried forward. That is why questions about its structure and practice have theological weight.

Against this background, we may identify necessary functions. As beneficiary of God's redemptive work, one of its necessary functions is worship, understood in the broadest sense of liturgy as service. The church offers itself up to God, seeking conformity with his outgoing love. Its praise is articulated in word and life. Second, as witness to and agent of God's redemption, it is committed to mission, to be defined not only as evangelism but also as any activity that engages with the dominion of evil in the individual and in human society.

Thus far, the Methodist statements already summarised. Perhaps, however, the definition of mission is too activist. Mission is also passively exercised by the church in faithful witness, by the quality of its life, its fidelity to the truth it has received and its bearing under attack, supremely by martyrdom. Certainly, to these two necessary functions – worship and mission – a third should be added. Because the church is recipient as well as agent of God's redemptive work, we must add to the list the necessary function of sustaining its life. The church must be so ordered that it is constantly reminded that it is not autonomous but dependent upon God. Ministries, pastoral and diaconal, interpersonal as the Incarnation is interpersonal, directed to the benefit of the church itself and not only to those outside, are a manifestation of its identity. Such ministries are, of course, activities of the church itself; they are not exercised from without, but the church is not free to dispense with ministry.

There is a distinction between those necessary functions of the church and their appropriate representation, however. There are, as history shows, many patterns, all of which may lay claim to be faithful representations of the church's worship, mission and ministry. There may come moments when function and representation are in conflict. John Wesley, for example, regarded himself as a committed Anglican, and many Methodists today would regard the historic episcopate as an appropriate sign of the church's continuity in time and its dependence upon the apostolic tradition. They would nevertheless regard Wesley's decision, in defiance of canon law, to ordain his preachers in 1784 and later years as a justified response to pastoral need in the circumstances of his time. Although he might not have put it so, there was an overriding theological requirement that the people of God should be furnished with persons authorised to preach the word and administer the sacraments; the manner of their authorisation, though important, was secondary.

Whether all this has a bearing on a church's national, as distinct from local, administrative structures will depend on the answer one gives to another ecclesiological question, arguably the fundamental ecumenical issue and, in the long term, the most difficult to resolve. A thoroughgoing congregational polity will assert that there are no intermediate manifestations of *ecclesia* between the local and the universal. Structures outside the local congregation are arrangements of mutual convenience and are voluntary. Questions of appropriateness will of course arise. Collaboration between autonomous local churches ought not to be tainted by unethical practice, for example; more fundamentally, it must not encroach upon local autonomy. In not doing so it will appropriately represent a congregational ecclesiology.

Here, however, a Methodist will show his or her colours. If we are serious both about *koinonia* and about incarnation, the implication is twofold. The first is that the local church manifests its true identity as church only in so far as it is linked by bonds of reciprocal support and interdependence with other local churches. The second is that there can be no true fellowship of local churches (any more than of individual Christians) that holds back from irrevocable commitment. That is the ultimate indictment of our current ecumenical disunity. Mere expressions of mutual goodwill between autonomous churches are not unity incarnate. It then becomes a necessary function of the church to maintain a structured coherence that will enable that reciprocity to be sustained.

How that necessary function is appropriately represented will depend on many factors. Geographical and political realities will have an effect. What has come to be termed 'subsidiarity' will have its place. Traditionally the office of bishop has been seen as both a symbol of *koinonia* and a means to sustain it. In Methodist tradition (at least in its British, non-episcopal version) the Conference has fulfilled that role. The ultimate regulatory authority of the Conference over the church, holding local churches together in concentric circles of circuit, district and connexion, and both authorising and holding in common obedience the ordained ministry of presbyter and deacon, is the structural expression of *koinonia*, though the two concepts – connexion and *koinonia* – are not strictly co-terminous.[4] In this regard, however, two points need to be remembered. First, while the idea of connexion emphasises the formal structural links (connections) by which local churches are held together, there are many constitutional alternatives that might give expression to that principle. Connexion must not simply be identified with the current constitution of the Methodist Church; indeed, in recent years the constitution has undergone significant change. Second, connexionalism does not of itself resolve the question of the balance of jurisdiction or initiative between central and more local authorities, nor the question of the representation of local interests in central decisions. These are matters for continuing debate. It does mean, however, that for Methodists there are ecclesiological questions implicit in the scope and function of the church's central administration.

Clearly, there is also a diachronic aspect to all this. The contemporary church is related to its past, not merely in the sense that, like all other human institutions, it is the product of preceding events but by virtue of its dependence on the Incarnation as its defining event. The church's necessary functions will include preserving a continuity without which its identity as church would be lost. Scripture, creeds, sacraments and ministry are elements in that continuity, as is tradition in a more general sense, although incarnation also demands, as we have seen, a creative adaptation to the present.

In turning then to questions of church order and church organisation, necessity and appropriateness are significant tests to apply in evaluating what is happening. They permit a wide degree of latitude in adopting organisational patterns, but at the same time pose important questions that organisers must constantly answer: is the church enabled to fulfil its necessary functions and (ideally) fulfil them better, and do the management structures adopted appropriately represent what we understand the church theologically to be?

Questions that arise

As has been the case in the Church of England, the Methodist reorganisation was ushered in against a background of unease and, in some quarters, strong opposition. The changes will need to prove themselves in practice, and it is important that there should be scope for amendment. What follows are brief comments, by one who has been closely involved in the changes and keenly supportive of them, on some of the questions that have emerged from the Methodist experience, concluding with a discussion of a wider issue.

Is organisational need driving the theology?

The theological basis offered for the changes laid great stress on partnership and the sharing of resources, using the *koinonia* of the Holy Trinity as a model and ruling out hierarchical patterns. It so happens that the result is much in line with current management theory. If, on the other hand, a hierarchical structure had been sought it would no doubt have been possible to justify it theologically by beginning, say, from the sovereignty of God; different theological premises could no doubt have been supplied for other organisational patterns. So, is the organisational tail wagging the theological dog? On what basis is one theological model to be preferred to another? Is it all a matter of theological fashion?

Theological fashions do come and go, but to dismiss all such changes of emphasis as mere fad is to ignore the genuine insights that can emerge from a re-examination of neglected aspects of Christian tradition. Some theological affirmations, such as the sovereignty of God, are common to Judaism and Islam as well as Christianity, while others, particularly the doctrine of the Trinity, are not. Although, therefore, there has recently been widespread ecumenical interest in the concept of *koinonia*, one may legitimately argue that in appealing to it the authors of restructuring proposals were not merely following fashion but focusing on a central and distinctively Christian concept.

It ought to be remembered that that appeal is not without its difficulties. Although in the case of both traditions any bald statement needs to be carefully qualified, it is the case that the eastern tradition has laid greater stress than the western on the priority of the Father within the Trinity. To that extent, the western tradition offers a more secure foundation for ruling out hierarchy. What will be the long-term effect of the west dropping the *filioque* clause from the Niceno-Constantinopolitan Creed?

But behind this question is an important issue of theological method. Is it the function of theology to lay down axioms from which all else may be deduced, or is theological insight given at the point of interaction between tradition and contemporary questions and insights? For Methodists who 'do their theology on the move', the latter must be the case.

By invoking theological principle, do we preclude further change?

There is a danger in using theology to reinforce what is otherwise desirable. Institutions may thereby become sacralised, rendering them impervious to reform. This is an issue a subsequent generation will have to face. Certainly, the intention in the current Methodist changes is that they should remain flexible and open to modification. Moreover, if it is true that experience brings theological insight, we should not assume that a theological rationale offered

30 years hence would simply be a repetition of what is before us now. What will be important as time goes on is that a clear distinction is maintained between the values that the theology suggests ought to be incorporated and the precise organisational structure that at any point of time seeks to give effect to them.

What expectations are created in the workplace?

The thinking behind Methodist restructuring carried the idea of partnership derived from *koinonia* through to the creation of a single team of those employed by the central agency. In practice, that can lead to difficulty. While some may find multiple relationships in a large team difficult and look for simpler, clearer lines of accountability, others may resist line management, arguing that the theological basis of the changes points to collective leadership and responsibility. There is a danger that undergirding administrative structures by appeal to theological principles will lead to expectations that central offices will be 'run like a church'. The problems become sharper if questions of redundancy or discipline arise. There is a crucial difference, which needs to be acknowledged, between the essentially voluntary relationships of a local church and the contractual relationships of a place of employment.

What is the role of goals and strategies in the life of the church?

It has become increasingly common to employ such concepts in discussions of church life. Talk of planning and policy-forming is clearly appropriate in the context of the church's national institutions. Priorities need to be determined in relation to the adoption of budgets or the making of grants, in setting up commissions to study public issues and in allocating resources between ecumenical and denominational activities. But there is an obvious distinction between such institutions, which have many analogies with commercial corporations and public charities, and the ongoing life of a local congregation. What place do such methods have in a local setting? Moreover, what is the relationship between strategies developed by the church nationally (in relation to the millennium, say, or the Decade of Evangelism) and their implementation at local level?

There are some obvious local applications. A church may (arguably, should) commit itself to a rolling programme for the maintenance and upgrading of its buildings; it may adopt particular projects, such as to contribute to a particular charity for a specified period, or to 'adopt' a church or a worker in a Third World country; it may recognise along with other local churches a social need that has arisen in the neighbourhood and share in ecumenical action to meet it. Sometimes more far-reaching questions may arise. Has the time come to 'plant' another church as a missionary offshoot? Is the church no longer viable and should the premises be closed and the congregation merged with another? Has the time come to form a local ecumenical partnership? Such questions need research and evaluation before decisions are taken, and usually ways need to be found to monitor effectiveness and keep projects on course, or modify or abandon them.

There are dangers, however. One is that attention will be focused exclusively on corporate activity, with the result that the church's witness and service to the community through its individual members is disregarded and devalued. A second danger is an emphasis on projects to the detriment of ongoing life. The staple activities of any local church must include regular worship and nurture of the faith. Without these the church is little more than a society for the promotion of good causes. An attendant danger is that activity will be more highly valued than being. Being and doing belong inseparably together, and to stress one to the neglect of the other is a distortion. This point can be taken further in relation to the next question.

How is value to be measured?

There is little point in adopting business practice of setting goals and targets unless there are ways of measuring whether they have been achieved. In some areas, such as fund-raising, this is easy. In terms of specific programmes, such as the publication of a series of booklets or setting up training courses, success or failure can be identified. In relation to the life of the church overall, however, it is more difficult, if not impossible. What is a 'successful' church? What would be the implications of 'failure'? The danger is that what is measurable becomes the criterion. Is a church with a large and growing membership more successful than one that has survived with diminishing numbers under persecution? Can one evaluate a church's performance without considering the environment in which it is placed? There are echoes here of debates about league tables in health and educational provision, but for the church the questions are theological. What is the church's mission and are declared conversions an indication (or even *the* indication) of its success? How does one measure the spiritual depth of a congregation's life? One can set targets for the number of baptisms or confirmations to be recorded in a given year, and possibly by aggressive methods achieve them, but this will reveal nothing about the spiritual realities that may or may not lie behind them. What should be an indicator of a deeper reality may, by being turned into a measure of achievement in itself, become a substitute for such reality.

These questions surface especially in the exercise of ministerial appraisal, which is now becoming increasingly common and in many ways is long overdue. The allocation of one's time over a period can be monitored, priorities can be established and tested, criteria can be set for diligence in sermon preparation, but the quality of pastoral conversations is more elusive and often a matter of confidentiality, and every preacher knows the experience of being sincerely thanked for a sermon, because a particular phrase or idea touched the situation of one listener, when he or she – and most of the congregation – had regarded it as a write-off. The value of what is done with an unpromising group of young people may not become apparent until, in much later life, perhaps after retirement, they find a home in the church and its faith. Ministry (ordained and lay) has a long pay-off period.

What is the relation between individual and corporate oversight?

The most important issue raised in reflection on structural change is that of oversight in the church. The carefully drafted phrases of *Baptism, Eucharist and Ministry* about the need for personal, collegial and communal dimensions of ministry to find constitutional expression mask profound difficulties about the interaction between them.[5] These are highlighted by the kind of developments we have been considering. How do management and oversight interact in a context in which some have been ordained to the exercise of oversight?

These are questions that Methodists and Anglicans alike have to face, for they are not confined to the issue of episcopal authority. Both churches have an understanding of pastoral oversight, which presbyters and bishops are called to exercise. It is expressed both in official documents and informally in general attitudes and relationships. Recent revisions of the ordinal in both churches have moderated the language of shepherd and (apparently passive) flock that is so prominent both in the Anglican ordinal of 1662 and in the Methodist order of 1936 and its predecessors, which drew heavily upon 1662. There is now an evident attempt to relate the ministry of the ordained to that of the whole church and the other special ministries within it, and to avoid the implication that ordination conveys authority over all the affairs of the church.[6] But use of the term 'shepherd' persists, as does the language of 'pastoral charge', in liturgical and other documents.

Moreover, the culture – and, indeed, the theology – of a church is not expressed in official documents alone but in the expectations and assumptions of both ordained and unordained in their relations with each other. Among the former, at least among those ordained with the use of the older books, these attitudes will have been reinforced by the liturgical language then used and the training they received. Many will feel that ordination has imposed upon them not only a cure of individual souls but a general responsibility for the welfare of the church. How does this relate to a culture that looks for the governance of the church to be in the hands of representative persons, ordained and lay, conferring on equal terms?

It is a matter, incidentally, that requires to be addressed sensitively in the current conversations between the Methodist Church and the Church of England. Although the underlying issue is similar for both churches, experience reveals that there is a subtle difference between the relationships of parish priest and parishioners and those of Methodist minister and church members. Assumptions that are made by both ordained and lay about their respective roles turn on questions of leadership and authority in oversight.

We need the complementarity of ordained and lay in the government of the church. All alike share the experience of pilgrimage in Christian faith, of joy, temptation and suffering, of being nourished by the church's sacraments, prayer and fellowship, and in various ways of ministering to and receiving ministry from others. For lay and ordained alike, the church is 'their' church, for which they must take responsibility. At the same time lay and ordained come to that responsibility with different perspectives and make different contributions, the one bringing the gifts and experience of life in the world, the other the training and experience of ministry in holy things.[7] The question is: are these equal contributions? What is to happen if there is conflict?

In language that can equally apply to the broader question we are addressing, the Turnbull Report and other General Synod documents elaborate carefully on the concept of 'the bishop-in-synod', which is presented as a model for the Archbishops' Council.[8] Leadership is not about the imposition of the leader's will upon others but about enabling them. Conciliarity implies the recognition of the different gifts that God distributes in the church. Decisions are taken in consultation.

We all long for such a scenario in both churches. Happily, it is often the case. As a result of careful consultation, the identification of common ground and goodwill all round, consensus is formed. Much depends on the level of trust established between the various parties and proper provisions (whether by periodic elections or by procedures for trial and dismissal) to ensure that everyone is seen to be accountable. But good experience may conceal constitutional flaws and discrepancies between practice and deeply held beliefs. What happens when, as in any community of pilgrim sinners sooner or later it will, something goes wrong? To an outsider, the phrase 'bishop-in-synod' signals a conflict waiting to happen. Is the synod advisory only and whom does it advise? What if the advice is not taken?

The concept of enabling leadership, welcome as it is, does not resolve the problem. Visionary insight and a prophetic voice are necessary to the health of the church, and think tanks, whether constituted of bishops or otherwise, have their place, but such leadership depends on the quality of what is offered. An occasional disagreement can be coped with, but leadership that is consistently not followed is ultimately discredited. One hopes, too, that those in positions of constitutional leadership will exercise it in an 'enabling' way, but one cannot avoid the question: is the leadership expected of the ordained, whether bishop or presbyter, a matter of moral authority or of constitutional right?

It may be that in practice the problem areas, at least at the national level, are limited, but they are potentially painful. It does not help to draw a distinction between 'practical' matters and 'doctrine', or between 'administration' and 'pastoral oversight', for these things interlock. Who is to decide, for example, which applicants, and how many of them, are to be accepted as ordinands when such decisions are dependent on policy concerning the opening and closing of churches, the deployment of clergy and the allocation of financial and other resources for their training and support? Of course, particular activities may be reserved or delegated to specified individuals or groups, but if a Methodist Council or Archbishops' Council, a Synod or a Conference, is genuinely to be responsible for policy across the whole life of the church then those individuals and groups will have to be constrained by the policy decisions taken. Perhaps the most obvious and painful examples of potential conflict at national level, for Methodists and Anglicans alike, concern the ordination and appointment of women and of those who are practising homosexuals, when corporate decisions already are, or may in the future be, in conflict with the conscientious objections of those expected to carry them out. At the local level there is oft-repeated experience of the will of two congregations, expressed through their constitutional procedures, to engage together in ecumenical cooperation being frustrated by the obstructiveness or neglect of one or both local ministers. The fundamental question in such matters is always: who holds the veto?

Broader issues

Two church order questions thus arise: how, humanly speaking, is the church to be governed ('humanly speaking' because in no ecclesiastical polity is it ever a matter of 'what the people want' but of what the church, by whatever means, discerns to be the will of God); and to what ministry or ministries and with what authority are bishops and presbyters ordained? It is the second question that makes the answer to the first so difficult. There is a neatness in the answers given by those traditions that locate authority exclusively in a council of bishops. For traditions that affirm a more inclusive polity, the answers, I suggest, are less clear.

In nineteenth-century Methodism these questions were fought over in relation to the powers of the Wesleyan Conference, composed as it was until 1878 entirely of presbyters. It was a major cause of many of the schisms that occurred in the first half of that century. The early Wesleyans interpreted the pastoral office as involving responsibility 'to teach, to feed and to rule'. As Richard Watson expressed it, 'Certain powers are inseparable from the duties of the ministry and cannot be transferred or put into commission with those who have not this calling.'[9] In practice, 'mixed committees' – that is, including laymen (*sic*) – were appointed for financial matters; after all, the laity raised the money! Given the premise from which they began, the early Wesleyans had logic on their side. Only gradually did the old system break down, and there has been tension over the matter ever since as, progressively, authority has shifted from the exclusively ministerial (presbyteral) session of the Conference to the ('mixed') representative session. Today the reserved powers of the ministerial session relate to certain decisions about the oversight of those in training for the ministry and to certain disciplinary appeals, while in other matters relating to ministerial status, including the acceptance of candidates and the final decision for ordination, a recommendation of that session to the representative session is indispensable.

These changes have been driven in part by pragmatic decisions and in part by an alternative theology that has stressed the 'ministry of the whole people of God', derived partly from the non-Wesleyan traditions that entered into Methodist Union in 1932 and partly from ecumenical studies of recent decades. But the problem persists. It is difficult for those who have been ordained to be 'shepherds to the flock of Christ'[10] to avoid the sense that they have a special interest in the welfare of the church as a whole. Moreover, the fourth paragraph of the doctrinal standards of the Methodist Church states:

> Christ's ministers in the church are stewards in the household of God and shepherds of his flock. Some are called and ordained to this sole occupation and have a principal and directing part in these great duties but they hold no priesthood differing in kind from that which is common to all the Lord's people and they have no exclusive title to the preaching of the gospel or the care of souls. These ministries are shared with them by others to whom also the Spirit divides his gifts severally as he wills.[11]

That statement was the product of theological compromise at Methodist Union, but it cannot be said to resolve the matter. What in constitutional terms is a 'principal and directing part' and what is the theological ground for that assertion? Any relocation of authority over the life of the church that involves a genuine partnership between ordained and lay must call into question assumptions about leadership roles traditionally exercised by those who are ordained and the theological justification offered for them.

The enterprise of restructuring, therefore, upon which both the Methodist Church and the Church of England have embarked raises questions about the government, not just the management, of the church and the theological justification given for it. If the *koinonia*–partnership model is right then other patterns are called into question throughout the life of the church. If, to use currently unfashionable legal terminology, jurisdiction rests with a synod or conference, not only does it require careful theological grounding but attention needs to be given, both in official statements and in popular attitudes, to the meaning of ordination.

Notes

1 Originally published in Gillian R. Evans and Martyn Percy (eds.), *Managing the Church? Order and Organization in a Secular Age* (Sheffield: Sheffield Academic Press, 2000). Used by permission of Bloomsbury Publishing plc.
2 *Working as One Body: The Report of the Archbishops' Commission on the Organisation of the Church of England* (London: Church House Publishing, 1995).
3 See my brief comparison in the *Epworth Review*, vol. 23, no. 2, 1996, pp. 6–8.
4 See Chapter 6 above.
5 *Baptism, Eucharist and Ministry*, 'Ministry', paras. 26–7.
6 In this respect, as in some others, the proposed ordinal of the Anglican–Methodist Unity Commission of 1968 now seems to be backward- rather than forward-looking.
7 To some extent theological expertise also, but this is now much less the preserve of the ordained than once it was.

8 *Working as One Body*, paras. 1.16ff.; '*Working as One Body*: Theological Reflections', House of Bishops Discussion Document no. GS Misc 491 (London: General Synod of the Church of England, 1997), paras. 27ff.; *Working as One Body: A Framework for Legislation*, House of Bishops Occasional Paper no. GS1188 (London: General Synod of the Church of England, 1996), paras. 24ff.

9 Watson, 'An Affectionate Address' (1828), *Works*, vol. 7, p. 98.

10 *Methodist Service Book*, 1975, p. G12, para. 16.

11 Clause 4 of the Deed of Union, in *The Constitutional Practice and Discipline of the Methodist Church*, vol. 2, 7th edn, 1998 rev., p. 214.

18 What is a divinity school for?[1]

What is a divinity school for? What purpose does it serve? What may the church expect of it? What obligations, if any, does it owe the church?

A divinity school, by its very name, signals a Christian commitment. No other religious tradition, so far as I know, uses the term 'divinity'; it is part of the vocabulary of the Christian heritage. A divinity school therefore differs from other types of academic institution dealing with religious questions; not necessarily in the range of subjects studied, but in the fact that it has a specific focus on the Christian faith and is committed to the study of it from within. It cannot be neutral.

What is more, the churches look to the divinity schools for the education of those who are to become their ministers, whether lay or ordained, and most of the students are likely to be in that category. So, for both church and students, the question is important.

The answer can be given in terms of what is taught and learned. If a divinity school is to produce ministers (lay or ordained), then church and students alike have a right to expect the output of effective practitioners of Christian ministry. So there are skills to be learned. For example, there is the conduct of Christian worship and the preaching of sermons; there is counselling and work in support of different age groups; there is engagement with the needs of society, in its deprivation and its affluence; there are the administrative duties that go with holding a large and complex congregation together. Such skills need to be acquired, and there is relentless pressure to add to the list, as needs become more diverse and new fields of expertise open up.

But what constitutes an effective practitioner of ministry? The distinguishing mark of the church is that it is a community of faith. It has a set of beliefs, and seeks to live by those beliefs. Practical ministry that is not informed and controlled by the beliefs – ministry that is not driven by the faith commitment that inspires the church itself – is not effective ministry. Alongside the getting of practical skills, therefore, must go theological engagement with the Christian tradition and the development of personal faith. A skilled communicator, whether in the pulpit or one to one, who has no theological insight or personal faith to communicate is like a blank television screen: all equipment and no message. A divinity school needs to be not only a school of ministerial practice but also a centre for theological exploration and a community where Christian discipleship is nurtured.

But that programme has its limits. The temptation of the church – and, I suspect, of many students – is to expect that the education provided by a school will be complete. The very process of assessment, grading and graduation suggests that. There may indeed be further specialisation, doctoral programmes and the like, but the expectation frequently is that graduates are 'trained'. Like a motor car, they roll off the assembly line ready to go. That expectation cannot be fulfilled.

The reason is not simply that new practical needs arise and new skills in ministry are called for that have to be learned after leaving college, nor is it that theology itself never stands still because theologians keep up the debate. The true reason is more fundamental. The human being is a learning animal. For many, that capacity becomes dormant and atrophied, and one encounters such people all too often: narrow in their interests, bigoted in their views, resistant to change. But those who believe that human beings are created in the image of God are committed thereby to lifelong learning. Intellectually, there are always questions to ask and answer; spiritually, life is a pilgrimage of growing maturity in communion with God. The best gift a divinity school can give to the church, and to its students, is to affirm that truth and to produce people with a lifelong capacity and desire to learn. It might not look well in the prospectus, but it would be to the credit of a school that had the courage to say: 'We turn out an unfinished product!' On the church's part, this means providing opportunities and resources by which lifelong ministerial education may be continued.

Conformity and freedom

Having made that point, however, about education embracing practical skills, theological exploration and the development of personal faith, we need to narrow the focus of the question to one component. In terms of theology, what should the church expect of a divinity school, and what does the school owe to the church? It is an area fraught with tension and conflict, as the history of all the denominations shows. The church likes to control the schools, to make sure the product is doctrinally sound. The schools fight for their freedom and intellectual self-respect. What can be said about this issue? Are divinity schools to be merely indoctrination centres, to use a pejorative term? Is their task simply to expound and advocate the received tradition, or are they to be places where that tradition is explored and challenged? The answer may seem obvious when put in those terms. But we have to remember that prevalent fashions in the schools can leave their stamp on a generation of students going out as the church's ministers and enrich or impoverish the church for years to come. There are many situations around the world in which the theological stance of the schools is manifestly out of touch with the prevailing theological stance of the church at large. Mistrust abounds and theology itself is discredited.

A teaching authority

The first thing to be said is that all the churches do need what is often called a teaching authority. Whether it is located, as in the Roman case, in the Bishop of Rome in communion with his fellow bishops, or, as in the Methodist tradition, in annual or quadrennial conferences, or, as in some other traditions, in the local congregation, every church needs – and in fact develops – a mechanism by which it can corporately say: 'This we believe, that we do not believe.' What is included in such statements may be detailed and comprehensive or very broad and only in outline, but there has to be some degree of corporate self-definition.

I do not underestimate the difficulty of the task. The last century or so has seen an explosion of diversity in the life of the church. With rapid changes in social structures, with increasing interaction between different cultures, with the liberation of voices long silenced, with the pressures of secular philosophies and with the breakdown of consensus on how to view the world around us and how to behave in it, it is not surprising that Christianity now expresses itself in a bewildering variety of theologies, patterns of worship and styles of living. Moreover, although there are manifest tensions in the church, the present age is by comparison a tolerant one. The ecumenical spirit amongst us encourages us to make room within the fellowship for those who differ from us. The task of self-definition, as I have called it, is therefore very difficult. What may legitimately be called Christian and what may not? Yet without some mechanism by which a church can identify what is true to the faith and what is not, without some limits to diversity, 'church' becomes co-terminous with 'world' and the word ceases to have meaning. Identity entails definition.

That definition must refer to tradition and be strongly influenced by it. Precisely because the central thesis of Christian faith is that God's self-revelation comes to us in Jesus Christ, the past represents for us not merely what happened long ago but a key part of our self-understanding. Now tradition is not a fossilised, dead thing, though it has its fixed elements. It includes the canonically fixed and authoritative tradition of scripture and the text of the Creeds, but also the more fluid tradition of the church's life and thought from earliest times to today. It is more than the handing on and development of doctrine. Tradition embraces the whole of Christian faith and life as that is handed on in the worship and corporate activity of the Christian community. Tradition, paradoxically, is not only what is preserved from the past. It leads us on to the faith of the people of God as it is now. Moreover, tradition does not exist in a vacuum. Every element, including the text of the Scriptures, has arisen in a particular time and place, out of a particular cultural setting, and carries the mark of that. To evoke tradition, therefore, is not an easy thing. It requires historical and contextual analysis and critical evaluation. The church's teaching authority therefore (to return to where we began) needs to be sensitive, not only to the past but to the present, to be alert not only to the scholars but to the ordinary people who keep the faith, to reflect the faith of the church today as well as to form it.

Teaching the tradition

The second thing to be said in this discussion of the tension between freedom and control is that it is the responsibility of a divinity school to teach the tradition. Precisely because of the importance of the tradition for the identity of the church, it must be a responsibility of those involved in the education of the church's future ministers to make them aware of what that tradition is and help them to an understanding of its dynamic. That includes both trying to uncover the underlying threads that hold the various elements together and recognising the provisional quality imparted to it by the particular historical circumstances in which it developed.

But the theological task cannot stop there. There must be evaluation and challenge. Faith itself requires it: Christianity was born out of a theological critique within first-century Judaism and the controversy it generated. Historically, as the church moved out into different cultures it came to understand itself by engagement with its environment. That engagement has not only been with those outside the Christian community. There has also been an inner dialogue, as faith and contemporary culture meet within each of us. For the Christian tradition to be a living tradition today, a tradition of faith and life that engages the hearts and minds of believers and is able to present itself credibly to those outside the Christian community, it requires the ongoing rigour of self-examination, exploration and challenge. That is a necessary activity for a divinity school, precisely because it works from within its commitment to the Christian tradition.

A tension between church and school is therefore inevitable. It is eased when each recognises the role of the other. The role of the teaching authority of the church is to conserve the tradition and protect it from misrepresentation and distortion. The church does that best when it takes a long-term view. The heresy hunters who leap in with doctrinal charges at the slightest provocation generally discredit their own cause. Most of the peculiar doctrinal aberrations in the history of the church have been successfully dealt with over time, not by the authority of the church but by the arguments of theologians who have met them on their own ground, or by the church standing back and letting the thing run out of steam. The important thing is to ensure that there is debate in which the real issues can be exposed.

On the other hand, the tradition lives by constant self-review. It is a task of a divinity school to help stimulate that process, and that needs to be recognised by the church. But there is a corresponding discipline. A divinity school needs to be sensitive to the church at large and the potential danger of becoming distant from its life. After all, the faith as it is believed by the people of God, the *sensus fidelium*, is itself an ingredient of Christian tradition; and those who are academically trained and theologically sophisticated can easily forget how hard it is for those who lack those benefits to follow their lead with confidence and understanding.

There is a further point: in today's immensely diversified church, schools of divinity are faced with an alternative. They may take the easier path of aligning themselves with a particular school of thought and becoming a flagship for a theological emphasis, conservative or radical, attracting and producing students formed in their own image and thereby increasing the polarisation within the church; or they may take the braver and harder line of embracing the polarities within their own community, continuing the dialogue in their own midst, and thus enabling the church in turn to deal creatively with sharp theological difference. A school of divinity should surely be a place where no expression of Christian theological conviction is excluded or denied a voice, and where the possibilities of a properly Christian inclusiveness are explored.

Faculty members

So far I have considered the school as a corporate entity, which can publish its statement of aims and take a stance on these issues as a matter of collective policy. The governing body then has the responsibility of seeing that that stance is maintained. But, at the end of the day, an institution comprises individual faculty members and students, each of whom has a personal intellectual quest to pursue and a personal life story to work out. Not all may share a school's corporate commitment to Christian faith. What does all this say about academic freedom and integrity?

First, it needs to be said that the task of re-examining the Christian tradition needs the engagement of those who will address it, as it were, from outside. It needs the insights and scepticism – sometimes sympathetic, sometimes hostile – that those from other religious traditions and life commitments may bring. A divinity school is enriched by their presence. All that is required of such persons is willingness to work in that setting.

Second, every Christian scholar, no matter how deeply committed, knows that, in a sense, he or she is like a chemist handling corrosive materials. Their work has the potential for destruction. There can come a point at which the questions one asks, or the answers one feels driven to accept, undermine one's faith to the point of destroying it. Working within an institution with an explicit Christian commitment may then become intolerable, and the alternative of working in a broader academic setting may be preferable for that individual. It happens to some, thankfully only to a few; and, be it noted, it can happen the other way. If there are those who think their way out of faith there are also those who think their way into it. An institution founded on Christian values, particularly, must respect the liberty of its members.

But there is more to be said. It is a particular temptation of intellectuals to imagine that intellectual questions comprise the whole of life, and, specifically, that Christian believing is exclusively, or even primarily, an intellectual matter. I recall the comment made years ago about a friend of mine in theological education, who suddenly declared himself an atheist and renounced all connection with the church. The comment was: 'Too much *language, truth and logic* (the philosophical preoccupation of the time), and not enough contact with the church.' One's faith commitment, whatever it may be, is never exclusively intellectual. It takes up all the dimensions of personality and is stimulated and nourished by all kinds of experiences, and particularly by worship and contact with other believers. It is easy for those with academic interests to become somewhat dismissive of the church – and sometimes a local church can be a bit of a trial – but it is important to maintain involvement with the church's normal life if the more specifically intellectual work is to be seen in its proper, rounded context.

Students

Finally, what do these reflections imply for those who come to a divinity school as students? It is a risky thing to embark on a course of education for Christian ministry. All learning involves risk: it leads into unfamiliar country; there is un-learning as well as learning to do. When theology is the subject there is the added threat, lurking in the mind and surfacing in the conversation of well-meaning friends, that it may destroy one's faith. A student's attitude to the scriptural text and its authority, or the importance to that student of certain doctrines expressed in certain ways, may be challenged by what he or she reads and hears. Such a student may feel under pressure to change his or her accustomed positions in order to gain acceptance; put crudely, to toe the approved line in order to get the necessary grades. Such pressures may well lie more in the fears and suspicions of students than in the actual attitudes of faculty members.

The point, surely, is that the faith once delivered to the saints is a dynamic thing, not static. It lives by growth. It is important that a student should feel threatened by what is encountered in a divinity school. Those who run away from disturbing questions never learn to answer them; those who never change their mind about anything have learned nothing; those who leave a school the same person as when they arrived have wasted time and money. From the time when Jesus called the first disciples, Christian commitment has implied a willingness to change. Yet the change required is not one imposed externally, to secure conformity, but one that arises from within, by working out the issues for oneself. Such learning is only a beginning, not only because the world is constantly changing but because human beings are learning animals, and Christian human beings are called to a pilgrimage of faith and understanding. So the most important thing to learn at a divinity school is how to go on learning, and go on wanting to learn, after one has left.

Note

1 Adapted from the Convocation Address given at Vanderbilt Divinity School, Nashville, Tennessee, on 27 August 1999.

Index